# POVERTY: THE FACTS

Carey Oppenheim

CPAG LTD 1-5 BATH STREET, LONDON EC1V 9PY

CPAG promotes action for the relief, directly or indirectly, of poverty among children and families with children. We work to ensure that those on low incomes get their full entitlements to welfare benefits. In our campaigning and information work we seek to improve benefits and policies for low income families, in order to eradicate the injustice of poverty. If you are not already supporting us, please consider a donation, or ask for details of our membership schemes and publications.

Child Poverty Action Group
1-5 Bath Street, London EC1V 9PY



ISBN 0 946744 49 1

Poverty Publication 84



A CIP record for this book is available from the British Library

Cover: Liz Redgate
Artwork: Devious Designs, Stafford Road, Sheffield
Typesetting: Boldface Typesetters, 17A Clerkenwell Road, London EC1
Printing: Bath Press

# Contents

# Acknowledgements

Many thanks to all the people who contributed to this book. Thanks to Fran Bennett, Joan Brown, Peter Golding, David Piachaud and Robin Simpson for their very valuable comments on the manuscript. In particular thanks to David Piachaud who patiently helped with my queries, and to Mary Shirley, Eileen Dacey and Fran who kept my ordinary work at bay.

We consulted people on the difficulties of choosing a poverty line. Many thanks to Jonathan Bradshaw, John Hills, Ruth Lister, David Piachaud, Garry Runciman, John Veit Wilson and CPAG's Executive Committee for their wisdom and advice. The responsibility for the final text lies, of course, with us.

Thanks are also due to Paul Johnson and Steve Webb at the Institute for Fiscal Studies for their help, Jo Roll, Robert Twigger and to HMSO for allowing us to adapt data from various publications, in particular *Households below Average Income, A Statistical Analysis, 1979-1988/89.*

Special thanks to Richard Kennedy and Julia Lewis who spent enormous amounts of time and energy suggesting ideas for the book and editing it. Many thanks to Peter Ridpath for the promotion of the book, Nigel Taylor for the beautiful work he has done on the design and graphs, Liz Redgate for the cover and to Boldface Typesetters and Bath Press for producing the book at breakneck speed. And finally thank you to Bill Norris and Maya and everyone at CPAG for their patience and all their support.

# Preface

In CPAG's twenty-fifth anniversary year, 1990, we produced a special, expanded edition of a publication which had previously appeared as a regular but slim pamphlet. This is the second edition of that publication, *Poverty: the Facts*, which has been fully revised and updated to replace the first edition (which sold out and had to be reprinted). We are planning to produce a new edition at regular intervals in future years.

The preface to the 1990 edition of *Poverty: the Facts* reads rather oddly now. It talks of the growing prosperity of the country and of the minority excluded from that prosperity by their poverty. Since 1990, we have seen the tentacles of the recession touching parts of the country, and sections of the population, which other recent recessions have not reached. We now know that between 1990 and 1991 there was a fall in real terms in average disposable income per household. House repossessions, the 'negative equity' trap (in which home-owners find that their house is worth less than their outstanding mortgage) and the growing burden of debt – both individual and national – have regularly made the headlines. There is a pervading sense that the consumer boom of the late 1980s was a bubble which burst, and that we are now back to a harsher reality.

This kind of climate creates a testing time for groups such as CPAG. On the one hand, as Carey Oppenheim says in this edition, it is more difficult to deny that real poverty exists. On the other hand, fear and insecurity do not naturally go hand-in-hand with generosity. What is indisputable is that the UK in 1993 does not feel like a nation 'at ease with itself', to use the Prime Minister's election campaign phrase.

At such a time, it is even more important that CPAG produces and publicises the facts and figures about poverty in this country to inform public debate. CPAG has always been clear what poverty means: people live in poverty when they are excluded from participating in the accepted way of life in the society in which they live because of the low level of their resources. But this does not provide the answer to the question posed so regularly by students and journalists in particular: 'what is the poverty line?' The question is crucial, because to use the word 'poverty' about the state in which some people are living is to make a moral judgment – and, implicitly at least, to call for something to be done. This is why there is such controversy about the definition of 'poverty', but why no such feelings are aroused by the terms 'on low income' or 'below half average income'; and this is why those less in favour of redistribution will tend to be those who put forward a minimalist meaning for the term 'poverty', such as not having enough to eat.

In *Poverty: the Facts*, we argue unambiguously that any 'poverty line' must relate to the rest of society and the position of people in poverty within that society.

No 'poverty line' is unproblematic. But they all tell roughly the same story – that is, that in the late 1980s/1990, there were some 11 to 12 million people in the UK, or one in five of the population, living in poverty. These are the people who by any commonly accepted definition of poverty are being deprived of access to the goods and resources needed for full participation in today's society. And the lives of the children involved are being damaged in ways which will make it much more likely that they will be unable to participate fully in tomorrow's society as adults either; some, of course, will not see that future at all, because poverty not only damages lives but also kills.

*Poverty: the Facts* also looks at the texture of poverty – the frustrations, the fears and often the feelings of failure involved, as well as the daily grind which the full-time job of living in poverty actually represents, especially perhaps for women with children.

In a recent research study, published in association with the Family Service Units, several of the claimants interviewed conveyed clearly that they felt that their most important role in life was to be a good parent to their children; and that they felt a failure in this role, despite their constant best efforts, because they were undermined in their ability to carry out their responsibilities by not having the resources to do so. This does *not* represent failure on the part of these parents. And to point it out is *not* – as some would say – to deny them any part in overcoming their poverty. In fact, of course, as they told the researchers, their daily lives are already made up of trying to minimise, as far as they can, the effects of poverty on their children.

But to make this point *is* to argue that the causes of poverty are rooted in the way society is organised, rather than in individuals' personal characteristics. This is particularly important at a time when, with insecurity increasing amongst a much wider group, the tendency to distance yourself from those below you on the ladder may also be increasing – and when a common practice amongst commentators is the labelling of a whole section of society as an 'underclass', virtually beyond hope of redemption.

Believing that poverty is primarily about injustice rather than inadequacy inevitably leads to questions about what can be done. It is not the purpose of *Poverty: the Facts* to provide answers to these questions; that is for other publications, and in particular the submissions which CPAG will be making to the Commission on Social Justice which has recently been established. But part of CPAG's wider task is to show that change *is* possible, whether through a legal test case in the Courts or a CPAG branch's successful lobbying of its local authority on anti-poverty policies.

Nearly half the population (compared with only 4% nearly 30 years ago) now thinks that young people will find it 'almost impossible' to get a job, and more than two in three people think Britain is *not* 'going forward along the right lines' (Gallup poll for *Daily Telegraph*, 5 February 1993). The time is ripe to put forward imaginative proposals for public debate about how these trends can be reversed, and about what kind of society we want our children to grow up in. A society in which it is poverty, rather than people in poverty, which is left behind.

Fran Bennett
*Director, Child Poverty Action Group*

February 1993

# Introduction

In the summer of 1992, Lucy and Natalie Godfrey, aged 5 and 3, were killed in a fire, started by a candle in their bedroom. Their mother, Denise, was living on income support and could not afford to pay for tokens for their electricity meter. Instead, they used candles.[1] Denise Godfrey was not officially disconnected by Eastern Electricity; she had in effect disconnected herself because she was unable to afford to buy fuel to heat and light her home. Her poverty was invisible, unknown and unrecorded by the Electricity Board; the difficulties she endured were hidden, until the fire created this unbearable havoc in her life.

Poverty is sometimes obvious – whether it is the poverty of beggars in the street, young homeless people bedded down for the night under the arches, or people rummaging in rubbish bins. At other times it is hidden inside homes, workplaces and institutions. It is not just a feature of the North or of inner cities, but widespread through affluent and rural areas. In 1988/89, the latest figures show that between 11 and 12 million people – around a fifth of the population in the United Kingdom – were living in poverty measured by either of the most common definitions. In 1979, less than half this number were living in poverty (defined as living below half average income after housing costs).[2]

In the last decade, the living standards of the poor and affluent marched in opposite directions. For the first time in recent years, there is official evidence that the real disposable incomes of the poorest actually fell. Between 1979 and 1988/89, the poorest tenth of the population saw their real income (after housing costs) fall by 6%; the average rose by 30%, while the richest tenth enjoyed a staggering rise of 46%.[3]

These figures tell the story of the 1980s, which, despite the recession of the early years, symbolise growth, economic confidence, sparkling affluence and the denial of poverty. But the boom proved to be ephemeral. The 1990s tell a different story. This recession has claimed some 3 million unemployed at the latest count. Its effects have been felt in corners of the UK which have been untouched by earlier recessions.

According to the latest *Social Trends*, between 1990 and 1991 average household spending and income fell for the first time for years. Reports of burglary, robbery and theft, often connected to deepening deprivation, all rose between 1990 and 1991.[4] Riots have erupted in impoverished inner city areas and outer estates, born of desperation and frustration induced by joblessness, exclusion, and hopelessness.

## Why have poverty and inequality increased so rapidly?

Firstly, unemployment has soared. It has almost tripled since 1979. It is predicted by some commentators to rise to around 4 million by the middle of the decade. The fear of unemployment and with it insecurity, poverty and demoralisation, hangs over many. But despite the spread of unemployment to new areas and new occupations, unemployment does not occur at random – it is shaped by class, occupation, race and gender. A construction worker is ten times more likely to be made redundant than a lawyer.

Manufacturing industry has continued to contract. Whole towns have been and will continue to be devastated by the closure of a steel foundry, a textile factory, or more topically a coal mine. Many inner cities have been emptied of their old industries and crafts. Large-scale redundancies have brought poverty in their wake: associated industries close down and small shopkeepers shut up shop when people cut their spending. Alongside these long-term changes are new sources of unemployment: the construction industry has all but ground to a halt because of the stagnant housing market, local authorities are implementing widespread redundancies, and service industries are also shedding labour, with the result that there are few new jobs to mop up those abandoned by the old industries.

Secondly, the nature of employment itself has changed radically. The industrial transformation which brought such stubbornly high levels of unemployment has reshaped the labour market. The recent announcement by Burtons, the clothing department store, of substantial losses of full-time jobs, to be replaced by part-time jobs, is but the latest indicator of a broad trend. Part-time work and self-employment have grown substantially. Temporary and casual work have also increased. This type of work is frequently low paid with poor working conditions and few employment and social security rights. This has particularly serious implications for women who make up the majority of part-time employees. Policies which have abolished employment rights and protection for wages have contributed to the proliferation of low pay. It is harder to capture the reality of poverty in work – long hours, cramped working conditions, juggling two jobs, coping with working and looking after children and meagre rates of pay. For many, poverty is about grappling with the insecurities and frustrations associated with spells of unemployment interspersed with low-paid work. Such work patterns taint the present with poverty and offer no respite for the future.

Thirdly, these profound economic changes have gone hand in hand with shifts in family patterns. In 1987-89, 16% of all families with children were lone parents – a rise from 12% in 1979 and 8% in 1971.[5] Nine out of ten lone parents are women. Frequently trapped by the combination of low wages and the difficulty of finding childcare, many lone mothers face a bleak future reliant on inadequate benefits.

Fourthly, the social security system has become an increasingly inadequate tool to deal with today's problems. Designed for a full-time male workforce, it discriminates against those who have been low paid, or unemployed, against those who have worked part time and people who have come to this country from abroad. The most radical reform of social security since Beveridge was fully implemented in 1988. It swallowed up rights and reduced benefits for some of the poorest in the country, weakening social security protection still further.

The official denial of poverty which was such a prominent feature of the 1980s is now largely discredited. For a country in the grip of recession, it is harder to write off the experiences of millions. However, poverty is still seen by many as the fault of the poor; there is growing emphasis in social security policies on individual responsibility for poverty rather than on structural causes. As Melanie Phillips writes in the *Guardian*: 'Poverty became the necessary spur to work rather than a condition from which all citizens should be protected.'[6] But as the pages which follow demonstrate, the facts about poverty speak for themselves; and the causes of poverty are primarily structural rather than personal.

> My name is Bijon. I am coming up to nine years of age . . . poverty means not having what you need. You have outer needs and inner needs, such as your body needs a house and food and toys and your soul needs friendship and happiness and prayer and meditation. We are poor in money compared to most people in our town. But we are rich compared to homeless people and starving people . . . For us being poor means you have less and less. When things break you can't mend them or get new ones. First the lawnmower broke so the grass is all long. I call it the field. Then the van failed the MOT. I miss the van most. No more adventures or weekends at Gran's unless she sends the fare.[7]

Poverty means going short materially, socially and emotionally. It means spending less on food, on heating, and on clothing than someone on an average income. But it is not what is spent that matters, but what isn't. Poverty means staying at home, often being bored, not seeing friends, not going to the cinema, not going out for a drink and not being able to take the children out for a trip or a treat or a holiday. It means coping with the stresses of managing on very little money, often for months or even years. It means having to withstand the onslaught of society's pressure to consume. It impinges on relationships with others and with yourself. Above all, poverty takes away the tools to create the building blocks for the future – your 'life chances'. It steals away the opportunity to have a life unmarked by sickness, a decent education, a secure home and a long retirement. It stops people being able to plan ahead. It stops people being able to take control of their lives.

So poverty widens the gap between reality and potential. But despite poverty, people struggle to make do and survive with strength, resilience and dignity in the face of immense difficulties.

In *Poverty: the Facts* we can only touch on some of these issues, yet the themes we explore lie at the heart of CPAG's work. CPAG fights for a society free from poverty. Part of our role is to act as both witness and reporter, to explain the causes of poverty and to portray poverty to a wider audience. Armed with the facts we can argue for a society which puts an end to the exclusion of millions from society; we can argue for a society which recognises the right of all to an adequate income from employment or benefit, allowing people to participate in society as full members.

This book is intended to guide the reader to the most important facts and figures about poverty today. It does not attempt to explain in detail the range of possible solutions to poverty. It looks at official and independent data on poverty and low incomes, the causes and reality of poverty, poverty for women and for black and minority groups, disparities between the countries and regions of the United Kingdom, inequalities, and how we compare to the rest of Europe. In doing so, it draws on the work of researchers, academics and government statisticians, as well as the views of ordinary people.

## NOTES

1. N. Davies, 'Suffer Little Children', *Guardian*, 21 December 1992.
2. DSS, *Households below Average Income: a statistical analysis 1979-1988/89*,

Government Statistical Service, HMSO, 1990, and Social Security Committee, Second Report, *Low Income Statistics: Low Income Families 1979-1989*, 359, HMSO, 1993.

3. *See* note 2.
4. *Social Trends 23*, Government Statistical Service, HMSO, 1993.
5. K Kiernan and M Wicks, *Family Change and Future Policy*, Family Policy Studies Centre and Joseph Rowntree Memorial Trust, 1990 and *Population Trends 65*, OPCS, HMSO, autumn 1991.
6. M Phillips, 'The New Road to Wigan Pier', *Guardian*, 21 November 1992.
7. Bijon Chaudhuri, winner of CPAG/Young Guardian competition in April 1989, printed in *Poverty*, No 73, CPAG Ltd, summer 1989.

CHAPTER ONE

# Definitions and debates

## Definitions: what is poverty?

> *Poverty is not about shortage of money. It is about rights and relationships; about how people are treated and how they regard themselves; about powerlessness, exclusion and loss of dignity. Yet the lack of an adequate income is at its heart.*
>
> Faith in the City[1]

Homeless people sleeping under the arches, pensioners counting out the pennies in the supermarket. A family crowded into a single room in a bed and breakfast hotel, mothers stretching out child benefit until their next giro comes. The fear of the debt collector, the queues for a housing transfer, for benefit, for advice . . . there is no doubt that these are the manifestations of poverty. However, in other respects poverty is difficult to define. For example, how does poverty in Britain compare to poverty in Somalia? How is the perception of poverty modified from one generation to the next? Is poverty for one family the same as poverty for another? Is poverty experienced in the same way by men and women?

British governments of all political persuasions have refused to define an official 'poverty line'. As a consequence, there is no *official* yardstick for measuring the rise or fall in poverty under different governments. This said, we can identify two broad approaches to defining poverty.

### Absolute poverty

An *absolute* definition of poverty assumes that it is possible to define a minimum standard of living based on a person's *biological* needs for food, water, clothing and shelter. The emphasis is on basic physical needs and not on broader social and cultural needs. Absolute poverty is when people fall below this level – when they cannot house, clothe or feed themselves.

Seebohm Rowntree used such a definition in his study of poverty in York in 1899. He devised a 'primary' poverty line based on a standard of minimum needs for food, clothing, heating and rent, to show that many families had incomes below this level. But, as he himself wrote:[2]

> My primary poverty line represented the minimum sum on which physical efficiency could be maintained. It was a bare standard of *subsistence* rather than living . . . such a minimum does not by any means constitute a reasonable living wage.

The absolute view of poverty is still a definition valued by many commentators. For example, Lord Joseph (former Secretary of State for Social Services) argued:[3]

> An absolute standard of means is defined by reference to the actual needs of the poor and not by reference to the expenditure of those who are not poor. A family is poor if it cannot afford to eat . . . A person who enjoys a standard of living equal to that of a medieval baron cannot be described as poor for the sole reason that he has chanced to be born into a society where the great majority can live like medieval kings. By any absolute standards there is very little poverty in Britain today.

This tougher definition of poverty is also one which appears to be shared by the general public. The *British Social Attitudes Survey* found that 60% of people agreed that poverty was about subsistence; 95% agreed that poverty was about living below minimum subsistence; and only 25% thought that poverty was relative to the living standards of others.[4]

The appeal of an absolute definition of poverty is its apparent clarity and its moral force. If there is not enough to eat there is poverty. However, the absolute definition is flawed, for two main reasons. Firstly, it is very difficult to define an 'adequate' minimum when standards of living themselves change over time. Beveridge recognised this in *Social Insurance and Allied Services* in 1942:

> determination of what is required for reasonable human subsistence is to some extent a matter of judgement; estimates on this point change with time, and generally in a progressive community, change upwards.[5]

How we house, clothe and feed ourselves has changed drastically over the years. Living standards also vary radically in different cultures. People's expectations also change because of the demands society makes of them, so that a minimum standard of living is shaped by the way society as a whole behaves and spends its money. Thus, an adequate minimum is itself defined by what is socially acceptable. Secondly, an absolute definition takes no account of social and cultural needs.

Sometimes the term 'absolute' poverty is used to refer to the use of a 'fixed' or 'static' poverty line (see Chapter 2). However, this approach also has its shortcomings. As Jo Roll points out in *Understanding Poverty: a guide to the concepts and the measures*:[6]

> There is no reason why an arbitrary date in the past should be taken as the relevant definition of poverty today. Even if it is considered desirable to pick a particular year for certain purposes it may not in practice be possible to define equivalent living standards at different dates or in different societies. David Donnison has argued that luxuries in one era may be necessities in another, not because of 'keeping up with the Jones family' but because people cannot eat or keep warm otherwise.[7]

Such considerations demand a more sophisticated approach to the definition of poverty.

## Relative poverty

> Poor people in Britain are not, of course, as poor as those in the Third World. But their poverty is real enough nonetheless. For poverty is a relative, as well as an absolute, concept. It exists, even in a relatively rich Western society, if people are denied access to what is generally regarded as a reasonable standard and quality of life in that society. (*Faith in the City*)[8]

In this instance poverty is defined in relation to a generally accepted standard of living in a specific society at a specific time and goes beyond basic biological needs. This view of poverty has a long heritage. Adam Smith, the eighteenth century economic philosopher, commented:

> By necessities I understand not only commodities which are indispensably necessary for the support of life but whatever *the custom of the country* renders it indecent for creditable people, even of the lowest order, to be without.
> (Adam Smith, *The Wealth of Nations*, our emphasis)[9]

In 1979, Peter Townsend's definitive work, *Poverty in the UK*, provided a forceful presentation of a relative view of poverty which echoed Smith's concerns:

> Individuals . . . can be said to be in poverty when they lack the resources to obtain the types of diet, participate in the activities and have the living conditions and amenities which are customary, or at least widely encouraged or approved, in the societies to which they belong.[10]

Thus poverty is not simply about lack of money but also about exclusion from the customs of society. While there are a number of difficulties inherent in this approach – for example, how do we establish what the norms of our society are, or what people *choose* to manage without? – such a perspective has played a crucial role in establishing a new agenda for contemporary debates about poverty.[11]

The relative view of poverty has been shared by people across the political spectrum. For example, when she was Conservative social security minister, Lady Chalker said:

> It is not sufficient to assess poverty by absolute standards; nowadays it must be judged on relative criteria by comparison with the standard of living of other groups in the community . . . beneficiaries must have an income which enables them to participate in the life of the community.[12]

Relative poverty is about social exclusion imposed by an inadequate income. It is not only about having to go short of food or clothing, it is also about not being able to join a local sports club, or send your children on a school trip, or go out with friends, or have a Christmas dinner:

> Christmas is not a time for celebrating for our family as we can only manage to buy the bare basic things to tide us over the holiday period. We do manage to buy a chicken for Christmas Day, that's all. After that it's back to basic meals – egg and chips, sausage and mash etc. We cannot even afford trivial things like jellies, mince pies, crackers etc to brighten up the festive season.
>
> (Mother of two, London)[13]

As Jo Roll argues, a relative definition of poverty encompasses the view that:

> It is not just that the physical needs have a social aspect but that social needs should be recognised in their own right.[14]

In a development of the relative approach, Joanna Mack and Stewart Lansley adopted an innovative approach to poverty which has been described as consensual or democratic.[15] They defined being in poverty as a situation in which people had to live without the things which society as a whole regarded as necessities. Using public opinion surveys, they found that there was general agreement about what constituted a minimum standard of living. At least two out of three people thought the following were necessities in 1991:

- Self-contained damp-free accommodation with an indoor toilet and bath;

- three daily meals for each child and two meals a day for adults;
- adequate bedrooms and beds;
- heating and carpeting;
- a refrigerator and washing machine;
- enough money for special occasions like Christmas;
- toys for the children.

In 1990, they found that around 11 million people – 1 in 5 of the population – lacked three of these necessities or more, which they defined as living in poverty.[16]

The limitations of the traditional debates about poverty have obscured crucial aspects of poverty, in particular poverty *inside* families. Recent research has found that women are much more vulnerable to poverty than men, but that their poverty has been hidden by surveys which have ignored individual living standards within the home (see Chapter 5).

CPAG has always supported the view that poverty should also be seen in relation to the standard of living in a particular society. People should have a right to an income which allows them to *participate* in society, rather than merely exist. Such participation involves having the means to fulfil responsibilities to others such as partners, sons and daughters, to care for elderly or sick relatives, to help neighbours and friends, and to be able to join in as workers and citizens:

> People should be given enough money so that they can actually live a life that's reasonably comfortable – so they can do things they enjoy and not just survive, because everybody has a right to more than survive.
>
> (Unemployed worker)[17]

## The Political Context

One of the hallmarks of the Thatcher era was the fierce debate over the nature of poverty. The more apparent poverty became the more strongly its level and indeed its very existence were denied. In 1989 John Moore MP, then Secretary of State for Social Security, made his famous speech 'The end of the line for poverty'.[18] In the course of that speech he argued that economic success had put an end to absolute poverty and that relative poverty – an invention of academics in the 1960s – could be dismissed as simply meaning inequality. The speech caused a storm of protest. Margaret Thatcher joined the controversy when she argued that to call people living on income support 'poor' was to denigrate them.[19] The word 'poverty' had already all but disappeared from official documents. Instead, the poor were often described as 'dependent'. Some people argued that poverty was caused not by low wages or unemployment but by long-term dependency on state support. Welfare itself generated poverty.

Since the autumn of 1990 when John Major became prime minister, the debate has shifted and the language changed. But how far and to what extent is difficult to assess. There is a crisis of the 'big idea' – whether it is on the right or the left. The political ground is much more uncertain. On the government side, the language is less obviously ideological and more pragmatic. There is more scope for differences of view within government. On the opposition side, the Labour Party has set up an independent Commission on Social Justice to investigate past changes and future policies in the fields of employment, tax and social welfare. The political context has changed: the government has a small majority of 21 and thus legislation has to be framed within a more responsive setting. It also has to be framed with one eye on the European Community, which is increasingly shaping our economic and, to a degree, our social policy agenda. The economic context has also changed: the depth and persistence of the recession make it more difficult for the government to write off poverty as the experience of an irrelevant minority. Below, we look at a number of current themes: we consider the government agenda and what it means for poverty; we then focus on key issues in social security policy and, finally, we explore the discussion around the concept of an 'underclass'. These debates are not intended to be comprehensive; instead they aim to provide a context for the examination of poverty today.

## John Major: opportunity, choice, ownership and responsibility?

'Opportunity, choice, ownership and responsibility' is the clarion call of the present Conservative government. The themes run throughout the Prime Minister's speeches, the Conservative manifesto and the Citizen's Charter. At the same time, the government is committed to a market-driven economy, reducing the size of the public sector, lowering taxes, maintaining low inflation as a central economic goal and extending privatisation. Below we assess what this agenda means for those in poverty.

*Opportunity . . .*

John Major, unusually for a Conservative Prime Minister, has staked his claim to creating a 'classless society':

> I have spoken of a 'classless society'. I do not mean by that a bleak uniformity, or a rejection of our rich tapestry of traditions . . . I mean one in which *opportunity is not confined to the fortunate few, but wide open to all.* (our emphasis)[20]

He has committed himself to 'policies that will turn more of Britain's Have-Nots into Haves',[21] to defending the ordinary man and woman,[22] to not forgetting 'those with their foot on the first rung of the ladder of opportunity or those who have been knocked off it by misfortune'.[23]

Echoing one nation Toryism, Major has called for a 'nation at ease with itself', which means, in his own words, 'removing as far as any government can, the fear that people have about their prospects . . . *maintaining a welfare safety net* . . .' (our emphasis)[24]

But, significantly, giving people opportunities is not equated with giving them support from the state:

> For our Conservatism is about developing personal independence. It is designed to give people a hand up, not a hand out. And it is about placing a restraining hand on the power of the State.[25]

*Choice . . .*

A second prominent theme has been to extend choice; to do away with the 'old divide between those who choose and those who have to take what's given':[26]

> In the 1990s we mean to widen the avenues to choice and freedom. We mean to empower not just the enterprising, but all people – the least well-off – those most dependent on public services as well . . . Where once Socialism nationalised or municipalised personal choice, taking it away from the individual and the family, we will give choice back to them and extend it further. Of all the privatisations that this Conservative Government conducts the greatest and most far-reaching and the one to which I am most committed is the *privatisation of choice*. (our emphasis)[27]

Underpinning the 'privatisation of choice' is a belief in low taxation:

> I believe in low taxes not just because they ignite enterprise – the spark of economic growth – but because they put *power and choice where it belongs – in your hands*. (our emphasis)[28]

*Ownership . . .*

One of the cornerstones of Thatcherism was the creation of a society of homeowners. This is strongly echoed by John Major; 'opportunity' and 'choice' rest on a foundation of 'ownership':

> We need, in all aspects of national life, a full sense of involvement. And we gain this, most of all, through personal ownership. That is why for me, no principle is more crucial than what I call the Right to Own. To have a home of your own. Savings of your own. A pension of your own.[29]

> *The widening of ownership* isn't an index of greed . . . Indeed, *it is the very foundation of personal security, the keystone of independence*, the gateway to opportunity and prosperity for generations to come. (our emphasis)[30]

*Responsibility . . .*

The notion of 'responsibility' runs through the government's philosophy and policies. The launch of the Citizen's Charter outlines what is meant by 'responsibility':

> The Citizen's Charter is about giving more power to the citizen. But citizenship is about our responsibilities – as parents, for example, or as neighbours – as well as our entitlements. The Citizen's Charter is not a recipe for more state action; it is a testament of our belief in people's right to be informed and to choose for themselves.[31]

There are a number of policies which are aimed at enforcing responsibility – for example, the imposition of fines on the parents of 'delinquent' children, the introduction of the Child Support Act which enforces the payment of maintenance by the absent parent, and the tightening of the 'actively seeking work' rules for so-called New Age Travellers, to name but a few.

What are the difficulties with 'opportunity, choice, ownership and responsibility' and what do they mean for people living in poverty? We look first at the concepts themselves and then at the conflict between the ideals and economic reality.

No one can argue against extending opportunity and choice to all. However, 'opportunity' and 'choice' are conceived of as solely about the 'individual' or 'family', in contrast to the state which is seen as taking these away from people. This goes to the heart of the Conservative paradox: the purpose of the state is to ensure the freedom and liberty of the individual. But freedom is conceived of as freedom *from* the state. In fact, despite a now general acknowledgement that public services can sometimes be bureaucratic and paternalistic, the state can and very often does provide the route to choice and opportunity – for example, by guaranteeing a pregnant woman a right to return to work after the birth of her child, or providing a state pension or childcare facilities.

The emphasis on 'ownership' is problematic for people in poverty. If ownership is the gateway to involvement, personal security, independence, opportunity and prosperity, it will of necessity exclude a core section of society who cannot afford to own their own homes or pensions. If ownership is held up as the ideal, as the means of having a stake in society, many will be compelled to regard themselves as second class citizens. More recently, the government has partly recognised the difficulty in the indefinite extension of owner occupation and has suggested ways of developing the rented sector and of reducing the resources devoted to mortgage interest tax relief. However, these are, as yet, straws in the wind.

There may be a conflict between encouraging, extending and ultimately enforcing 'responsibility' and, on the other hand, decreasing the power of the state in principle and in practice. The government has increased the powers of government agencies in the social security field in order to enforce certain responsibilities. In addition, just as 'opportunity' and 'choice' are seen as primarily being about the 'individual', so too is responsibility. The Citizen's Charter is the tool for the individual to be more informed, to have the opportunity to complain, to receive compensation in order to make public services more accountable. These goals are laudable, if limited. But as CPAG's Fran Bennett points out in *Windows of Opportunity*, redress for disappointed customers is of no value if you have no access to the service in the first place (for example, childcare facilities). There is considerable evidence to show that a person's social and economic resources influence their capacity to act politically. In *British Social Attitudes*, Ken Young shows how certain political actions such as contacting an MP or a government department, or speaking to an influential person, are strongly related to class – in other words, the middle class tend to undertake these activities much more frequently than the working class.[32] Thus initiatives like the Citizen's Charter tend to empower those who are already empowered. A 'classless society' would involve not just a transfer of economic and social resources, but also political tools:

> Perceptions of Britain as an unequal society are deeply embedded and no portrait of social division in Britain would be complete that did not take them into account.
>
> Moreover, because these inequalities extend to the political realm, the

> prospects for change are remote – unless, that is, the determination to create a classless society extends beyond the eradication of overt discrimination and self-limitation to the expansion of political resources to the 'dispossessed' . . . The commitment to a Citizen's Charter would on this analysis certainly help but it will require a far wider and more rigorous application if it is to address the class inequalities in political influence. Birth, wealth and connection will surely continue to have a main bearing on political power as long as they are expected – and thus permitted – to do so.[33]

We now turn to the clash between the ideals of 'opportunity, choice, ownership and responsibility' and the economic reality.

While some commentators report that the 'green shoots' of recovery are in sight, the consequences of the recession continue unabated. Unemployment has already reached 3 million and will continue to rise for several years. The government is pursuing an economic policy which has the restraint of inflation as its key goal and, in Norman Lamont's unfortunate words, unemployment as a 'price well worth paying' for this objective.[34] Rapidly increasing unemployment brings with it sharp rises in the numbers of people who have to rely on means-tested benefits like income support. The rise in repossessions is a nightmare that has hit thousands of people. Alongside this trend, the government faces a rising public sector deficit with strong pressures to reduce public spending. In such a climate, taking away people's fears about their prospects and maintaining an adequate welfare safety net become almost impossible to achieve. The broader goals of extending 'opportunity, choice and ownership' seem but a pipe-dream to a significant percentage of the population.

The government's commitment to reducing the public sector's share of national income and extending privatisation puts universal public services (both national and local) under threat. Access to universal services of high quality – be it at a national or local level – is crucial for everyone, but of particular importance to people in or close to poverty. 'Benefits in kind' make up a much higher proportion of poorer people's total income than they do for the more affluent.[35] At a local level, local authorities are currently implementing stringent cuts in services such as childcare, school meals, community education and leisure services. At national level, many fear that the health and education reforms will create a two-tier service. Under such circumstances, it is hard to see how opportunities and choices for people in or close to poverty will be enhanced.

The government remains pledged to low taxation; but such a goal will inevitably mean fewer resources which could otherwise be used to extend services and financial support to those who are currently denied choice and opportunity.

## Social Security Issues

### The future of universal benefits

> The chill wind of recession is still hitting many homes. They depend on us for support. They will receive it. But to escape recession we must curb public spending, including social security. But improving benefits is not just a question of spending more money. It's how we spend it that counts.
>
> (Rt Hon Peter Lilley MP, Secretary of State for Social Security)[36]

This quotation sums up the government's dilemma – to protect the unemployed, but to cut spending. One of the ways it proposes to square the circle is 'to focus benefits on the most needy'.[37] At the same time, the government is tied by its manifesto pledges to retaining universal retirement pension and child benefit. However, there are several signals from a number of sources which suggest that universal benefits are far from secure.

The government has just announced a long-term review of social security alongside other parts of the welfare state. This follows a number of rumours. A report in *The Times* (23 January 1993) suggests that the right-wing No Turning Back Group (which includes Peter Lilley MP and Michael Portillo MP, the Chief Secretary to the Treasury) plans to produce a report calling for the welfare state to be reduced to a safety net for the poor and recommending an end to universal child benefit and retirement pension. The Institute of Directors has said that it will be making proposals about means-testing universal benefits in its submission for the December Budget.[38] According to the *Daily Telegraph* (24 January 1993), the government is considering a radical proposal to allow opting out of the basic state pension, along the lines of the current system for opting out of the State Earnings-Related Pension Scheme. People would pay lower rates of national insurance and divert their cash into private insurance instead. This may provide a model for other benefits such as unemployment and sickness benefits. Such a step would represent a dramatic change in the existing system; although retirement pension would not be means-tested, it would cease to be 'universal', as many pensioners would provide for themselves. There are a number of objections to such an approach: the inevitable undermining of the state pension as more and more people fear that its level would not be protected and thus opt out of the state scheme; the high administrative costs associated with private schemes; and the difficulty of ensuring adequate protection through private cover and the resulting increase in the numbers of people on means-tested support in retirement.

Such proposals engender a climate in which it becomes feasible for the government to make more fundamental changes in social security policy.

The challenge to universal benefits comes not only from the government side, but also from the Labour Party. The pledge to increase universal child benefit and retirement pension alongside increases in taxation for the better-off were the key public spending commitments made at the time of the last election. The fourth election defeat in a row encouraged the Labour Party to start to re-think its employment, tax and social welfare policies by setting up an independent Commission on Social Justice headed by Sir Gordon Borrie QC.

Many commentators have argued forcefully for a rejection of universal benefits:

> The lesson is that benefits paid to everyone are ineffective in tackling poverty. They cannot be high enough to meet real need without unacceptable taxation levels. Universal benefits are also inefficient – too much money goes to those who have no need of it . . . Sir Gordon's Commission must convince Labour that providing sufficient help for those with the greatest need cannot be done with universal benefits. Instead, means-testing must be used to target resources on pensioners with inadequate occupational pensions, one-parent families and families with low-paid breadwinners.[39]

Despite the bandwagon for means-testing, the case for universal benefits remains compelling. A social security system in a modern society should be multi-purpose; its function is not only to relieve poverty once it has struck, but also to prevent it. Thus retirement pension and child benefit are, in a sense, 'targeted', not on the basis of income, but at times in the lifecycle when there is a risk of falling into poverty – retirement and childhood are just such times. Child benefit is the only recognition of the costs of children in our tax and social security system. It replaced the child tax allowance and thus also functions as a recognition of the fact that people with children have less taxable capacity than those without children.[40]

Means-tested benefits have persistent problems of take-up which result from their inevitable complexity; they are expensive to administer;

they increase the poverty trap and create stigma for those who claim them. By contrast, child benefit has virtually 100% take-up, is cheap to administer, and provides a building block on which to enter and leave the labour market (because it is not withdrawn as earnings rise), and a buffer against changes in family life such as divorce or separation and remarriage. Above all, universal benefits guarantee that everyone, not only the poor, has a stake in the welfare state. It is this which ensures public support for the principle. Thus, just like the universal health and education services, universal benefits reinforce and foster solidarity in our society. To go down the route of means-testing will undermine political support for the welfare state. Martin Linton, writing in *Fabian Review*, describes the Swedish restructuring of the welfare state which has retained universal benefits:

> The moment [benefits] are made selective one is on a slippery slope. The cost of the welfare state might be reduced, but so would the willingness of the middle classes to pay for it . . . the middle classes start to look for private insurance solutions, then they no longer want to pay for universal services because this would be seen as paying twice, and finally the welfare state becomes a safety net for the poor.[41]

Those who advocate means-testing assume that there is only one source of extra cash, namely universal benefits; but in fact there are far more obvious sources of money, including the extensive tax reliefs and allowances which could fund an attack on poverty.

## Rights and Responsibilities

The government's encouragement of personal responsibility is echoed in its social security policy. The introduction of the Child Support Act – which enforces the payment of maintenance from absent parents, usually fathers, to the caring parent – is couched in the language of responsibility:

> We back parents' rights. But with rights go duties. All parents have a duty to support their children. Yet only one in three absent fathers pays a penny towards the maintenance of his children. That must and will change. So I am pressing ahead with the new Child Support Agency. We will insist that absent parents contribute to the upkeep of their children. That will have the overwhelming support of parents throughout the country.[42]

In order to achieve this goal the government has had to give the Child Support Agency widespread powers to investigate people's circumstances and to enforce substantial penalties if they fail to cooperate. For example, if a mother on benefit refuses to cooperate with the pursuit of maintenance without an adequate reason, 20% will be deducted from her personal allowance for a period of six months and 10% for the remaining 12 months. This example highlights the conflict between encouraging responsibility and reducing the power of the state.

The issue of rights and responsibilities has surfaced in debates about workfare. Workfare originates from the United States and is a system whereby those in receipt of 'welfare' have to work to pay off their benefit. Rumours about the possible introduction of similar schemes in the UK have abounded. The prime minister has thrown his hat into the ring. In his speech to the Carlton Club, outlining the Conservative agenda for change, he argued:

> I increasingly wonder whether paying unemployment benefit, without offering or requiring any activity in return, serves unemployed people in society well.[43]

However, the case for workfare-type schemes is not shared by all within the Conservative Party. For example, the Rt Hon Kenneth Clarke MP argues against:

> the more authoritarian approaches being pioneered in the United States, which commentators there have styled 'the New Paternalism'. In some States single mothers are required to live in controlled and supervised housing as a condition of receiving support. Parents of welfare families must prevent truancy and satisfy child support requirements if they are to receive benefits . . . In our secure and civilised society we see measures like those as a move away from the idea of a nation of free and independent citizens. We are not attracted by the prospect of a substantial number of citizens being, as it were, wards of the state.[44]

## Fraud

> Be in no doubt. This Government and this Secretary of State will not tolerate fraud. It's an insult to the law-abiding majority. I have set a target of tracking down £500 million. And I mean to get it back. I'm closing down the something for nothing society.[45]

The strong emphasis on fraud is a prominent feature in current social security policy. The government intends to introduce new controls on invalidity benefit and provide incentives for local authorities to track down fraud in housing benefit payments. In the government's view, clamping down on fraud will save money. But as social security becomes associated in the public's mind with scrounging rather than entitlement, this may also discourage rightful claims. Take, for example, Peter Lilley's reference to the New Age Travellers:

> Most people were as sickened as I was by the sight of these spongers descending like locusts, demanding benefits with menaces. We are not in the business of subsidising scroungers.[46]

Moreover, the attack on scroungers has been extended to include so-called 'bogus' asylum-seekers. The stigma which these groups already experience will only be reinforced by the association with fraud.

On the one hand, the government makes the identification of fraudulent claims a key element of its social security strategy. On the other hand, it pays scant attention to the equally serious problem of low take-up of benefits.

## The 'underclass'

> I see the growth of a so-called underclass as the most formidable challenge to a secure and civilised way of life throughout the developed world. Our society cannot afford to alienate and exclude significant numbers of the poor, the black and the young.
>
> (Rt Hon Kenneth Clarke QC MP, Secretary of State for Home Affairs)[47]

The term 'underclass' has proved to be of enduring use. A broad cross-section of leader writers, academics and journalists seem to hold the belief that Britain is characterised by the growth of an 'underclass' which is cut off from the rest of society.[48]

There are broadly two approaches to the 'underclass' debate. One approach which is usually, though not entirely, associated with the political right sees the underclass primarily as a 'cultural' phenomenon. The other approach, associated with the left, sees the 'underclass' as a structural phenomenon – the result of social and economic changes.[49]

Chief amongst those who see the 'underclass' as a cultural phenomenon is American political scientist Charles Murray.[50] In an article in the *Sunday Times*, Murray defined the characteristics of the 'underclass': high rates of illegitimacy, of crime and of drop-out from the labour market.[51] Thus the term 'underclass' describes a type of poverty that is defined by *behaviour*:

> When I use the term 'underclass' I am indeed focusing on a certain type of

FORMAT PHOTOG LTD/PAM ISHERWOOD (8658/23)

***To do without the things that the rest of society regards as essential – a fridge, toys for the children, being able to give a birthday present – is to experience real poverty.***

> poor person defined not by his condition – eg, long-term unemployed – but by his *deplorable behaviour in response to that condition* – eg, unwilling to take the jobs that are available to him. (our emphasis)[52]

In the United States, the discussion of the 'underclass' is dominated by the issue of 'race'. In the UK, such an approach is less pervasive. However, as Fred Robinson and Nicky Gregson note in *Critical Social Policy*, using the term 'underclass' has

> a veneer of liberal racial tolerance (by not explicitly referring to race) but . . . may serve both to promulgate racism and conceal the issue of racial discrimination.[53]

From the point of view of their exponents, both 'dependency' and 'underclass' appeal because they create a distinction between different groups of people in poverty. A new lease of life is given to the old distinction between the deserving and undeserving poor. For example, Digby Anderson, director of the Social Affairs Unit, argues:

> A more common sense morality would distinguish between those in difficulty through no fault of their own . . . and those who contributed to their circumstances. For, increasingly, low incomes are associated with behaviour, such as irresponsible sexual habits and unstable family formation, lack of commitment to work or training and failure to save or to spend prudently . . . It is time to bring back the notions of deserving and undeserving poor, to restore moral discrimination to social policy.[54]

For Murray and others, the solution to the problem of the 'underclass' is not money, or training, or education. Instead, they suggest that the answer lies in a radical dose of 'self-government', whereby the views of local communities determine welfare policy. Digby Anderson presents the case rather more starkly than most by arguing for the return of social stigma:

> The fundamental dispute is whether the welfare of a society including the poor may need the disincentives, stigma and other unpleasantnesses which arise naturally in local communities to dissuade people from poverty-producing behaviour.[55]

By contrast, other commentators have used the term in a quite different way. For example, Garry Runciman places the 'underclass' in his overall schema of social classes:

> That there is below the two working classes an underclass which constitutes a separate category of roles is . . . readily demonstrable . . . But the term must

> be understood to stand not for a group or category of workers systematically disadvantaged within the labour market . . . but for those members of British society whose roles place them more or less permanently at the economic level where benefits are paid by the state to those unable to participate in the labour market at all.[56]

Frank Field adopts a similar approach.[57] For Field, the creation of such a class is primarily the consequence of structural factors and in his terms comprises the long-term unemployed, lone parents and those elderly people who are dependent solely on state benefits. He sees the 'underclass' as excluded from the rights of citizenship, separated from the rest of society in terms of 'income, life chances and aspirations'. He believes that, alongside other measures, policies on maintenance, pensions and availability for work will help to reduce its numbers.

Ralf Dahrendorf straddles the two approaches, seeing the 'underclass' as rooted in economic and social changes – ie, that modern societies can have satisfactory rates of growth while substantial minorities remain unemployed.[58] But he also argues that

> the underclass is the living doubt in the prevailing values which will eat into the texture of the societies in which we are living. In fact, it has already done so, which is why there is a very strong moral case for doing something about it.[59]

For Dahrendorf, the solution to the problem is to extend social citizenship to the 'underclass' by creating a basic income guarantee which does not rely on having employment.

So how useful is the term 'underclass'? Its key strength is that it is an attempt to capture an intensity of poverty. It conveys the ways in which different aspects of poverty – such as low quality housing, a bleak urban environment, social isolation, exclusion from the world of work and lack of participation in political life – compound one another. However, despite this advantage there are several objections to using the term.

Firstly, it is imprecise. Murray has used it to describe behaviour. Others, such as Frank Field, have placed the 'underclass' in the context of social and economic trends. It is not clear whether the 'underclass' describes all the poor, or sub-groups of the poor. If the latter, precisely which sub-groups fall into this category and why? Is the underclass defined by its economic status or its 'deviance' from the norm?

The 'underclass' has proved to be very difficult to define empirically. In *Understanding the Underclass* Nick Buck attempts to define an 'underclass' by looking at the numbers of 'inactive and long-term unemployed' households. He found an increase in this group from 5% to 10% between 1979 and 1986. However, as he himself states, it is not clear whether this group should be called an 'underclass'. As yet, there is no evidence that this group was continually unemployed over the period and thus it does not necessarily represent a stable class. However, Buck suggests that repeated periods of large-scale unemployment may increase the number of people who are never employed and thus risk becoming unemployable.[60]

Secondly, there is little empirical evidence to support the cultural interpretation of the 'underclass'. In a study of attitudes of families who had been long-term unemployed, Antony Heath found that their values and attitudes were very similar to the employed.[61] This is borne out by a study of people on benefit in Newcastle-upon-Tyne. In short, there is no clear evidence that such a class exists:

> At a time when British poverty is again being discussed in terms of an underclass, it is of crucial importance to recognise that these families and probably millions more like them living on social security benefits, are in no sense a detached and isolated group cut off from the rest of society. They are just the same people as the rest of our population, with the same culture and aspirations but with simply too little money to be able to share in the activities and possessions of everyday life with the rest of the population.
>
> (*Living on the Edge*)[62]

Thirdly, the predominance of 'cultural' or 'behavioural' interpretations of the underclass is profoundly worrying. It allows poverty to be explained away by personal and moral considerations, while allowing social and economic factors to be conveniently overshadowed. This is not to suggest that people's behaviour does not matter, but that poverty cannot be explained *solely* or mainly in terms of that behaviour.

Fourthly, the term 'underclass' is often heavy with negative resonance. It brings to mind the underworld, the sub-human, 'Hobbesian savagery',[63] the underbelly of society, the wayward, drunken, feckless, 'dangerous' classes that the Victorians inveighed against.

> The underclass *spawns* illegitimate children without a care for tomorrow and *feeds* on a crime rate which rivals the United States in property offences. Its able-bodied youths see no point in working and feel no compulsion either. They reject society while *feeding* off it; they are becoming a lost generation giving the cycle of deprivation a new spin . . . No amount of income redistribution or social engineering can solve their problem. Their *sub*-lifestyles are

> beyond welfare benefit rises and job creation schemes. They exist as active social outcasts, wedded to an anti-social system.
>
> (*Sunday Times* editorial – our emphasis)[64]

The 'underclass' is described as though it were a parasite, spawning off-spring, and feeding off the rest of society. Thus, the term expresses more about the *fears* of the rest of society than about the reality it seeks to describe. As Ruth Lister has suggested:

> The danger is that the more certain groups in poverty are described in such value-laden language, the easier it becomes for the rest of society to write them off as beyond the bonds of common citizenship.[65]

A more fruitful approach to this debate would be to focus on the ways in which poor people are excluded and marginalised by society itself; to identify the barriers to participation rather than blaming the people beyond the barriers.[66]

## Conclusion

We have looked at different approaches to poverty and have argued that it is crucial to consider poverty in relation to the living standards of the rest of society. To do without the things that the rest of society regards as essential – a fridge, toys for the children, being able to give a birthday present – is to experience real poverty. We have touched on the political debates which provide the context for the discussion of poverty: the ways in which the government's ideals of 'opportunity, choice, ownership and responsibility' clash with its economic policies and the economic reality; the debate between universal and selective benefits, rights and responsibilities and the new attack on fraud. We have argued that the concept of the 'underclass' in many of its uses cannot be sustained. The pages which follow concentrate on the facts about, and the causes of, poverty. They show that despite society's prosperity, the number of people living in poverty has increased and that this poverty is the outcome not of inadequacy but of broader social and economic factors.

### NOTES

1. The report of the Archbishop of Canterbury's Commission on Urban Priority Areas,

*Faith in the City, A Call for Action by Church and Nation*, Vol. 15, Part 1, Church House, 1985.

2. Quoted in J Veit Wilson, 'Paradigms of poverty', *Journal of Social Policy*, January 1986.
3. K Joseph, *Stranded on middle ground*, Centre for Policy Studies, 1976.
4. Peter Taylor Gooby, 'Social Welfare: the unkindest cuts', eds., R Jowell et al, *British Social Attitudes, the 7th Report*, Gower, 1990.
5. Sir William Beveridge, *Social Insurance and Allied Services*, Cmnd 6404, 1942, quoted in J Roll, *Understanding poverty, A guide to the concepts and measures*, Family Policy Studies Centre, 1992 .
6. J Roll, *see* note 5.
7. D Donnison, quoted in J Roll, *see* note 5.
8. *See* note 1.
9. Adam Smith, *The Wealth of Nations*, 1812.
10. P Townsend, *Poverty in the UK*, Penguin, 1979.
11. *See* debate between David Piachaud and Peter Townsend in *New Society*, 10 and 18 September 1981.
12. House of Commons, 6 November 1979.
13. S McEvaddy and C Oppenheim, 'Christmas on the Breadline', CPAG Ltd, 1987.
14. J Roll, *see* note 5.
15. J Mack and S Lansley, *Poor Britain*, Allen & Unwin, 1985. This work is updated in *Breadline Britain – 1990s*, the findings of the television series, Domino Films, LWT, 1991.
16. *See* note 15.
17. 'Fair Shares?', CPAG video, 1984.
18. Speech by the Rt Hon John Moore MP, to the Greater London Area CPC, 11 May 1989.
19. Letter from the Prime Minister, Rt Hon Margaret Thatcher MP, to Rt Hon Neil Kinnock MP, 30 May 1989.
20. Speech by the Prime Minister, Rt Hon John Major MP, to the Conservative Party's Women's Conference, 27 June 1991.
21. *See* note 20.
22. Speech by the Prime Minister, Rt Hon John Major MP, to the Adam Smith Institute, 16 June 1992.
23. Speech by the Prime Minister, Rt Hon John Major MP, to the Young Conservatives Conference, 8 February 1992.
24. Transcript of an interview with the Prime Minister, Rt Hon J Major, Radio 4, 3 December 1991.
25. *See* note 20.
26. *See* note 22.
27. *See* note 22.
28. The Conservative Party Manifesto, *The Best Future for Britain*, Conservative Central Office, 1992.
29. *See* note 20.
30. Speech by the Prime Minister, Rt Hon John Major MP, to the Annual Conservative Central Council Meeting, 23 March 1991.
31. The Citizen's Charter, *Raising the Standard*, HMSO, Cmnd 1599, 1991.
32. K Young, 'Class, Race and Opportunity', *British Social Attitudes, the 9th Report*, Dartmouth, 1992. *See* also S Ward, 'Power, Politics and Poverty', in ed P Golding, *Excluding the Poor*, CPAG, 1986.

33. *See* note 32.
34. Rt Hon Norman Lamont MP, House of Commons *Hansard*, 16 May 1991 Col 413.
35. 'The Effects of Taxes and Benefits', *Economic Trends*, January 1993, HMSO, 1993.
36. Speech by the Rt Hon Peter Lilley MP, Secretary of State for Social Security, to the Conservative Party Conference, 7 October 1992.
37. *See* note 36.
38. *The Times*, 15 January 1993.
39. Leader, *Financial Times*, 18 January 1993.
40. For more detail on these debates *see* JC Brown, *Child Benefit: Options for the 1990s*, Save Child Benefit, 1991.
41. *Fabian Review*, Vol 104, No 6, 1992.
42. *See* note 36.
43. Speech by Prime Minister, the Rt Hon John Major MP, to the Carlton Club, 3 February 1993.
44. Speech by Rt Hon Kenneth Clarke QC MP to the Tory Reform Group, 24 November 1991.
45. *See* note 36.
46. *See* note 36.
47. *See* note 43.
48. C Oppenheim in *Social Work Today*, 26 October 1989.
49. Ed D Smith, *Understanding the Underclass*, Policy Studies Institute, 1992.
50. The full exposition of some of Murray's views can be found in C Murray, *Losing ground*, Basic Books Inc (USA), 1984.
51. *Sunday Times*, 26 November 1989.
52. C Murray, 'Rejoinder', *The emerging British underclass*, Institute of Economic Affairs, 1990.
53. F Robinson and N Gregson, 'The "Underclass" ', *Critical Social Policy*, No 34, summer 1992.
54. D Anderson, *Sunday Times*, 29 July 1990.
55. D Anderson, *Sunday Times*, 20 May 1990.
56. G Runciman, quoted in ed D Smith, *see* note 49.
57. F Field, *Losing Out: the emergence of Britain's underclass*, Blackwell, 1989.
58. R Dahrendorf, quoted in ed, D Smith, *see* note 49.
59. *See* note 58.
60. N Buck, quoted in ed, D Smith, *see* note 49.
61. A Heath, quoted in ed, D Smith, *see* note 49.
62. J Bradshaw and H Holmes, *Living on the Edge: a study of the living standards of families on benefit in Tyne and Wear*, Tyneside CPAG, 1989.
63. T Dalrymple, 'The underclass: nasty, brutish and short of human hope', *Daily Telegraph*, 25 January 1993.
64. *Sunday Times*, 26 November 1989.
65. R Lister, *The Exclusive Society: citizenship and the poor*, CPAG Ltd, 1990.
66. *See* Ed, P Golding, *Excluding the Poor*, CPAG, 1986.

CHAPTER TWO

# Poverty: the facts

*Measuring poverty is an exercise in demarcation. Lines have to be drawn where none may be visible and they have to be made bold. Where one draws the line is itself a battlefield.*

(Meghnad Desai, *Excluding the Poor*)[1]

## Introduction

CPAG is in no doubt about the existence, growth and nature of poverty in the United Kingdom today. At its heart, poverty is about exclusion from social participation. However, unlike other countries – such as the United States – in the United Kingdom there is no official poverty line, no government-sanctioned marker which admits the existence of poverty. Nevertheless, since our task is to estimate the extent of poverty, we need to establish such a line – one which divides those who are poor from those who are not poor.

We have chosen to look at two possible poverty lines.

The first poverty line is based on the *Low Income Families* (LIF)[2] statistics which were originally published by the DSS (for the years 1972-85), subsequently by the independent Institute for Fiscal Studies and now under the auspices of the House of Commons Social Security Committee.[3] This series shows the numbers of people living on, below or just above the supplementary benefit income support level. CPAG uses supplementary benefit/income support as a proxy for the poverty line.

The second poverty line is based on the *Households below Average Income*[4] statistics with which the government replaced LIF. We use 50% of average income after housing costs as a proxy for the poverty line.

Each approach has its strengths and weaknesses and by examining the two side by side we are able to present a more comprehensive picture of poverty (see Appendix 1 for more detail).

The first approach, which uses supplementary benefit/income support as a poverty line, allows us to assess how many people are on or below what the state deems a minimum level of income for people who are not in 'full-time' work. Supplementary benefit/income support is set each year by Parliament and is supposed to function as a 'safety net'. Thus, it is a crucial way of assessing the effectiveness of the government's own minimum income guarantee.

The second approach, which uses half of average income after housing costs as a poverty line, draws on official data and is an explicitly relative measure which looks at how people at the bottom of the income distribution have fared in relation to the average.

## Key Results

As we shall see, despite their different approaches, what both methods reveal is crystal clear – that the income represented by either poverty line is unacceptably low in an affluent and civilised society. Living on such levels of income excludes people from the basic goods, resources and services which they have a right to expect. The statistics demonstrate that:

- in 1989, 4,350,000 people (8% of the population) were living *below* income support level. In 1979, 6% of the population were living below the supplementary benefit level;[5]
- in 1989, 11,330,000 people (20% of the population) were living on or below the income support level. In 1979, 14% of the population were living on or below the supplementary benefit level;[6]
- in 1988/89, 12 million people (22% of the population) were living below 50% of average income after housing costs. In 1979, 9% of the population were living below 50% of average income.[7]

*So, whichever way you measure it, poverty has grown significantly over recent years and by 1988/89 between 11 and 12 million people in the United Kingdom – around a fifth of our society – were living in poverty.*

## Context

What is the context in which we are looking at the changes in poverty? The figures from both series cover the period 1979 to 1989. During that time there were major economic and social changes. Between 1979 and 1989 such changes included:[8]

- a rise in the Gross National Product (GNP) of 30% in real (ie, after inflation) terms, although real GNP fell by 2% to 3% between 1979 and 1981 because of the recession;
- very substantial rises in average incomes – a rise of around 30% in real personal disposable income;
- average earnings rose by 26% in real terms, but the earnings of the rich and poor became more dispersed;
- prices increased by 103% (with a peak of 22% in 1980);
- a very sharp rise in unemployment which rose from just over 1 million to around 3 million in 1983 and stayed at that level until 1986, falling to 1.8 million by mid-1989;
- increases in the proportion of the population receiving means-tested benefits from 17% in 1979 to a peak of 24% in 1987 and then a fall to 20% in 1988/89;
- the weakening of some contributory parts of the social security system such as unemployment benefit, leaving many more people to fall back on means-tested benefits;
- a gradual change in employment patterns, with the growth of part-time and self-employed labour;
- bonuses for the average earner and windfalls for the rich through reductions in income tax. However, national insurance contributions and indirect taxes were increased;
- increases in the number of single adults below pension age without children, pensioners and lone parent families; all these groups tend to have lower than average incomes;
- decreases in the number of couples with children and children as a whole.

In short, the persistence of high unemployment coupled with increased average incomes forged a much wider gap between the people who were dependent solely on benefits (which generally rise by the level of inflation only) or reliant on low wages and people on average earnings and above.

## What the figures miss out

Both *Low Income Families* (LIF) and *Households below Average Income* (HBAI) are derived from the same source – the Family Expenditure Survey (FES) – an annual government survey of around 10,000 households in the UK. Due to the nature of the FES, both LIF and HBAI *exclude* the following from their figures:

- people living in institutions – eg, hospitals, nursing homes, residential homes and prisons;
- homeless people.

Neither do they provide an analysis of the data by sex or ethnic origin. The exclusion of homeless people and people living in institutions means that *all* the figures we present below are likely to be an *underestimate*. This is because homeless people and many people living in institutions often have very little money.

## The first source: Low Income Families statistics

### What are the Low Income Families statistics?

The *Low Income Families* statistics 1979-1989 (LIF), produced by the Institute for Fiscal Studies (IFS), were published by the House of Commons Social Security Committee in early 1993.[9] LIF show the numbers of people living on, below and up to 140% of supplementary benefit/ income support. Income support replaced supplementary benefit as part of the 1988 social security changes. Like its predecessor, supplementary benefit, it is a means-tested benefit for people who are not in 'full-time' work (see Appendix 2 for full definition). However, it has a different structure from supplementary benefit. Instead of scale rates and extra weekly additions for certain needs such as heating and diet, income support consists of personal allowances and premia for certain groups such as families with children, pensioners, lone parents, disabled people and carers. This change in the social security system has created some difficulties in looking at these figures over time. However, the IFS has attempted to create a continuous series.[10]

CPAG defines all those living on and below supplementary benefit/income support as living in poverty. It also looks at those people living between 100% and 140% of supplementary benefit/income support and describes them as living on the *margins* of poverty.

## What is the poverty line in the Low Income Families statistics?

The poverty line is measured by the level of income support. It shows that in 1988/89 a two-parent family with two children below 11 years of age were living in poverty if they had an income (after paying for their housing costs) of £79.10 a week. In 1993/94 the same type of family were living in poverty if they had an income (after housing costs) of £108.75 a week. In Table 1 we show what the poverty line is for different families using income support to define poverty.

**TABLE 1**

**The poverty line using income support (after housing costs)**

| Family type | Income support rates April 1988-March 1989[1] | April 1993-March 1994[1] |
|---|---|---|
| **Non-pensioners** | | |
| Single person: aged 18-24 | £26.05 | £34.80 |
| aged 25+ | £33.40 | £44.00 |
| Lone parent with 1 child aged under 11[2] | £54.00 | £73.60 |
| Couple[3] | £51.45 | £69.00 |
| Couple with 2 children[4] (aged under 11) | £79.10 | £108.75 |
| **Pensioners** (aged 60-74) | | |
| Single person | £44.05 | £61.30 |
| Couple | £67.70 | £95.25 |

*Note:*

1. *These figures are the levels of benefit that were paid at the time (ie, they are cash figures which are not adjusted for inflation).*
2. *Lone parent is aged 18 or over.*
3. *At least one member of the couple is aged 18 or over.*
4. *See note 3.*
5. *In 1988/89 income support had to cover a contribution of 20% to the poll tax; from 1993/94 no contribution has to be made to the council tax.*

*SOURCE: National Welfare Benefits Handbook 1988/89 and Welfare Rights Bulletin 111, CPAG Ltd., 1988 and 1992*

## What do the figures from Low Income Families statistics show?

The *Low Income Families* statistics show that in 1989 in the UK:[11]

- 11,330,000 people – a fifth (20%) of the population – were living in poverty (on or below income support). Of these, 4,350,000 people – 8% of the population – were living *below* the poverty line;
- a total of 16,520,000 people – 29% of the population – were living in or on the margins of poverty (up to 140% of income support).

Figure 1 shows the rises in the numbers of people living in poverty or on its margins between 1979 and 1989. Although there is some discontinuity between the figures, it is nevertheless possible to identify the broad trends.

**FIGURE 1: Numbers of people living in or on the margins of poverty in 1979 and 1989 (defined as 140% of supplementary benefit and below).**

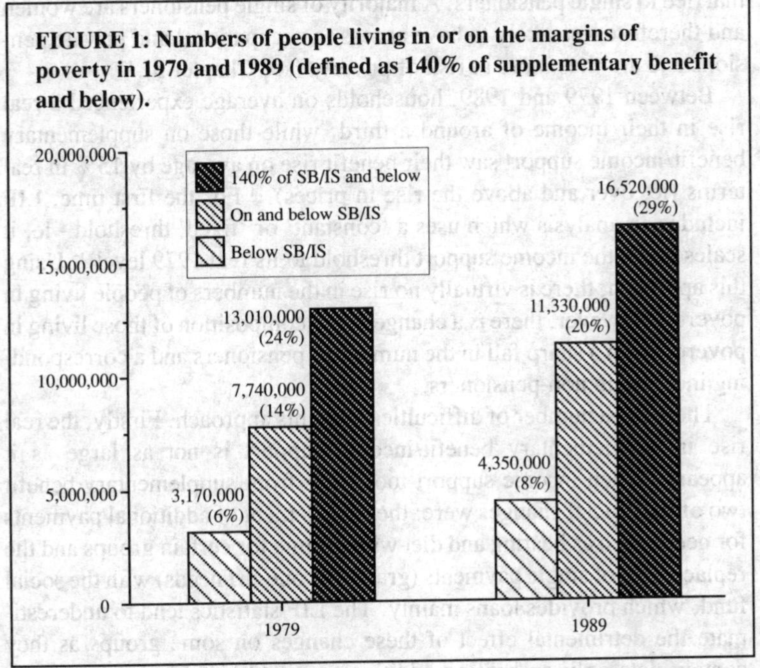


In 1979, 14% of the population was living in poverty, but by 1989 this had risen to a fifth (20%). The bulk of this increase occurred in the early part of the decade due to the sharp rise in unemployment. Since 1987, there has been a slight decline in the numbers in poverty, again reflecting the change in patterns of unemployment – in this case a slight fall. However, there has been a change in the relationship between those living below supplementary benefit/income support and those receiving the benefit. The former group continued to increase between 1987 and 1989 while the latter decreased.[12]

The Social Security Committee looks at the period between 1979 and 1989 as a whole. It shows that the number of pensioners on supplementary benefit/income support has fallen. However, non-pensioners – in particular, couples with children, lone parents, the unemployed and the long-term sick – have increased, and account for most of the rise in the numbers of people living on supplementary benefit/income support over this period. Turning to the numbers living below supplementary benefit/income support, it is single people without children who account for most of the increase between 1979 and 1989. Although the pensioner group has remained relatively stable, there has also been a shift from married to single pensioners. A majority of single pensioners are women and therefore less likely to have access to occupational and private pensions and are thus more at risk of poverty (see Chapter 5).[13]

Between 1979 and 1989, households on average experienced a real rise in their income of around a third, while those on supplementary benefit/income support saw their benefit rise on average by 15% in real terms (ie, over and above the rise in prices).[14] For the first time, LIF includes an analysis which uses a 'constant' or 'fixed' threshold – ie, it scales down the income support threshold to its real 1979 level.[15] Using this approach, there is virtually no rise in the numbers of people living in poverty. However, there *is* a change in the composition of those living in poverty, with a sharp fall in the number of pensioners and a corresponding increase in non-pensioners.

There are a number of difficulties with this approach. Firstly, the real rise in supplementary benefit/income support is not as large as it appears. When income support took over from supplementary benefit two of the crucial changes were: the replacement of additional payments for needs such as heating and diet with premia for certain groups and the replacement of single payments (grants for one-off needs) with the social fund, which provides loans mainly. The LIF statistics tend to underestimate the detrimental effect of these changes on some groups as they contain data only on heating additions available in the supplementary benefit scheme, but no others and do not take into account the change to the social fund at all. (In *Households below Average Income*, the inclusion of the effects of the introduction of the social fund produced a drop of 1% in the average real income of the poorest 10% between 1979 and 1989,[16] see p48). Secondly, using a 'constant' or 'fixed' poverty line is to adopt an 'absolute' approach to poverty. As we saw in Chapter 1 this approach is flawed because it assumes that standards of living and our notions of what is essential or necessary do not change and adapt over time. Such an approach assumes that the poorest should not share in rises in living standards that the rest of society experiences. As the Social Security Committee itself says:

> The long-term rate of supplementary benefit, and the new income support rates together with the range of premiums, provide one guide to society's view on the minimum acceptable living standard for a family who are not in full-time work and who have no other resources. If, over time this minimum standard increases, the number of families deemed to be living on minimum income will also rise. To argue otherwise opens up the notion that as the decades go by the minimum acceptable living standard should not rise at all.[17]

## How many children?

- In 1989,[18] there were 2,760,000 children – 22% of all children – living in poverty (on or below the income support level). Of these 760,000 (6% of all children) were living below the poverty line. In 1979 there were 1,500,000 children living in poverty (11%); of these 520,000 (4% of all children) were living below the poverty line;
- in 1989 there were 3,780,000 children – 30% of all children – living in or on the margins of poverty (below 140% of income support). In 1979 there were 2,580,000 children living in or on the margins of poverty (19%).

A child's risk of falling into poverty depends on the type of family s/he grows up in. In 1989 over three-quarters (76%) of children growing up in lone-parent families were living in poverty compared to 13% of children in two-parent families.

Figure 2 below shows how the number of children in poverty has grown between 1979 and 1989 and how in 1989 there were more children in poverty in lone-parent families than in two-parent families.[19]

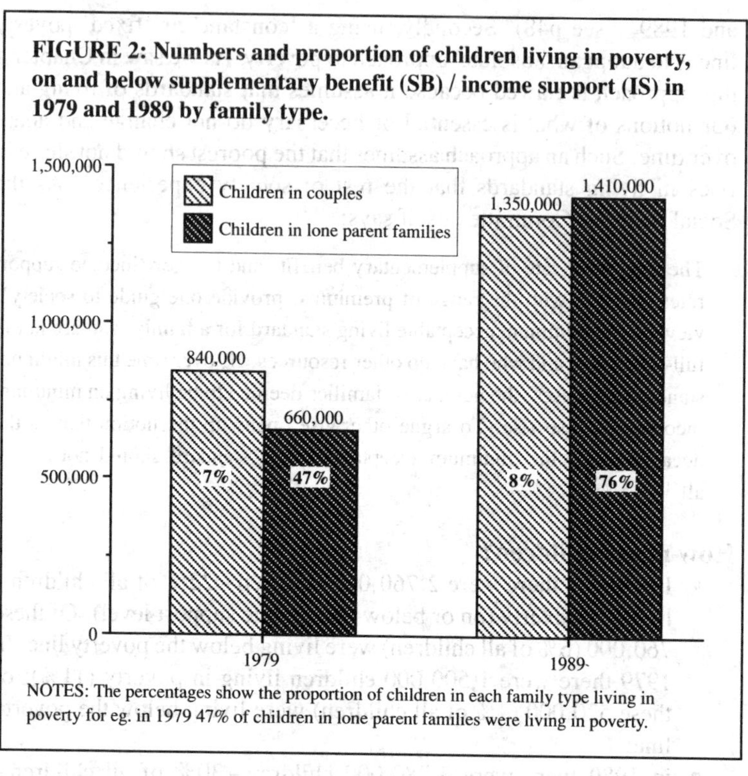


**FIGURE 2: Numbers and proportion of children living in poverty, on and below supplementary benefit (SB) / income support (IS) in 1979 and 1989 by family type.**

NOTES: The percentages show the proportion of children in each family type living in poverty for eg. in 1979 47% of children in lone parent families were living in poverty.

## Falling through the safety net

One of the most important things that the LIF figures reveal is how many people fall through the 'safety net' of income support. In 1989, there were a total of 4,350,000 people (including children) living below income support. The largest groups among this total were single people without children and couples with children (the former accounted for 31% of people falling through the safety net and the latter 28%). Many of the single people living below income support were living in households with other adults; they may have been sharing some of their resources and thus might not have been as poor as they appeared to be. Looking at economic status: 22% of people falling below income support level lived in families with a full-time worker; a further 7% of people lived in families with one or more persons working part time.[20] For many of these people, low earnings play a big part in their poverty.

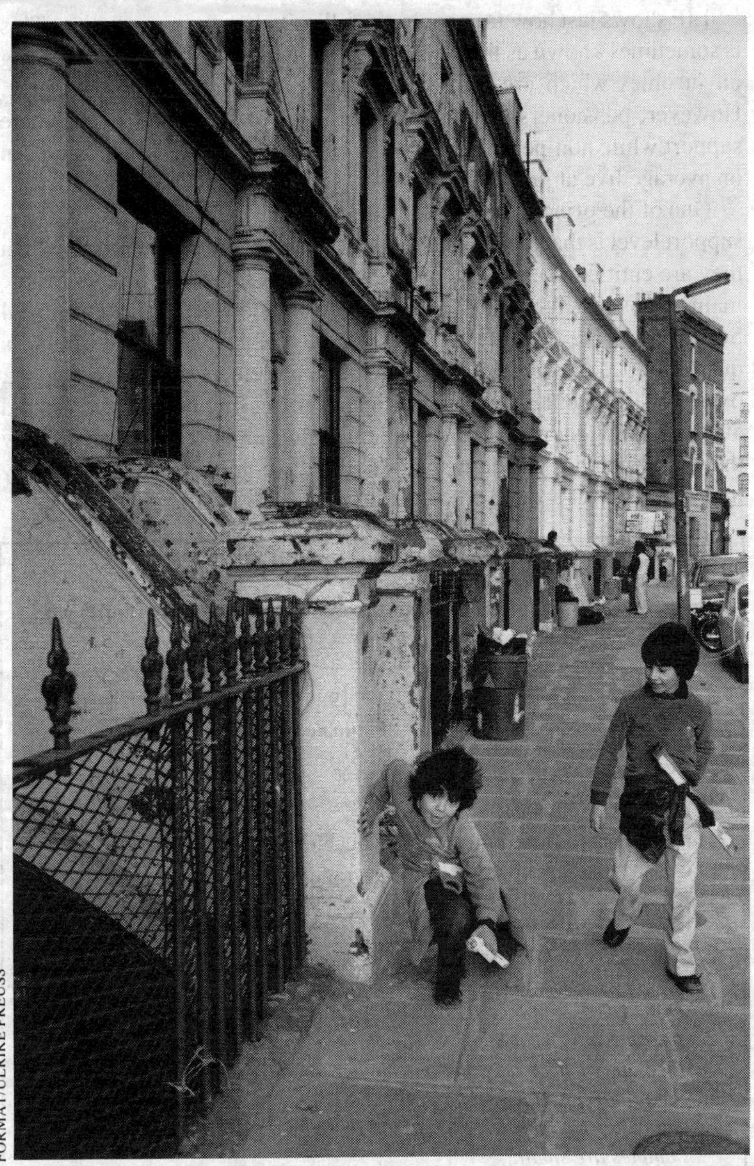

FORMAT/ULRIKE PREUSS

***Children are more vulnerable to poverty than the rest of society. In 1989, over 2.75 million children, close to 1 in 4, were living in poverty.***

LIF shows just how far people are falling below the poverty line. This is sometimes known as the **poverty gap**. On average, families are living on incomes which are around a quarter lower than income support. However, pensioners tend to have resources of around 80% of income support while non-pensioners have around 60%. Couples with children on average live at just under two-thirds of income support.[21]

One of the principal reasons that people are living below the income support level is that they are not taking up means-tested benefits to which they are entitled. Table 2 below shows the latest take-up figures for the main means-tested benefits, produced by both the Department of Social Security and the Institute for Fiscal Studies.[22] It reveals that around a quarter of people were not claiming their entitlement to income support, over 30% of people were not getting their housing benefit and around 50% were not claiming their entitlement to family credit. Research by the Policy Studies Institute suggests that take-up of family credit may now be higher at around 64% in 1991.[23]

**TABLE 2**

**Proportions of people entitled to the main means-tested benefits who were not claiming in 1989 and 1990**

| | 1989 Estimate by: | | 1990 Estimate by: |
|---|---|---|---|
| | DSS[1] | IFS[2] | IFS[2] |
| Income support | 25% | 27% | 25% |
| Housing benefit (for those not on income support) | Not available | 35% | 33% |
| Family credit | 43%[3] | 50%[3] | Not available |

*Notes:*

1. *DSS, Take-up of income related benefits, HMSO, 1993.*
2. *Institute for Fiscal Studies. The IFS have produced two estimates of take-up; we have used the one closest to DSS estimates (though these tend to over-estimate take-up).*
3. *Estimates for family credit should be treated with caution as the samples are small.*

*SOURCES: V Fry and G Stark, The Take-up of means-tested benefits, 1984-1990, IFS, 1993 and DSS, Take-up of income-related benefits, HMSO, 1993.*

## The second source: Households below Average Income

### What are the Households below Average Income statistics?

*Households below Average Income* (HBAI) was published for the first time in 1988. It is now the major source of official information about people living on a low income. The latest edition, *Households below Average Income, a statistical analysis, 1979-1988/89*, was issued quietly in the summer of 1992 just before MPs went off on their summer holidays.[24] It examines the living standards of people in the lower half of the income distribution. The series shows:

- the number of individuals in households with incomes below various thresholds, from 40% average household income to average household income;
- the number of individuals living in households in the bottom 10%, 20%, 30%, 40% and 50% of the income distribution (these are known as decile groups), and the rises in real income for each of these groups.

Following a *Stock-taking Report on Households below Average Income* published in 1991, a number of methodological changes were made to the series.[25] The result is that the data contained in this latest edition use different assumptions and thus produce different results from earlier editions.

### What is the poverty line in Households below Average Income?

*Households below Average Income* does not contain an obvious poverty line. We have chosen 50% of average income as a poverty line, a definition which is widely used by commentators and in international studies.

HBAI presents figures both before and after housing costs. There are arguments for using both measures.[26] We have chosen in most cases here to use figures which show numbers and income after housing costs for the following reasons: firstly, the figures are more comparable with supplementary benefit/income support (as these are also after housing costs); secondly, housing expenditure is different from other kinds of

**TABLE 3**

**The poverty line in 1988/89 and 1993: defined as 50% average income (after housing costs) £ per week[1]**

| | 50% of average income | |
|---|---|---|
| | 1988/89[2] | 1993[3] |
| | £ per week | |
| single person | £46 | £59 |
| couple | £83 | £107 |
| single person with 1 child (aged 3) | £61 | £79 |
| couple with 2 children (aged 3 and 6) | £115 | £148 |

*Notes:*

1. *These figures are cash figures which are not adjusted for inflation.*
2. *These figures are based on half average equivalised income after housing costs in January 1989 of £83 a week. This is adjusted for different family types using the equivalence scales in HBAI.*
3. *Figures for 1993 are based on uprating the figures for 1988/89 by the rise in personal disposable income per head between the first quarter of 1989 and the first quarter of 1993 (29%).*

*SOURCE: DSS, Households below Average Income, A Statistical Analysis, 1979-1988/89, Government Statistical Service, HMSO, 1992, supplemented by information from the DSS; Economic Trends (annual supplement 1993 edition, HMSO, 1993) and forecasts from the London Business School.*

expenditure – it varies widely depending on the area in which you live, and the time in your life; and thirdly, it is also a fixed cost for many families, particularly those on low incomes, who often have little choice about the amount they spend on their housing and therefore about the money they have left, for example, to spend on their children's needs.

For the first time, HBAI amalgamates two years' data for 1988 and 1989. We show in Table 3 what a poverty line measured by 50% of average income after housing costs was in 1988/89 (the date of the latest set of figures) and updated to 1993 for different types of family. In 1988/89 a two-parent family with two children (aged 3 and 6) on an income of less than £115 a week (after paying for their housing costs) was living below the poverty line (defined as below 50% of average income). In 1993 a similar family with an income of less than £148 a week was living below the poverty line defined in the same way.

## What do the figures show in Households below Average Income?

*Households below Average Income* (HBAI) presents the official figures on low income. HBAI shows that in the UK in 1988/89:

- 12 million people were living in poverty (below 50% of average income after housing costs) – over a fifth of the population. This is well over double the number in 1979 – 5 million – 9% of the population.

### Who is in poverty?

The global figure of 12 million hides within it important patterns. We can look at the composition of the poor – which groups make up the bulk of those in poverty; we can also assess the risk of poverty – which groups are most likely to be poor. These two things are different – eg, lone parents only make up a small proportion of the total number of people in poverty as they are a small group; however, they have a high risk of poverty.

First we look at the composition of the poor, by economic status and family status. The pie charts on page 42 illustrate how poverty is distributed among different groups (see Figure 3).

Looking at economic status first, unemployment is a crucial cause of poverty, accounting for nearly a fifth of those in poverty. For the first time, the data look both at the different work patterns within couples and at differences between full- and part-time work. Not surprisingly, couples where both partners are working full time and single people in full-time work make up only 6% of those in poverty. The growing importance of two wages coming in to protect couples and families against poverty is illustrated by the figures which show that couples where only one member is working full time and one not at all make up some 13% of those in poverty. People in families where one or more is in part-time work make up 7% of those in poverty.[27]

Turning to family status, couples with children account for the largest group in poverty – 35%. The next largest group is pensioners who make up 30% of those in poverty.[28] Single people with and without children account for smaller proportions of those in poverty.

The risk of poverty for different groups is illustrated clearly in Figures 4 and 5.

**FIGURE 3:**
**The composition of the poor (defined as living below 50% of average income after housing costs) in 1988/89:**

**by family status**

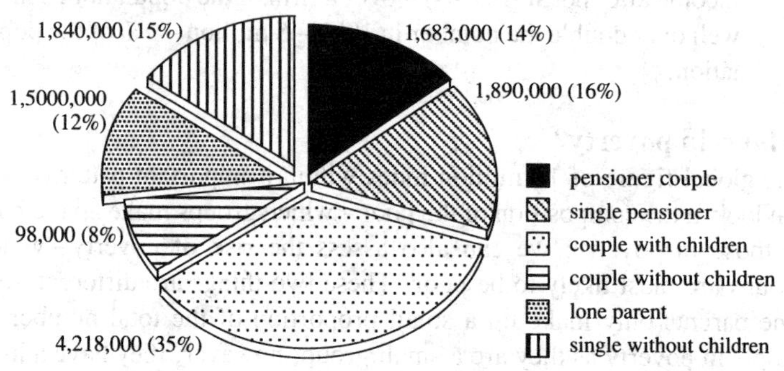


**by economic status**

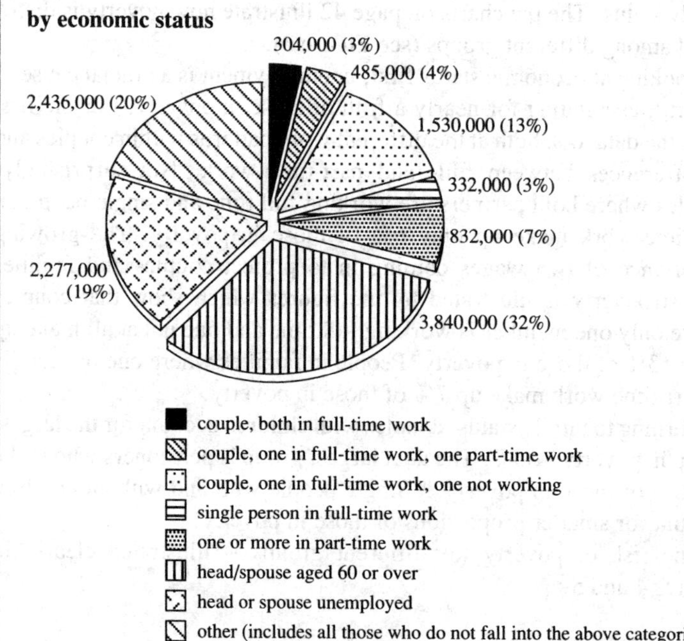

**FIGURE 4: The risk of poverty by economic status in 1988/89**

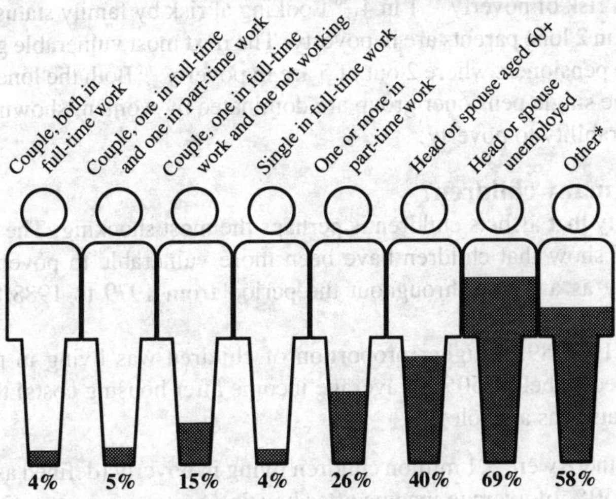


Proportion living in poverty
(below 50% average income after housing costs)

*NOTE: Other = all those not included in previous groups.

**FIGURE 5: The risk of poverty by family status in 1988/89**

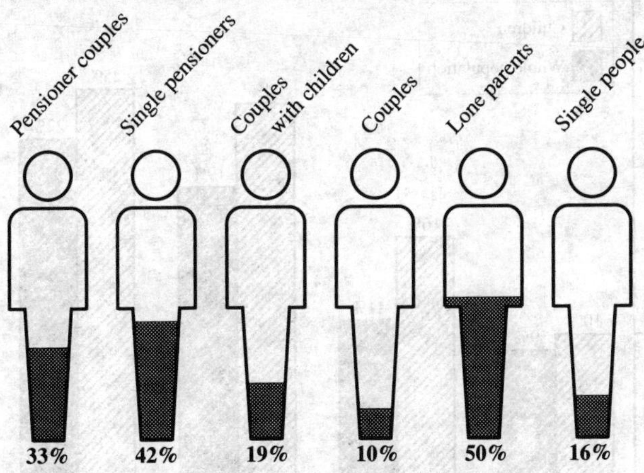


Proportion living in poverty
(below 50% average income after housing costs)

The group with the highest risk is the unemployed – 7 out of 10 are in poverty. People in families where there is only part-time work also carry a high risk of poverty – 1 in 4.[29] Looking at risk by family status shows that 1 in 2 lone parents are in poverty. The next most vulnerable group is single pensioners where 2 out of 5 are in poverty.[30] Both the lone parent and the single pensioner group are dominated by women, showing their vulnerability to poverty.

## How many children?

Poverty that afflicts children is perhaps the most shocking. The figures below show that children have been more vulnerable to poverty than society as a whole throughout the period from 1979 to 1988/89 (see Figure 6).

In 1988/89, a higher proportion of children was living in poverty (defined as below 50% of average income after housing costs) than the population as a whole:[31]

- there were 3.1 million children living in poverty (defined as below 50% of average income after housing costs) – a quarter (25%) of

**FIGURE 6: Proportion of children and population living in poverty between 1979–1988/89 (living below 50% average income after housing costs).**

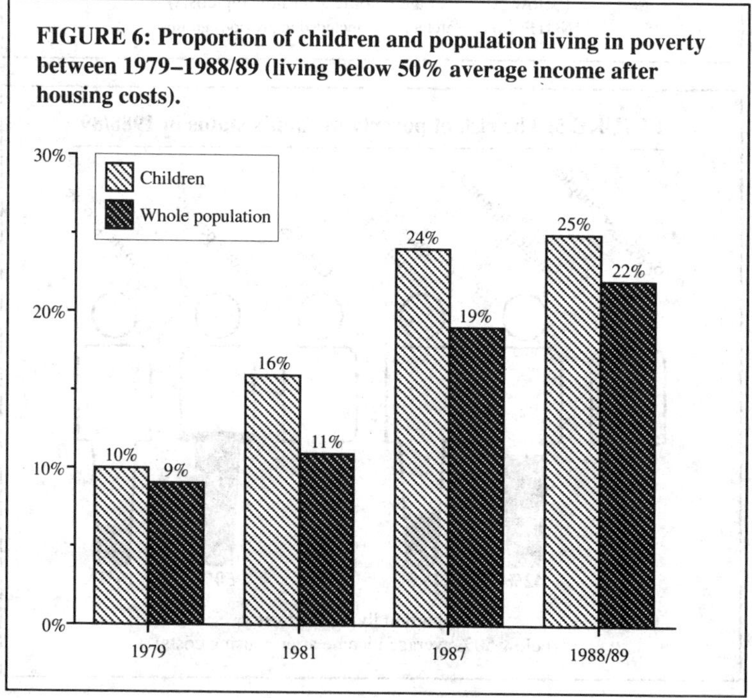

all children. This compares to 1.4 million in 1979 – 10% of all children.

## Which children are in poverty?

Of the 3.1 million children living in poverty (defined as below 50% of average income after housing costs) in 1988/89:[32]

- 1,076,000 were living in families where there was one or more full-time workers – 35% of all children living in poverty;
- 2,034,000 were living in families where there was no full-time worker – 65% of all children living in poverty. Within this group the largest category was children growing up in lone-parent families who numbered 896,000, some 29% of the total number of children living in poverty.

Children at greatest risk of poverty were those living in families where there was no full-time worker, particularly in large families:

- 86% of children in couples with no full-time worker and with 3 or more children were living in poverty;
- 67% of children in couples with no full-time worker and with 1 or 2 children were living in poverty;
- 64% of children in lone-parent families were living in poverty.

The risk of poverty was much lower for children in families where there was a full-time worker; however, there was still an increased risk of poverty for large families:

- 8% of children in families with one or more full-time workers and with 1 or 2 children were in poverty;
- 19% of children in families with one or more full-time workers and with 3 or more children were in poverty.

## What has happened since 1979?

*Households below Average Income* only provides comparative data as far back as 1979, so we cannot make comparisons over a longer time span. But poverty increased dramatically between 1979 and 1988/89 whether measured before or after housing costs (see Table 4).

The HBAI statistics also use a 'constant'/'fixed' threshold in the same way as the LIF statistics (see p34). Even using this approach poverty has increased. Using 50% of average income at its 1979 real level (after housing costs), poverty has increased from 5 million to 5.3 million – a rise of 6%.[33] Some groups show an increased risk of poverty – eg,

**TABLE 4**

**Numbers and proportions of individuals living below 50% of average income before and after housing costs**

| | Before housing costs | | After housing costs | |
|---|---|---|---|---|
| | Nos: millions | % | Nos: millions | % |
| 1979 | 4.4 | 8 | 5.0 | 9 |
| 1981 | 4.7 | 9 | 6.2 | 11 |
| 1987 | 8.7 | 16 | 10.5 | 19 |
| 1988/89 | 10.4 | 19 | 12.0 | 22 |

*Note: figures for individuals include children*

couples with children and single people without children. Using this constant poverty line, the number of children in poverty has also increased from 1.4 to 1.6 million – a rise of 14%.[34] However, as we outlined earlier we do not believe that this is the right approach to looking at changes in poverty over time.

By considering the poorest 10% of the population in 1979 and 1988/89 (after housing costs), we can see how the *composition* of the poorest groups has changed.[35] Figure 7 shows how pensioners made up a much smaller proportion of the poorest 10% in 1988/89 than in 1979 (down from 31% to 14% of the bottom 10%); couples with children made up a slightly larger proportion (up from 41% to 44%); and in particular single people without children leapt from making up 10% of the bottom 10% in 1979 to 22% in 1988/89 (largely due to higher unemployment and changes in benefit rules). Looking at *economic* status, the effect of unemployment is directly apparent – in 1979 only 16% of the bottom 10% were unemployed, but by 1988/89 the figure had risen to 30%. Even the proportion of couples and single people in full-time work in the bottom 10% increased by a few percentage points, despite the fact that average earnings over the period had risen substantially (see Figure 7).

## Growing divisions

*The figures also show a stark picture of poor people falling further and further behind the rest of society since 1979.* Between 1979 and 1988/89 the poorest 10% (known as decile group – see Appendix 2) experienced a *fall* in their real income after housing costs of 6%, while the average had an increase of 30%. Incomes before housing costs also show a very large gap between the poorest and the average – the real incomes of the

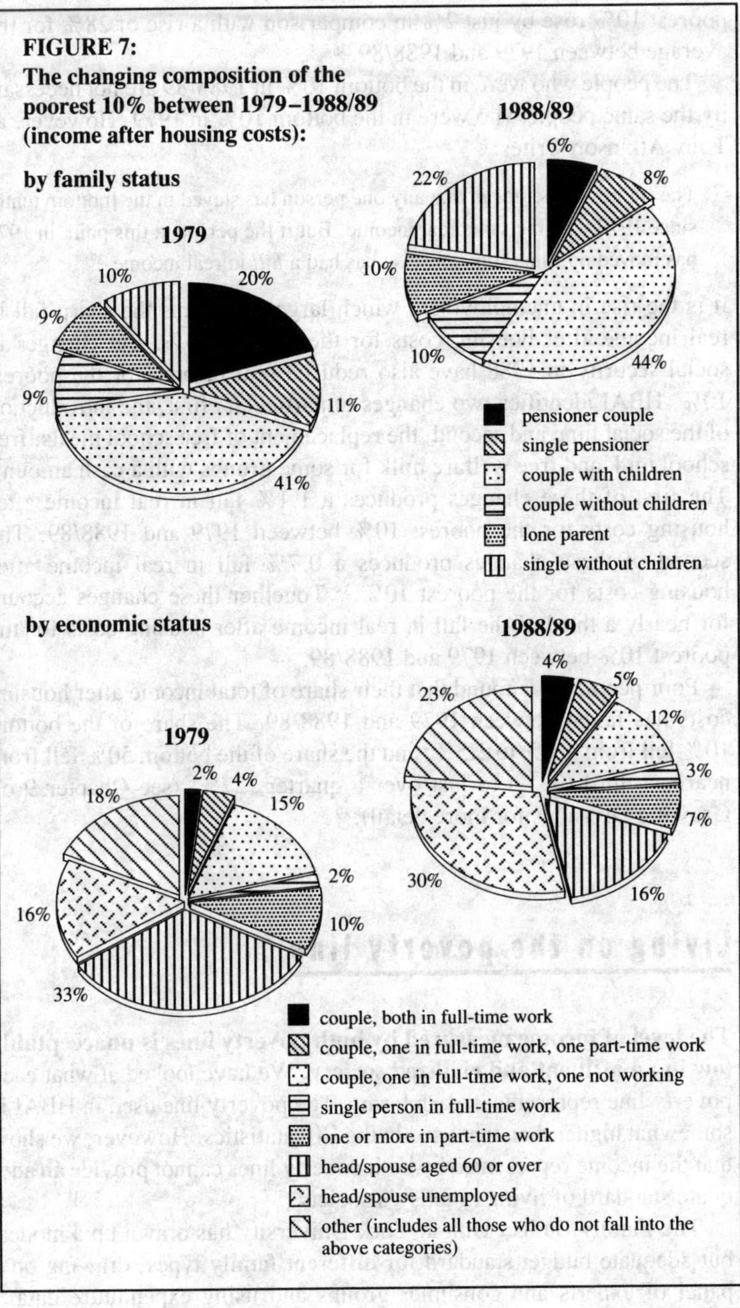
FIGURE 7:
The changing composition of the poorest 10% between 1979–1988/89 (income after housing costs):
by family status
1979
20%
11%
41%
9%
9%
10%
1988/89
6%
8%
44%
10%
10%
22%
pensioner couple
single pensioner
couple with children
couple without children
lone parent
single without children
by economic status
1979
2%
4%
15%
2%
10%
33%
16%
18%
1988/89
4%
5%
12%
3%
7%
16%
30%
23%
couple, both in full-time work
couple, one in full-time work, one part-time work
couple, one in full-time work, one not working
single person in full-time work
one or more in part-time work
head/spouse aged 60 or over
head/spouse unemployed
other (includes all those who do not fall into the above categories)

poorest 10% rose by just 2% in comparison with a rise of 28% for the average between 1979 and 1988/89.[36]

The people who were in the bottom 10% in 1988/89 are not necessarily the same people who were in the bottom 10% in 1979. However, as Tony Atkinson writes:

> The figures do not mean that any one person has stayed in the [bottom tenth] since 1979 with the same real income. But if the person at this point in 1979 has moved up, then someone else has had a *fall* in real income.[37]

It is the rise in unemployment which largely explains the sharp fall in real income after housing costs for the poorest 10%. But changes in social security in 1988 have also reduced real income for the poorest 10%. HBAI identifies two changes in particular: first, the introduction of the social fund and second, the replacement of free school meals, free school milk and free welfare milk for some groups with a cash amount. The first of these changes produces a 1.1% fall in real income after housing costs for the poorest 10% between 1979 and 1988/89. The second of these changes produces a 0.7% fall in real income after housing costs for the poorest 10%.[38] Together these changes account for nearly a third of the fall in real income after housing costs for the poorest 10% between 1979 and 1988/89.

Poor people have found that their share of total income after housing costs has fallen between 1979 and 1988/89. The share of the bottom 10% fell from 4.0% to 2.5%, and the share of the bottom 50% fell from nearly a third (32%) to just over a quarter (27%) (see Chapter 9 on Growing Divisions for more detail).[39]

## Living on the poverty line

**The level of income measured by both poverty lines is unacceptably low in an affluent and civilized society.** We have looked at what each poverty line represents in cash terms. The poverty line used in HBAI is somewhat higher than that used in the LIF statistics. However, we show that the income represented by both poverty lines cannot provide an adequate standard of living in today's society.

The Family Budget Unit at York University has drawn up a modest but adequate budget standard for different family types, drawing on a panel of experts and consumer groups and using expenditure data.[40]

**TABLE 5**

**Modest but adequate budget**

| Examples of items included | Examples of items excluded |
|---|---|
| Basic designs, mass manufactured furniture, textiles and hardware | Antiques, handmade or precious household durables |
| Prescription charges, dental care, sight test | Spectacles, private health care |
| Fridge-freezer, washing machine, microwave, food-mixer, sewing machine | Tumble-dryer, shower, electric blankets |
| Basic clothing, sensible designs | Second-hand, designer and high fashion clothing |
| TV, video hire, basic music system and camera | Children's TVs, compact discs, camcorders |
| Second-hand 5-year-old car, second-hand adult bicycle, new children's bikes | A second car, caravan, camping equipment, mountain bikes |
| Basic jewellery, watch | Precious jewellery |
| Basic cosmetics, haircuts | Perfume, hair perm |
| Alcohol – men 14 units, women 10 units (2/3 HEA safety limit) | Smoking |
| One week annual holiday | Holiday abroad |
| Walking, swimming, cycling, football, cinema, panto every two years, youth club, scouts/guides | Fishing, water sports, horse-riding, creative or educational adult classes, children's ballet/music lessons |

*SOURCE: Social Policy Research Findings, No. 31, Joseph Rowntree Foundation, November 1992, derived from J Bradshaw et al, Summary Budget Standards for Six Households, Family Budget Unit, 1992*

Items are included in the budget if more than half the population have them or they are regarded as necessities in public opinion surveys. The kinds of items which are included and excluded in this budget standard are listed in Table 5. For example, it includes one week's annual holiday

**TABLE 6**

**A comparison of the modest but adequate (MBA) budget with the income support and 50% of average income[1] poverty lines (£ per week, 1993 prices)[2]**

| | Single Man | Two Adults | Lone Mother Two younger children[3] | Two adults Two younger children[3] |
|---|---|---|---|---|
| Housing (tenants) | 33.65 | 36.76 | 44.95 | 48.88 |
| Food | 27.11 | 40.70 | 40.64 | 60.67 |
| Fuel | 5.99 | 7.47 | 13.84 | 15.32 |
| Alcohol | 7.86 | 13.47 | 5.62 | 13.47 |
| Clothing | 7.10 | 15.24 | 23.20 | 30.27 |
| Household goods | 9.35 | 17.61 | 29.04 | 30.62 |
| Household services | 5.56 | 8.64 | 5.87 | 8.57 |
| Personal care | 3.76 | 8.90 | 7.75 | 10.99 |
| Motoring | 34.71 | 34.74 | 35.24 | 37.57 |
| Fares | 3.24 | 5.36 | 5.13 | 10.57 |
| Leisure goods | 6.39 | 8.82 | 15.85 | 16.08 |
| Leisure services | 10.73 | 20.33 | 11.70 | 17.26 |
| Child care costs[4] | - | - | 65.27 | 26.99 |
| **Total for Tenants** | **155.45** | **218.04** | **304.10** | **327.26** |
| Less housing costs[5] | 121.80 | 181.28 | 259.15 | 278.38 |
| Income support poverty line | 44.00 | 69.00 | 88.65 | 108.75 |
| % of MBA budget met by income support | 36% | 38% | 34% | 39% |
| 50% average income poverty line | 59.00 | 107.00 | 103.00 | 151.00 |
| % of MBA budget met by 50% of average income | 48% | 59% | 40% | 54% |

*Notes:*

1. *After housing costs.*
2. *The MBA budget has been updated to 1993 prices using a projection for the third quarter of 1993 from an average of independent forecasters.*
3. *Children aged 4 and 10.*
4. *Includes childcare costs which are not incurred by everyone.*
5. *Housing costs are deducted for the purposes of comparison with the poverty lines which are after housing costs.*

*SOURCE: Social Policy Research Findings, No 31, Joseph Rowntree Foundation, derived from J Bradshaw et al, Summary Budget Standards for Six Households, Family Budget Unit, 1992.*

in the UK, but excludes a holiday abroad; it includes a sight test but excludes the cost of spectacles.[41] The modest but adequate budget standard can be seen as representing a level of income which allows people to participate fully in society rather than simply exist.

In Table 6 we compare the poverty lines represented by income support and 50% of average income after housing costs with the modest but adequate budget standard. It shows that both poverty lines fall far below this standard, in particular for families with children. For example, income support for a couple with two children represents only 39% of the modest but adequate budget; 50% of average income represents only 54%.

The 11-12 million people who are living in poverty according to either definition are foregoing many of the things that more than half of society takes for granted, whether it is a varied and healthy diet, enough money for transport, new but basic clothing, or treats such as going to the pantomime once every two years. They also fall so far below this level that they are going without many of the most basic essentials.

## Conclusion

This chapter has looked at bare facts and figures about poverty in the UK. The task of estimating the extent of poverty is made much more difficult because no government of any political colour has established an official poverty line; there has been no attempt to relate rates of benefit to research into people's basic needs; and government statistics which measure low income have been delayed and changed, thus breaking continuity over time.

The government has made improvements in how it produces information on low income. It is undertaking a new Family Resources Survey which will provide new and valuable material. It is now committed to producing HBAI each year and has provided more extensive material modelling the effects of different assumptions. However, it has continued its usual practice of issuing the figures just before the parliamentary recess, minimising public debate. The issue of how and when statistics on low income are published is crucial. It is only when the facts are exposed to the glare of publicity and open scrutiny that we can discuss the policies and action which are so urgently needed.

Poverty has grown rapidly between 1979 and 1988/89. Whichever poverty line is used, around a fifth of our society was living in poverty in the UK in 1989. The poverty encountered by children is even greater than for society as a whole – around a quarter of children in the UK were living in poverty in 1988/89. Over 4 million people were living below the 'safety net' of income support in 1989. There have been important changes since 1979, with a decline in the proportion of pensioners in the poorest 10% and a rise in the proportion of single people without children and families with children. While the average person has found that their real income has grown very comfortably by 30% between 1979 and 1988/89, the poorest have seen a fall of 6% in their real incomes (after paying for their housing costs).

The figures we have looked at stop in 1989. Since then we have entered a full-blown recession. Average household income and expenditure have fallen between 1990 and 1991.[42] Unemployment is sharply rising once again. Between 1989 and 1993 unemployment rose by over 80%, from 1.6 million to 3 million people, according to official figures. It is likely to stay over 3 million for several years after the recession is over. Undoubtedly yet more people are in poverty today as a result of the unrelenting rise in unemployment.

## NOTES

1. M Desai, 'Drawing the Line', in ed P Golding, *Excluding the Poor*, CPAG 1986.
2. DHSS, *Low Income Families*, 1985, 1988.
3. Social Security Committee, Second Report, *Low Income Statistics: Low Income Families (LIF) 1979-1989*, 359, HMSO, 1993.
4. DSS, *Households below Average Income* (HBAI), *A Statistical Analysis, 1979-1988/89*, Government Statistical Service, HMSO, 1992.
5. LIF, *see* note 3.
6. LIF, *see* note 3.
7. HBAI, *see* note 4.
8. HBAI, *see* note 4.
9. LIF, *see* note 3.
10. LIF, Appendix 1, *see* note 3.
11. LIF, *see* note 3.
12. LIF, *see* note 3.
13. LIF, *see* note 3.
14. LIF, *see* note 3.
15. This is done using the 'Rossi' index, ie, the retail prices index minus housing costs.
16. HBAI, Appendix 6, *see* note 4.
17. LIF, para 63, *see* note 3.
18. Derived from LIF, *see* note 3. Note that LIF does not include a breakdown of those on SB/IS by family type for Northern Ireland. This leads to the anomaly that the figures for children *exclude those on SB/IS in N. Ireland*, but include those *below*

SB/IS in N. Ireland. They therefore underestimate the extent of child poverty in the UK.

19. *See* note 17.
20. LIF, *see* note 3.
21. LIF, *see* note 3.
22. DSS, *Take-up of income related benefits*, HMSO, 1993 and V Fry and G Stark, *The Take-Up of Means-tested benefits, 1984-1990*, Institute for Fiscal Studies, 1993.
23. A Marsh and S McKay, 'Supplementing Low Wages: 50 years after Beveridge', unpublished paper by Beveridge Conference, 1992.
24. HBAI, *see* note 4.
25. DSS, *Stocktaking Report, Households below Average Income*, 1991.
26. HBAI; refer to Appendix 1 for a fuller discussion of these issues, *see* note 4.
27. HBAI, Table F2 (AHC), *see* note 4.
28. HBAI, Table F1 ((AHC), *see* note 4.
29. *See* note 27.
30. *See* note 28.
31. HBAI, Table F3 (AHC), *see* note 4.
32. *See* note 31.
33. HBAI, Table E1 (AHC), *see* note 4.
34. *See* note 33.
35. HBAI, Tables D1 and D2 (AHC), *see* note 4.
36. HBAI, Table A1, *see* note 4. The changes in real income of the bottom decile are of less certain accuracy due to sampling error and the choice of equivalence scales.
37. AB Atkinson, 'DSS Report on Households below Average Income 1981-1987', paper for the Social Services Select Committee, 1990.
38. HBAI, Appendix 6, *see* note 4.
39. HBAI, Table A3, *see* note 4.
40. J Bradshaw, L. Hicks, H Parker, *Summary Budget Standards for Six Households*, Family Budget Unit, Working Paper No 12, 1992.
41. *Social Policy Research Findings, No 31*, Joseph Rowntree Foundation, November 1992.
42. *Social Trends 23*, Government Statistical Service, 1993.

CHAPTER THREE

# The causes of poverty

A factory closes its doors, casual workers are laid off, management is 'thinned out' – unemployment looms. A woman works a 50-hour week doing two jobs to scrape together a living. A lone mother struggles on benefit to meet the costs of her child – the only employment on offer would barely pay for her childcare. A man, prematurely retired because of chronic sickness, lives on invalidity pension which fails to cover the costs of his disability and his ordinary needs. *All these are instances of poverty.*

Poverty is caused by not having access to decently paid employment. It is also the result of the extra costs of having a child or a disability. Poverty is particularly acute when these two factors combine. Moreover, the social security system often fails to meet adequately the needs generated by unemployment, low pay, having a child or coping with a disability. Thus, poverty is also caused by social policy – ie, it is avoidable, not just the consequence of random misfortune. The risk of poverty is not shared out evenly – it depends on social class, on gender and on race. We look separately at women (Chapter 5) and race (Chapter 6). Below we explore some of the principal causes of poverty.

## Unemployment

> I mean we can manage now – we haven't got a right lot of choice but to manage, have we? We're not rock bottom, but I think if it goes on much longer we could be going that way . . . It's getting harder to manage each week . . . I'd love a holiday, really would love a complete break, but we haven't got much chance have we? I mean it's natural to want holidays and things isn't it? . . . I think everyone needs a holiday, I don't care who you are. There's no way we can . . . but if you're working you don't have this problem. (Mr Hawkins)[1]

The stubborn persistence of the recession has brought soaring unemployment once again and with it rapidly growing poverty. The UK now has an unemployment rate which is well above the European Community average.[2] In December 1992, the official rate of unemployment in the UK stood at 10.5% – 2,973,500 people.[3] This is well over two and a half times as high as the number in April 1979 when there were 1,089,100 unemployed people, a rate of 4.1%.[4]

The method of counting unemployed people is controversial. In the UK, the government uses the 'claimant count' – the number of unemployed people receiving benefits or signing on to get credited national insurance contributions. Any changes in benefit rules are translated immediately into changes in the number of people officially classed as unemployed. According to the Unemployment Unit, the government has changed the method of counting unemployed people 30 times since 1979.[5] These changes fall into four broad types: (i) statistical changes such as limiting the count to people actually receiving benefits or contribution credits; (ii) changes in benefit rules; (iii) administrative changes such as tightening up the availability for work test; and (iv) temporary work and training schemes.[6] According to the Unit, the true story of unemployment is much worse than the official version; it estimates unemployment at 14.2% in December 1992 – a total of 4,138,900 people.[7]

In many cases, the sharp divide between the worlds of unemployment and work is not an accurate reflection of reality. A 1987 survey by the Department of Employment of people who became unemployed confirms the picture of frequent bouts of unemployment: 63% of the unemployed had signed on in the previous five years; 41% of their last jobs had been held for less than six months; 24% left their last jobs because they were seasonal or temporary. A further 28% had left their last jobs through redundancy; 22% had left voluntarily and 11% had been dismissed.[8]

New research by Bill Daniel at the Policy Studies Institute suggests that the unemployed are not a fixed group, but rather one whose composition is constantly changing.[9] Increases in unemployment occur when inflows into unemployment outnumber the outflows into employment. The 'unemployed' can be divided into people who are recurrently unemployed and the long-term unemployed. This is how Daniel describes the patterns of recurrent unemployment:

> so far as the unemployed flow as a whole are concerned, they tended to work in low paid, low skilled and manifestly insecure jobs. They lost them with

> little notice and little or no compensation. Despite the fact that being in work furnished them with relatively poor rewards, they found being out of work was so much worse that they were generally prepared to take the first job offered them, however unsatisfactory, simply to be back in work. Again, although they tended to be low paid in their previous jobs, they took a pay cut, on average, in order to return to work. Moreover, and perhaps most importantly, for those who found new jobs relatively quickly, those new jobs proved to be only temporary in most cases.[10]

Unemployment is not shared evenly. Particular areas of the country and certain sections of society bear the brunt (see Chapter 7 for more detail). For example, in December 1992, unemployment ranged from 14.6% in Northern Ireland to 8.5% in East Anglia.[11]

As well as regional differences, the likelihood of unemployment is also determined by social class, race and sex. For example, in 1990 the unemployment rate was seven times as high for general labourers (16.3%) as for managerial and professional workers (2.3%).[12]

In a period of high unemployment, the numbers of people who are long-term unemployed (for a year or more) increases. Daniel divides the long-term unemployed into three groups: older workers who are near retirement; people who are prone to ill health or not fully fit; and people who are without skills and qualifications.[13] In October 1992, 955,600 people were long-term unemployed – over a third (34%) of all unemployed people.[14] In May 1991, there were 401,700 parents on income support who had been registered as unemployed for a year or more.[15] Families sometimes experience multiple unemployment. In 1992, 210,000 families contained two or more unemployed people.[16] Poverty is most intense amongst long-term unemployed families, because savings are used up, borrowing increases and household goods have to be replaced.

Unemployment means *poverty*. Daniel found that unemployment, however brief, caused both hardship and trauma. When people were asked how they viewed their experience of unemployment, the group as a whole ranked it close to the worst experience they had endured. When asked about the worst things about being out of work, 78% identified lack of money or not being able to afford goods or activities; 60% identified boredom or not having anything to do. Substantial minorities talked of depression and shame.[17] One survey on living standards during unemployment showed that after three months of unemployment the average disposable income of families dropped to 59% of what it had been before unemployment. Families immediately reduced their spending on food, clothing and entertainments. Unemployment was also likely to cause psychological distress: 38% thought that the worst thing about being unemployed was being short of money, but 53% identified being bored, depressed, feeling dependent or losing control as being the prime cause of stress (see Chapter 4).[18] If a man becomes unemployed there is a strong likelihood that his wife will give up paid work as well. This is because of the benefit rules – if the family is living on income support, a wife's earnings are offset against the benefit pound for pound (after a small amount of earnings is ignored). Thus, the woman would have to be able to command a high wage to make it worthwhile for the whole family to come off benefit. So unemployment in couples often means a sharp drop in income from a two-earner family to no earners at all.[19]

## Benefits for unemployed people

> Unemployed people, rightly or wrongly, accept that they must be content to manage on incomes substantially below those of most people in work. But social justice demands that the gap between earnings and benefits should not be so wide that those without jobs are condemned to an impoverished existence on the margins of society . . . The right to decent benefits paid in a dignified manner is no substitute for a job; but as long as jobs are not available for all who seek them, it is an essential requirement.
>
> (Tony Lynes, *The wrong side of the tracks*)[20]

According to the *British Social Attitudes Survey*, the public is less generous in its attitudes to unemployed people than to the elderly. In 1990 only 8% of people surveyed chose unemployment benefits as a priority for much more government spending in comparison with 30% for old age pensions. The survey also identifies public misconceptions about levels of benefits: only 12% thought that a hypothetical couple on unemployment benefit were 'really poor'; however, when they were told the amount that the couple were actually receiving the proportion rose to 42%.[21]

In recent years, while unemployment has soared, benefits for unemployed people have been cut. Unemployed people can rely either on *unemployment benefit*, a national insurance contributory benefit, or on *income support* which is means-tested, or on a combination of the two. The advantage of the former is that it is not means-tested and it is paid on an individual basis (so that an unemployed wife can receive unemployment benefit and her husband can continue to work without his earnings affecting her entitlement to benefit). However, because contributions have to be made and unemployment benefit lasts for only a year, many people have been forced on to means-tested income support. In 1991-92, unemployment benefit supported 29% of unemployed people in whole or part; the rest relied solely on means-tested income support.[22] Some of the cuts and changes made to benefits for unemployed people are listed here:[23]

- In 1980, 5% was cut from unemployment benefit and only restored in 1983.
- In 1980, the earnings-related supplement to unemployment benefit was phased out, and finally abolished in 1982.
- In 1984, the children's additions for unemployment benefit were abolished.
- In recent years, unemployment benefit has dropped as a proportion of average earnings: in 1971 for a single person it was 17.5% of average male earnings; this dropped to 16.2% in 1979 and then again to 14.2% in 1992.[24]
- The maximum period of disqualification from unemployment benefit when someone is 'voluntarily unemployed' has increased from 6 weeks to 26 weeks. During that time income support is *cut* by 20% or 40%.[25]
- On the means-tested side, the 1986 Social Security Act replaced supplementary benefit with income support which is made up of personal allowances with premia for certain groups, such as pensioners, people who are sick or who have a disability, families with children and lone-parent families. Unemployed people, however, receive no special premium to supplement their basic benefit.
- The Social Security Act 1986 also ushered in substantial cuts in benefit for young people. Young people aged 16 and 17 can only receive income support if they have a Youth Training place or if they fall into one of the strictly defined categories of severe hardship. Otherwise they have to fend for themselves with little or no support from the state. A lower rate of income support for 18- to 24-year-olds for single and childless claimants was also introduced.
- Since 1988, it has become more difficult to satisfy the contribution conditions for unemployment benefit because benefit rights rely on contributions paid in the two previous years (rather than one) and contributions must be paid rather than credited in at least one of those years. The latter measure particularly affects women who may have been caring for a child or elderly person.

- New rules on availability for work and actively seeking work for unemployed people have deterred many from claiming benefits. The process of claiming and receiving benefits for unemployment has become increasingly stigmatising.[26]

## Poverty in employment

> The pay is quite poor but it's better than unemployment benefit, even if it is only for a limited period . . . The problem I found with doing casual work is that you have no security, not knowing from one week to the next if your contract will be terminated . . . The insecurity of the casual job was the worst problem for me because of all my commitments at home.
>
> (Liz, lone mother of two)[27]

The poverty of low wages and poor working conditions is often still a hidden factor in the poverty debate. Recent government policies have specifically weakened employment rights. Rights against unfair dismissal have been made conditional on longer length of service (two years for full-time workers); many part-time workers fail to qualify at all. In 1982, the Fair Wages Resolution (which set minimum conditions of work for firms operating government contracts) was ended. In 1986, Wages Council protection for young workers was abolished, while, for adult workers, it was weakened. Legislation to abolish Wages Councils is currently passing through Parliament. In addition, the number of wages inspectors was cut substantially in 1986. The legislation to protect low-paid workers has been diluted and the means to enforce what remains of it weakened.

Alongside the deregulation of employment law, new patterns of employment have changed the profile of the workforce. There has been a marked increase in self-employment and in part-time and low-paid work and a small increase in temporary work. Women are more likely to be in both part-time and temporary work. Many of these jobs are low-paid with few employment and social security rights: a situation which not only creates poverty, but also stores it up for the future.

Between 1984 and 1991:[28]

- The number of self-employed workers grew by 27%.
- The number of full-time employees grew by 4%, while the number of part-time employees grew by 17%. In 1991, women made up 88% of all part-time employees;

- The number of permanent workers grew by 9%, while the number of temporary workers grew by 11%. In 1991, women made up 55% of the temporary workforce.

A survey of employers commissioned by the Department of Employment in 1987 found that part-time and temporary workers were less likely to have fringe benefits than permanent workers:[29]

- 96% of full-time workers had access to sick pay compared to 74% of part-time workers and 40% of temporary workers;
- 84% of full-time workers had access to a pension scheme compared to 36% of part-time workers and 19% of temporary workers.

High unemployment and the weakening of employment protection expose workers to low rates of pay. In 1991, over a third of full-time workers were living on low pay, according to the Council of Europe's decency threshold (£193.60 a week or £5.15 an hour).[30] The risk of low pay is much higher for women and black and other ethnic minority groups (see Chapters 5 and 6 respectively). Part-time workers are much more likely to be low-paid than full-time workers.

In 1991, using the Council of Europe's decency threshold:

- 4.3 million part-time workers (77% of the part-time workforce) were low paid.
- 5.72 million full-time workers (36% of the full-time adult workforce) were low paid. 2.92 million were women.

## Benefits for the low-paid

There are no social security benefits for the low paid as a whole. Housing benefit and community charge benefit (to be replaced by council tax benefit from April 1993) are paid to people in low-paid work to help meet their housing costs and their community charge/poll tax. However, expenditure on housing benefit for people in work has been reduced substantially over recent years. In addition, family credit is paid to families with children in low-paid work. Introduced from April 1988 under the 1986 Social Security Act, it is more generous than its predecessor (family income supplement), but there are still major drawbacks:

- A high proportion of people who are entitled to family credit do not claim. The latest official figures show that in 1989, 57% of those entitled to claim did so.[31] Preliminary research by the

Policy Studies Institute suggests that take-up may have been higher, at around 64%, in 1991.[32]

- Family credit claimants no longer receive free school meals for their children (family income supplement claimants were entitled to free school meals), although there is some cash compensation. This cash compensation sometimes falls short of actual school meal prices and is not earmarked for the children.
- Gains in family credit for many claimants are partially offset by losses in housing benefit and community charge benefit as the family credit is treated as income in the assessment of these benefits.
- Family credit claimants receive no help with mortgage interest payments, unlike income support claimants. This pushes some families into the unemployment trap because they are better off on income support than family credit.
- The poverty trap (where a large part of any rise in earnings is withdrawn through increased tax and reduced social security benefits) is a particular problem for family credit recipients. The most extreme example is a family which receives family credit, housing benefit and council tax benefit. They will retain only 3 pence of each extra pound that is earned – this is equivalent to a marginal tax rate of 97%.

In 1985/86, 290,000 families stood to lose between 70 pence and 99 pence out of every extra £1 they earned.[33] Although the most extreme form of the poverty trap (whereby someone could lose more than a pound for each extra pound of earnings) has been all but eliminated, the poverty trap now catches more people. By 1992/93 the figure had risen to 490,000, of whom 375,000 would receive family credit.[34]

## The cost of a child

> I struggle to hold down a full-time job, which is both physically and mentally tiring, and add to this the extra work involved in packing lunches, trying vainly to cook nourishing meals in the evening and daily trying to save money by cutting corners. (Lone mother of two)[35]

Poverty ebbs and flows through the lifecycle, but one particularly vulnerable period is when children are born into the family. Children bring extra costs for essentials and they usually mean that the mother stops work for a while.

The Family Budget Unit at York University has done important work in identifying the direct costs of children. Using a 'modest but adequate' standard of living as the benchmark, Nina Oldfield found that by October 1991 prices, the weekly cost of a child was on average:

- £56.50 for a child aged 4 or 10 and £57.82 for a child aged 10 or 16 assuming his/her parents are local authority tenants.
- £58.54 for a child aged 4 or 10 and £59.72 for a child aged 10 or 16 living in owner-occupied accommodation.[36]

Parents have experienced rising costs due to the reduction in free services such as transport and leisure. This is particularly so in education where parents are increasingly having to meet the costs of books, stationery, equipment and school trips. The combination of higher costs and lower income pushes families – and particularly lone mothers – into poverty. The evidence is stark. The income of the poorest quarter of the population *with* children is substantially lower than the income of those *without* children:[37]

- Using disposable income adjusted for family size, in 1990 the *Family Expenditure Survey* revealed that the poorest quarter of couples with no children had incomes of £221 a week on average. This fell to £162 for a couple with 2 children and £68 for a couple with 4 children in the poorest quarter.
- For lone parents, the effects were even worse. In 1990, the average income of the poorest quarter of single people without children was £155 a week. This was halved to £74 for a lone parent with one child in the poorest quarter (ie, less than 50% of the figure for those without children).

## Benefits for families with children

There have been a number of changes of policy in providing benefits for families with children over the last few years. In 'Child Benefit, Options for the 1990s', Joan Brown analyses the role of child benefit and its future.[38]

Following the 1987 general election, child benefit – a universal benefit paid to all families – was frozen in real terms for three successive years. However, in 1990 the government announced that child benefit would be increased (though by less than inflation) in April 1991 and its structure changed to include a higher payment for the first/eldest child. In the 1991 Budget the government announced a further increase for child benefit in October 1991 and a pledge to uprate it in line with prices in future years. Despite these welcome improvements, the cuts in child benefit have still not been made good.[39]

- If child benefit had been uprated in line with inflation from 1988 onwards it would stand at £10.30 for each child in April 1993. This represents a fall of 3% (30 pence) in real terms for the eldest child, and 22% (£2.20) for subsequent children.
- The real value of child support (that is, child benefit now, compared with the old family allowances and child tax allowances) for a standard rate tax-paying family is worth less now than 30 years ago (with the exception of a family with one child under 11).[40]
- The government's total saving in 1992-93 from not uprating child benefit in line with prices since 1979, and changing its structure, amounts to £240 million gross and £145 million net.[41]

While child benefit has undergone significant reductions, the government has increased support for children living in families on income support and family credit above the rate of inflation.

However, there is considerable evidence that income support falls far short of providing an acceptable living standard for families with children. The Family Budget Unit shows that in 1992 income support provided:

- Only 74% of a 'low-cost' budget (estimated at £141 a week) and 33% of a 'modest but adequate' budget (estimated at £317 a week) for a couple with two children aged 4 and 10.
- Only 77% of a 'low-cost' budget (estimated at £111 a week) and 29% of a 'modest but adequate' budget (estimated at £294 a week) for a lone mother with two children aged 4 and 10.[42]

The social fund was introduced in 1987/88 as part of the changes under the 1986 Social Security Act. It replaced the system of entitlements to single payments (one-off grants) with a cash-limited discretionary fund, consisting of interest-free loans and community care grants. Comparing the single payment budget in 1985/86 (before cuts had been introduced) with the community care grants budget in 1992/93 shows a fall from £504 million to £91 million in real terms.[43] The introduction of the social fund has had a detrimental effect on claimants of all types. However families with children have been hit particularly badly by the social fund because they were more likely to receive single payments under the old system. Many families have found that loans have created considerable hardship, pushing them below the income support level. The Department of Social Security commissioned research into the social fund by the Social Policy Research Unit at York University. Their report is highly critical of the social fund; amongst its many findings, it showed that people who were repaying loans suffered considerable hardship:

- Almost 70% said that repayments left them with insufficient money to live on.
- Over a third said that they had to cut back on food, clothing or paying bills.
- A fifth borrowed money from other sources to cope with their reduced incomes.[44]

## Disability and sickness

> To be disabled, therefore, is also to be disadvantaged. It means regularly being unable to participate in the social and economic activities which most people take for granted. It means confronting the negative attitudes of others and sometimes internalising those reactions until they become part of the psychological accoutrements of disability itself. However, at the same time it can also mean gaining the additional insight that comes from encountering a wider range of experiences. It can mean overcoming enormous challenges leading to a sense of achievement and fulfilment.
>
> (*Women and Disability*)[45]

Adults and children with disabilities are frequently locked out of society by a combination of poor employment opportunities, discrimination, lower earnings, high dependency on benefit, greater costs and inadequate services. Together this means people with disabilities have to live on very low incomes, often with little chance of being able to participate fully in society.

> One of the most significant factors undermining the rights of disabled adults to participate fully and equally in society is their systematic exclusion and marginalisation from the labour market.
>
> (Steven Smith, *Disabled in the Labour Market*)[46]

A report by the Employment Policy Institute found that people with disabilities experienced extensive discrimination in the labour market:

- Employers are six times more likely to turn a disabled person down for an interview, even if their qualifications and experience are identical to a non-disabled applicant.
- The official unemployment figures hide the true picture of unemployment among people with disabilities. Disabled people are at least two and a half times more likely to be unemployed than the non-disabled.
- Three-quarters of employers fail to meet the statutory quota of employing 3% of registered disabled people under the 1944 Disabled Persons Employment Act. But since 1944 there have only been 10 prosecutions under the Act.
- Disabled men earn on average about four-fifths of their non-disabled counterparts.[47]

The last survey of disability in Britain was carried out by the Office of Population Censuses and Surveys (OPCS) between 1985 and 1988 and constituted the most complete picture of disability in Britain today.[48] According to the survey, there are 6.2 million adults (14% of all adults) and 360,000 children (3% of all children) with one or more disabilities. The Disability Alliance believes that even this large figure is an underestimate.[49] According to the OPCS survey, in 1985:

- 34% of non-pensioner adults with a disability were living in poverty (below 50% of average income) in comparison with 23% of the general population. Only 19% had incomes above the average, in comparison with 42% of the general population.

(These figures are not the same as in *Households below Average Income*, as different assumptions are used.)[50]

It is not only having less money coming in which puts people with a disability at risk of poverty, but also the extra money they have to spend to cope with their disability. The report estimated that in 1985:

- 16% of adults with a disability had made a lump-sum purchase for special equipment or furniture related to their disability, averaging £78 over the past year.
- On average, adults with a disability were spending an extra £6.10 a week on regular extra costs such as prescriptions, home services, fuel, clothing, and bedding. This extra spending varied with the severity of the disability – £3.20 for people with the least severe disability, rising to £11.10 for people with the most severe disability. On average 8% of income was spent on disability-related expenses.[51]

## Benefits for people with disabilities

Poor employment chances often mean lifelong dependence on inadequate and patchy social security benefits. In 1985, the OPCS survey found that over half (58%) of the income of adults with a disability came from state benefits in comparison with 13% for the general population.[52] Although the government has made some improvements in benefits for people with disabilities, recent years have nevertheless seen a number of cuts:

- Many people with disabilities lost out substantially as a result of the 1988 social security changes. This is because under the supplementary benefit system many people with both mild and severe disabilities received extra weekly payments to help with special diets, extra baths, extra laundry and so on. These additions were replaced by disability and severe disability premiums. Some people with a mild disability – eg, a child with chronic asthma – find they are not entitled to a premium at all. For others, whose extra needs are considerable, the premiums are not sufficient to meet the demands.[53]
- Like other benefits, invalidity pension has not kept pace with earnings. In 1971, invalidity pension for a single person was 17.5% of male average earnings; in 1979 it had risen to 20.4%, but by 1992 it had fallen to 17.8%.[54] In 1992 the government announced a tightening up of administrative and medical control procedures with a predicted saving of £240 million.[55]
- The new disability benefits introduced as part of the government's response to the OPCS surveys only touch the surface of the problem. They help some 850,000 people out of the 6.5 million identified as having disabilities in the surveys. While they bring increases in some areas, they bring cuts in others.[56] Moreover, there have been considerable problems in achieving successful claims for the new disability living allowance and disability working allowance which came into operation in April 1992.[57]

Sickness and disability affect, in turn, how much relatives who take on caring responsibilities can earn, and often ensure that both carers and people with disabilities are pushed further into poverty. In 1985, one-fifth (20%) of adults aged 45 to 64 were looking after someone who was sick, elderly or had a disability. Women were more likely to be carers than men – nearly a quarter (24%) of women aged 45 to 64 were carers, compared with 16% of men.[58]

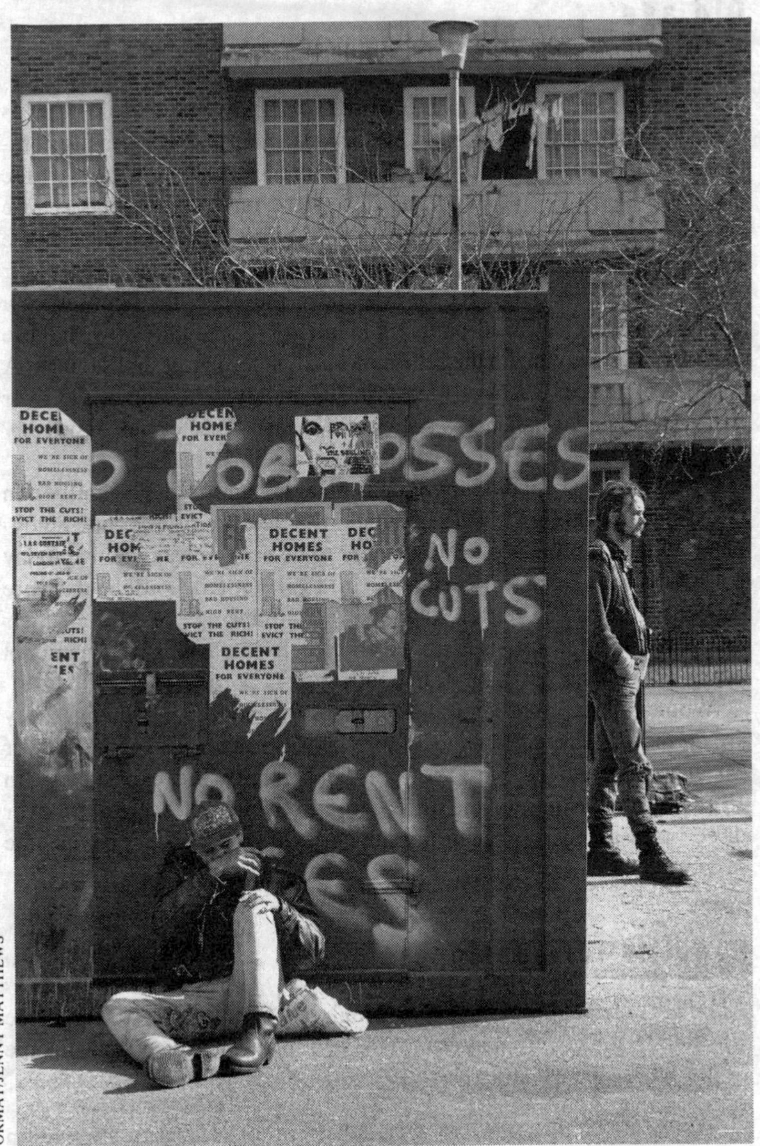


FORMAT/JENNY MATTHEWS

***The UK now has an unemployment rate which is well above the European Community average. In December 1992 the official rate of unemployment in the UK stood at 10.5% – almost 3 million people.***

## Old age

The inequalities in working life between employment and unemployment, low-paid and high-paid work, between men and women, are compounded in old age. Broadly speaking, there are still two nations of the elderly: elderly people who are dependent on income support (the replacement for supplementary pension), and in council or private rented housing without private or occupational pensions and with few or no savings; and elderly people who have the generous bonuses of a lifetime's secure and well-paid employment.[59] Some fall between these two extremes, relying on the return on small inheritances and savings. A number of factors such as long-term unemployment among the over fifties and changes in pension policy will create a greater risk of poverty for some groups of future pensioners.

In 1990, elderly people (over pension age) numbered 10.5 million in Great Britain, or 18% of the population.[60] Because of high unemployment, elderly people are far less likely to be economically active today than they were twenty years ago. In 1991 retired households were dependent on social security benefits for an average of 41% of their household income (the remainder coming from savings, occupational pensions and small earnings), in contrast to 11% for all households.[61]

Women make up around two-thirds of the elderly population. They are far more likely than men to be poor pensioners because of their lower earnings, interrupted work patterns and greater life expectancy. In 1991, even adjusting for the different retirement ages, there were over three times as many women pensioners as men dependent on income support.[62]

### Benefits for pensioners

Although elderly people have a very high risk of falling into poverty (see Chapter 2), the government has weakened financial protection for some of the poorest pensioners:

- The decision in 1980 to uprate the retirement pension by rises in prices alone (until that date retirement pension was uprated by earnings or prices, whichever was higher) has meant substantial losses for pensioners. In April 1993, the retirement pension would be £19.35 higher for a single person and £30.65 higher for a couple had it been uprated by this method since 1980.[63]

- Not surprisingly, the retirement pension has dropped as a proportion of earnings since 1980: the retirement pension for a single person under 80 was 17.5% of male average earnings in 1971; 20.4% in 1979 and 17.8% in 1992.[64]
- The new disability benefits proposals do nothing to help the 4.2 million pensioners with disabilities.
- The Social Security Act 1986 has both weakened the State Earnings Related Pension Scheme (SERPS) and increased incentives to take out a personal pension. In years to come, this will increase poverty for many elderly people. Private pensions mirror inequalities in the labour market, leaving those who have been unemployed, or low paid, or who have worked part time, in poverty in their old age, while providing large incomes for those who have had permanent and well-paid jobs.

## Rising Costs

A hidden cause of poverty is rising costs; whether it is housing, water rates, the contribution to the poll tax, transport, leisure and childcare services, educational materials or school meals. Some of these costs are *partly* covered by income support and housing benefit – eg, housing costs, water rates, and the 20% contribution to the poll tax. (For the first time in 1992/93, income-related benefits were uprated by an adjusted price index which takes account of rises in the poll tax and water rates. However, between 1988/89 and 1991/92 any rises in the poll tax and water rates were not reflected in the level of those benefits.) Children in families receiving income support are entitled to free school meals. Other costs are not covered by income support – eg, costs at school, leisure and childcare services.

The situation is particularly acute for those who are on low incomes, but not on income support. They find that they are facing a panoply of rising costs with no financial support. Costs have risen as a result of increasing the scope of the market, through deregulation, contracting out and privatisation, into areas that were once heavily subsidised by public money. For example, water prices have risen far above inflation since privatisation. Under strong financial and political pressure local authorities have cut subsidies and increased charges for childcare, leisure services and school meals. Rents have been de-regulated and housing benefit has failed to keep pace with the subsequent increases. The cost of public transport has risen sharply as government subsidies have been withdrawn. The cost of services, both national and local, forms a crucial element of people's living standards, particularly people living in or close to poverty.

## Conclusion

Poverty is largely determined by three factors – access to the labour market, and extra costs and the failure of policies to deal with them. Access to the labour market depends on a number of different factors – amongst them, class, gender, and race. We have seen how the rise in unemployment has pushed millions into poverty. Getting a job is not necessarily the answer to poverty if that job pays paltry earnings, has long hours and poor working conditions – the poverty of unemployment is simply translated into the poverty of work. Extra costs often come with changes in the lifecycle. For example, the extra costs of a child combined with being out of the labour market brings poverty to families with children and in particular to lone mothers. Disability and sickness also bring extra costs, but at the same time less or no opportunity to be in paid work. And finally, old age carries a high risk of poverty because it is a time of life when there are few earnings and as old age progresses no earnings at all. In each of these cases social security benefits have failed to pull people out of poverty, often leaving them to manage on the most meagre of incomes.

Coming to grips with the causes of poverty involves a commitment to a wide-ranging strategy. CPAG believes that some of the following policies would begin to set the agenda:

- An economic strategy which has the reduction of unemployment at its heart, and which aims to create worthwhile jobs.
- A strong commitment to training and re-training.
- A statutory minimum wage for full- and part-time workers, equal pay for men and women, pro-rata employment rights for part-time workers.
- A large increase in child benefit and a substantial increase in the availability of subsidised childcare.
- A comprehensive disability income which both meets the cost of disability and provides an income for people with disabilities who cannot work or whose ability to work is affected by their disability.

- Steps towards enacting civil rights legislation for disabled people which would outlaw discrimination against disabled people in and seeking employment.
- Steps towards a non-means-tested social security system without contribution conditions; individual entitlement to benefits and benefits paid at an adequate level.

## NOTES

1. Quoted in J Ritchie, *Thirty families: their living standards in unemployment*, DSS, HMSO, 1990.
2. Department of Employment, 'Labour Market Commentary', *Employment Gazette*, October 1992, HMSO, 1992.
3. Figures given orally from the Department of Employment, January 1993.
4. *Employment Gazette*, Historical Supplement No 1, Unemployment Statistics, Department of Employment, April 1989.
5. 'Creative Counting', Unemployment Unit, 1990.
6. T Lynes, *The Wrong Side of the Tracks*: Factsheet on Unemployment and Benefits, CPAG Ltd, 1992.
7. 'Working Brief', Unemployment Unit, February 1993.
8. A Garman, R Redmond, S Lonsdale, *Incomes in and out of Work: a cohort study of newly unemployed men and women*, Department of Social Security, Research Report No 7, HMSO, 1992.
9. WW Daniel, *The Unemployed Flow*, Policy Studies Institute, 1990.
10. *See* note 9.
11. Figures given orally from the Department of Employment, January 1993.
12. *Employment Gazette*, 'Characteristics of the unemployed', Department of Employment, May 1991.
13. *See* note 9.
14. Figures given orally from the Department of Employment, January 1993.
15. House of Commons, *Hansard*, 26 October 1992, cols 489-90.
16. House of Commons, *Hansard*, 26 October 1992, cols 496-7.
17. *See* note 9.
18. P Heady and M Smyth, *Living standards during unemployment*, Vol 1: The Results, HMSO, 1990.
19. For more detail, see J C Brown, *Why don't they go to work?: Mothers on benefit*, Social Security Advisory Committee, HMSO, 1989.
20. *See* note 6.
21. P Taylor-Gooby, 'Attachment to the welfare state' in eds., R Jowell, L Brook & B Taylor, *British Social Attitudes, the 8th Report*, SCPR, Dartmouth, 1991 and P Taylor-Gooby, 'Social welfare: the unkindest of cuts', in eds, R Jowell et al, *British Social Attitudes, the 7th Report*, SCPR, Gower, 1990.
22. *Social Security: The Government's Expenditure Plans 1992-93 to 1994-95*, Cmnd 1914, HMSO, 1992.
23. *See* T Lynes (see note 6) for full details on cuts to benefits for unemployed people and J C Brown, *Victims or Villains? social security benefits in unemployment*, Joseph Rowntree Memorial Trust, 1990.

24. *Abstract of statistics for index of: retail prices, average earnings, social security benefits and contributions*, Section 5, DSS, October 1992.
25. D Byrne & J Jacobs, *Disqualified from benefit*, Low Pay Unit, 1988.
26. *See* note 6.
27. Quoted in T Potter, *A temporary phenomenon*, West Midlands Low Pay Unit, 1989.
28. *Employment Gazette*, Department of Employment, April 1992.
29. Department of Employment, 'Employers and the Flexible Workforce', *Employment Gazette*, May 1992, HMSO, 1992.
30. *The New Review, No 13*, Low Pay Unit, December 1991/January 1992.
31. Department of Social Security, *Income Related Benefits – Estimates of take-up 1989*, Government Statistical Service, 1993.
32. A Marsh and S McKay, *Supplementing Low Wages: 50 years after Beveridge*, Unpublished Paper for Beveridge Conference, 1992.
33. *The New Review, No. 3*, Low Pay Unit Parliamentary briefing, April/May 1990.
34. *House of Commons Hansard*, 5 June 1992, col 659.
35. Quoted in S McEvaddy, 'One good meal a day', CPAG, 1988.
36. N Oldfield, *Using Budget Standards to Estimate the Cost of Children*, Family Budget Unit, Joseph Rowntree Foundation, September 1992.
37. Updated from D Piachaud, 'Poverty and Social Security', unpublished paper for the Select Committee on Social Services, 1990, using the Family Expenditure Survey 1990.
38. J C Brown, *Child Benefit. Options for the Future*, Save Child Benefit, 1991.
39. *Child Benefit: Looking to the Future*, Coalition for Child Benefit, 1991.
40. House of Commons, *Hansard*, 3 March 1992, cols 143-146.
41. House of Commons, *Hansard*, 7 December 1992, cols 506-7.
42. *Household Budgets and Living Standards*, Summary of research by the Family Budget Unit, in Social Policy Research Findings, No 31, Joseph Rowntree Foundation, November 1992.
43. House of Commons, *Hansard*, 10 December 1992.
44. M Huby and G Dix, *Evaluating the Social Fund* and R Walker, G Dix and M Huby, *Working the Social Fund*, HMSO, 1992.
45. S Lonsdale, *Women and disability*, Macmillan, 1990.
46. S Smith, *Disabled in the Labour Market*, Employment Policy Institute, Economic report, Vol 7, No 1 July/August 1992.
47. *See* note 46.
48. *Office of Population Censuses and Surveys, Surveys of disability in Great Britain*, Reports 1-6, HMSO, 1988/89.
49. Disability Alliance, 'Briefing on the "First Report" from the OPCS surveys of disability', 1988.
50. *See* note 48. Report 2, 'The financial circumstances of disabled adults living in private households'.
51. *See* note 48.
52. *Family Expenditure Survey 1985*, HMSO, 1986. We have used an earlier date for comparative purposes with the disability survey which took place in 1985 (*see* note 48).
53. *See* R Cohen et al, *Hardship Britain: Being poor in the 1990s*, CPAG Ltd in association with FSU, 1992, for case studies.
54. DSS, *see* note 24.
55. DSS press release, *Peter Lilley announces full uprating for benefits*, 12 November 1992.

56. Linda Lennard, *Welfare Rights Bulletin 97*, CPAG Ltd, August 1990.
57. *See* A Hadjipateras and M Howard, *Too Little . . . Too Late*, Disability Alliance and RADAR, 1992, for more information.
58. H Green, 'Informal Carers', *General Household Survey*, HMSO, 1988.
59. P Townsend, *Poverty in the UK*, Penguin, 1979.
60. *Population Studies*, HMSO, 1992.
61. *Family Spending, A Report on the Family Expenditure Survey, 1991*, HMSO, 1992.
62. *Social Security Statistics 1992*, DSS, HMSO, 1992.
63. CPAG updating of R Twigger, *The Pension and Pensioners' Income*, House of Commons Research Note No 90/67, 1990.
64. DSS, *see* note 24.

CHAPTER FOUR

# Dimensions of poverty

*Poverty curtails freedom of choice. The freedom to eat as you wish, to go where and when you like, to seek the leisure pursuits or political activities which others expect; all are denied to those without the resources . . . poverty is most comprehensively understood as a condition of partial citizenship.*

Peter Golding, Excluding the Poor[1]

Poverty filters into every aspect of life. It is not simply about doing without *things*; it is also about being denied the expectation of decent health, education, shelter, a social life and a sense of self-esteem which the rest of society takes for granted.

In this chapter we look at some dimensions of poverty: living on a low income, debt, poor health and homelessness.

## Living on a low income

Living on benefit or on low earnings creates material and social hardship. We look at just what it means to have to survive on a very tight budget for extended periods: going short of the essentials, being isolated, unable to meet children's needs, living with stress and dealing with the benefit authorities. But by highlighting the impact of poverty, the tendency is to ignore the countless strategies that claimants and others have for coping. These may be informal networks between women to share childcare, run toddlers' groups and set up small-scale cooperatives; or initiatives to recycle secondhand goods; or establishing credit unions and community enterprises; or running youth clubs and old people's lunch clubs.[2]

This section draws mainly on two reports: *Evaluating the Social Fund*, written by the Social Policy Research Unit (SPRU) at York

University, which conducted a survey of over 1,700 people living on low incomes in 1990[3] and a small qualitative study carried out by the Family Service Units and Bradford University's Social Fund Research Project called *Hardship Britain: Being poor in the 1990s*.[4] The quotations come largely from *Hardship Britain*.

## Going Short

> Some nights I just cry myself to sleep. We live in a three bedroomed house, but at this time of year we all sleep in the same double bed and throw Kirsty's duvet on top as well. It's warmer that way. I can't afford the heating.
>
> (Lone parent with two children in Gateshead, *Independent on Sunday*, 15 November 1992)

Many studies have shown how people on low incomes have to cut down on essentials such as food, clothing, fuel bills and household goods. We identify some key findings from the SPRU report:[5]

- Clothing, fuel and food and housekeeping needs had caused most concern among all groups: 30% mentioned clothing; 26% mentioned gas and electricity; 14% mentioned food and general housekeeping.
- Families with children identified beds (including cots and mattresses), washing machines and children's items such as nappies and baby clothes as needs which had caused concern.
- Providing enough food at each meal was the main difficulty, especially in households with children and pensioner households.
- 38% of respondents had problems with damp; 58% had problems with heating and 31% had a lack of hot water.
- Buying clothing or footwear created particular difficulties and often disrupted budgeting for several weeks.
- Many families were short of basic household amenities: 27% did not have adequate bedding for each member of the family (35% of lone parents); 14% did not have adequate floor covering in their main living area; 17% did not have enough beds or cots suitable for each member of the family; 30% did not have a washing machine.

> I try to put things together, you know, what's left in the cupboards, or sometimes I go to bed with a cup of tea or some bread . . . If I just have enough to give the kids I'll just have a cup of tea and that's it.
>
> (Mother quoted in *Hardship Britain*)

In 1991, the National Children's Home's, *Poverty and Nutrition Survey*, a study of 354 families with children on low incomes, found that one in five parents and one in ten children had gone hungry in the previous month because they did not have enough money to buy food.[6]

## Isolation

*Hardship Britain* describes the sense of isolation and exclusion that many people in poverty experience:

> Like the children, adults often found their social life severely limited. In general, people had very little money to socialise with friends and were therefore often deprived of much social contact outside the home. The exceptions were people who clearly had a strong network of local friends and/or family.[7]

Only a minority of families interviewed in *Hardship Britain* had any money left over for social activities; most could not afford to go out or invite people:

> It's very shameful when you can't treat your guests good and feed them well . . . The government only gives a little bit of money which isn't even enough to feed yourself, let alone anyone else that comes to the house.[8]

In *Young and Jobless* by Susan McRae[9] young unemployed claimants describe how both a shortage of money and the isolation inherent in unemployment affect the chances of making friends:

> Yes, it makes it harder . . . When you go out, you can only stay out for so long, because you can't afford to buy so many drinks. Yes it is hard, it's more difficult than normal because they're all showing you what they've bought and that's depressing again . . .
>
> (Adam, young unemployed man in Manchester)

> I don't see a lot of people, so I feel I'm boring in conversation sometimes. I think back on what I've done and talk about that, but nothing concrete about what I've been doing over the last few months, because it's all the same. Days become the same, unless you break it up and do something.
>
> (Katje, unemployed woman in Manchester)

## The impact on children

Living in poverty inevitably restricts the activities in which children can participate. *Hardship Britain* documents how many families could not afford to send their children on school trips or outings with friends.

Many said that there were few play facilities for children and they had no money to travel further afield:

> You can't go to the adventure playground over there because of the drug users, you can't go over there because of the neighbours, they can't play football in the streets because of the motors, there's nothing left for them . . .
>
> I feel rotten that I'm having to ground them for disobeying us, because they only want to play.
>
> (quoted in *Hardship Britain*)[10]

A National Children's Home survey of 347 families conducted in 1991, *Deep in Debt*, found that 89% of parents felt that they could not afford to give their children all the things they needed; in particular, they couldn't afford clothing, shoes and toys. Over half of the families felt a sense of injustice on behalf of their children, but around half also felt guilty about not being able to provide what they needed.[11]

## Stress

Many people who have had to live on low incomes for long periods talk of suffering from anxiety, strain and stress. Coping on very little money often created difficulties for relationships within couples and between parents and children.

> You end up pulling your hair out because you can't ever get away for a night out like working people . . . Tensions build when you get a bit of time on your own.
>
> The children are always asking for things – they say their friends have this and this . . . we have to say no, so the children get upset and we feel upset.
>
> (both quoted in *Hardship Britain*)[12]

Above all, some claimants talked of the way that lack of money brought a loss of control and diminished self-confidence:

> I think that the real problem of being on the dole is it destroys your self-esteem, you know, and your ability to provide for yourself . . . I said lack of self-esteem but I mean also, like, a lot of apathy. If you're on the dole for a long period of time you tend to get . . . quite apathetic in many ways.[13]

## Battling with the benefit authorities

Living on a low income, coming on and off social security, involves vast quantities of form-filling, visiting benefit offices, queueing and sorting out difficulties.[14] Benefit authorities, while they are there to help, all too often are a burden in themselves because of the demands they place on claimants. *Hardship Britain* documents the ways in which many claimants feel stigmatised because of their experience of the social security system and how some give up in the face of past failures to gain entitlement:

> Claimants emphasised that they found direct dealings with the DSS difficult and stressful, especially if they had to call at the office – often having to wait hours to be seen – rather than telephone. The atmosphere of the waiting rooms . . . discouraged many of them from going there.[15]

The Benefits Agency has replaced local DSS offices. While its commitment to providing a better service is a positive development, many of the difficulties are likely to remain: shortage of resources, rising unemployment and extensive and complex means-testing.

Living on a low income means cutting down on basics, it means no money for treats for the children, it means having to rely on friends and relatives to come to the rescue, it sometimes means being isolated and coping with a battered sense of self-esteem.

## Debt

> Debt results from either a sudden disruption to income (for example, as a result of unemployment or relationship breakdown or illness), where previous comitments are difficult to sustain, or from a slower, cumulative effect of a persistently low and inadequate income (for example, as a result of living on benefit for a sustained period), and it is these two processes that have been so pronounced during the 1980s. The processes of slow decline and sudden disruption are conceptually distinct, although in practice linked for many households.
>
> (Janet Ford, *Consuming Credit: debt and poverty in the UK*)[16]

### Indicators of debt

Debt is a major problem in the UK:

- In 1989, there were 2.8 million households with arrears, compared with 1.3 million in 1981. In 1989, there were 530,000 households in multiple debt (owing money to three or more creditors at the same time) compared to 130,000 in 1981.[17]

- In 1991, 75,540 homes were repossessed – up from 3,480 in 1980. In 1991, 191,280 homeowners were between six and twelve months in arrears with their mortgage payments compared with 15,530 in 1980.[18]
- One in five homeowners who bought their properties in the last five years now owe more than their property is worth.[19]
- In 1991/92, 21,282 domestic customers in England and Wales had their water supplies disconnected for non-payment of charges. In 1989/90, the comparable figure was 8,426.[20]
- In 1991/92, there were 23,693 electricity disconnections, down from 98,894 in 1979/80. In 1992, there were 15,707 gas disconnections, a fall from 35,166 in 1979. The decrease in disconnections has been accompanied by a substantial increase in pre-payment meters. Such meters allow customers effectively to disconnect themselves if they are short of money. Thus the official figures hide the extent of fuel poverty.[21]

Many income support claimants are living below the basic benefit level because of direct deductions for arrears. Deductions can be made for an increasing number of arrears: rent, water charges, fuel charges and the poll tax, mortgage and other housing costs, accommodation charges. On top of arrears, deductions can be made for current consumption (eg, for fuel and water), for repayment of social fund loans and for punitive sanctions such as fines for not cooperating with the Child Support Agency from April 1993. While there is a ceiling on the total amount which can be deducted for certain arrears (£6.60 from April 1993), the ceiling does not include the amount for current consumption. Up to 25% of benefit (excluding housing costs) can be deducted from the claimant without permission. Although there are no statistics which show how many claimants are facing multiple deductions, there are indicators of how many income support claimants have deductions for certain items.[22] In 1991:

- 96,000 income support claimants had deductions from their basic benefit to pay for electricity at an average weekly amount of £9.86 and 146,000 for gas at an average rate of £9.31 per week;
- 94,000 income support claimants had automatic deductions to pay their rent arrears/amenity charges at an average of £3.81 per week;
- 443,000 income support claimants had automatic deductions to repay social fund loans at an average of £5.53 a week;

- 34,000 income support claimants had direct deductions from their basic benefit to pay poll tax arrears at an average of £2.08 per week;
- 67,000 income support claimants had direct deductions for water and sewerage charges at an average of £4.55 a week.

## Who falls into debt?

Not surprisingly, many of the poorest households face acute debt problems. In *Credit and Debt*, the PSI report, Richard Berthoud and Elaine Kempson defined debts as difficulties in paying household expenses or consumer credit payments.[23] If a family said they had a problem meeting an expense, this counted as a problem debt, and three or more of these counted as multiple debt. The authors show how a third of households with net weekly incomes of less than £100 had debts, compared with 2% for households with incomes of above £400 a week (see Table 7):

**TABLE 7**

**Incidence of problem debts by income for non-pensioner households (%)**

| Net weekly income | Proportion with problem debts | Proportion with multiple debts |
|---|---|---|
| up to £100 | 33 | 10 |
| £100-150 | 22 | 4 |
| £150-200 | 13 | 4 |
| £200-250 | 9 | 2 |
| £250-300 | 10 | 1 |
| £300-400 | 8 | 1 |
| £400 or more | 2 | – |

*SOURCE: Credit and Debt, the PSI Report, R Berthoud and E Kempson, Policy Studies Institute, 1992*

However, some families are more likely to be in debt than others. Berthoud and Kempson identify three 'debt-inducing' factors: age, children and income. Any two of these factors brought a much higher risk of debt – eg, young households with low incomes or families with children on low incomes. Lone parents are particularly at risk: they had three times the number of problem debts as single people without children. The majority of debts faced by people living on low incomes are not the result of excessive consumerism – rather, as Berthoud and Kempson put it:

> Low income leads to indebtedness through the week-to-week budgeting problems it causes, rather than because poor people persist in buying consumer goods they cannot afford.[24]

## The impact of debt

> There is evidence of growing indebtedness to the fund, including multiple loans on the part of an increasing number of recipients.
>
> (National Audit Office, *The Social Fund* )[25]

Debt undoubtedly reinforces the hardship that people living on low incomes face. The research by SPRU into the social fund illustrates some of the problems of paying back loans from very low incomes. The study found that 69% of respondents thought that the social fund repayments did not leave enough to live on. There were a number of different ways of coping with repaying the loans: 46% juggled different expenses; 34% went without other things; 14% coped as usual; and 7% borrowed from friends. When asked on what areas spending was reduced, 61% said they had cut back on food and living expenses; 47% on clothing and 21% on bills.[26]

Debts often lead to yet further debt. The pressure of having to meet urgent demands often drives people into seeking 'secured' loans on their homes or borrowing from a loan shark. The first brings with it the danger of losing your home, the second exorbitant rates of interest. A survey in Birmingham of licensed money-lenders to the unemployed and people on benefit found that they had an average of 525% annual percentage rate interest.[27]

> We're getting deeper and deeper into debt. I mean that hurts as well . . . One week he'll go and tell them that we can't pay, the next week I'll go. There was a time I'd hide if anybody knocked on the door. And if I went to the door, I'd stand there shaking. But now I just stand there and face them and tell them we haven't got the money. (Mrs Ward)[28]

Debt is still frequently regarded by society at large as a sign of personal failure and it is this which adds to the stress, anxiety and stigma which accompany debt. *Deep in Debt*, the NCH survey of 347 families, looked at the effects of worries about money: 71% of respondents were depressed; 50% were unable to sleep; 40% felt that they could not cope; 39% smoked more; 21% felt that their relationship with their partner had been damaged. Many people felt embarrassed and guilty about being in debt.[29] Janet Ford sums up the impact of debt:

> The experience of debt magnifies and reinforces the experience of poverty – the watchfulness and anxiety over money; the calculation and moving around of limited funds. But debt may also alter the agenda. For example, social exclusion may increase; households become vulnerable to legal sanctions and to the loss of any property they possess; homelessness cannot be discounted.
>
> (Janet Ford, *Consuming Credit: debt and poverty in the UK*)[30]

## Poor health

> Analysis of the major advances in health . . . shows that these have been associated more often with improvements in social circumstances than with medical advances. Thus, where people are in a position to exercise greater choice in their housing, environment, employment, leisure activity and consumption generally this has tended to be beneficial to their health. By contrast, those not able to exercise greater choice because of low income, lack of education or lack of capacity to take the initiative tend to suffer more ill-health. (Chief Medical Officer, *On the State of Public Health*)[31]

### Indicators of inequalities in health

#### Unemployment and Health

> Unemployment begets poverty, which begets ill health and premature death. Any lingering doubts about this genealogy were settled in England and Wales by a longitudinal study of mortality and social organisation, which explains much of the excess mortality experienced by men seeking work.
>
> (R Smith, 'Poor Britain: Losing Out', *British Medical Journal*)[32]

> The evidence that unemployment kills – particularly the middle-aged – now verges on the irrefutable.
>
> (R Smith, 'Unemployment: here we go again', *British Medical Journal*)[33]

There is growing evidence of the health risks of unemployment. According to the *British Medical Journal*, death rates are particularly high from suicide, accidents, violence and circulatory diseases. International studies have confirmed this picture; a study in Finland in 1990 showed that mortality was 90% higher amongst the unemployed than the employed (after other factors were controlled for) and that mortality increased with longer durations of unemployment. A study in Sweden

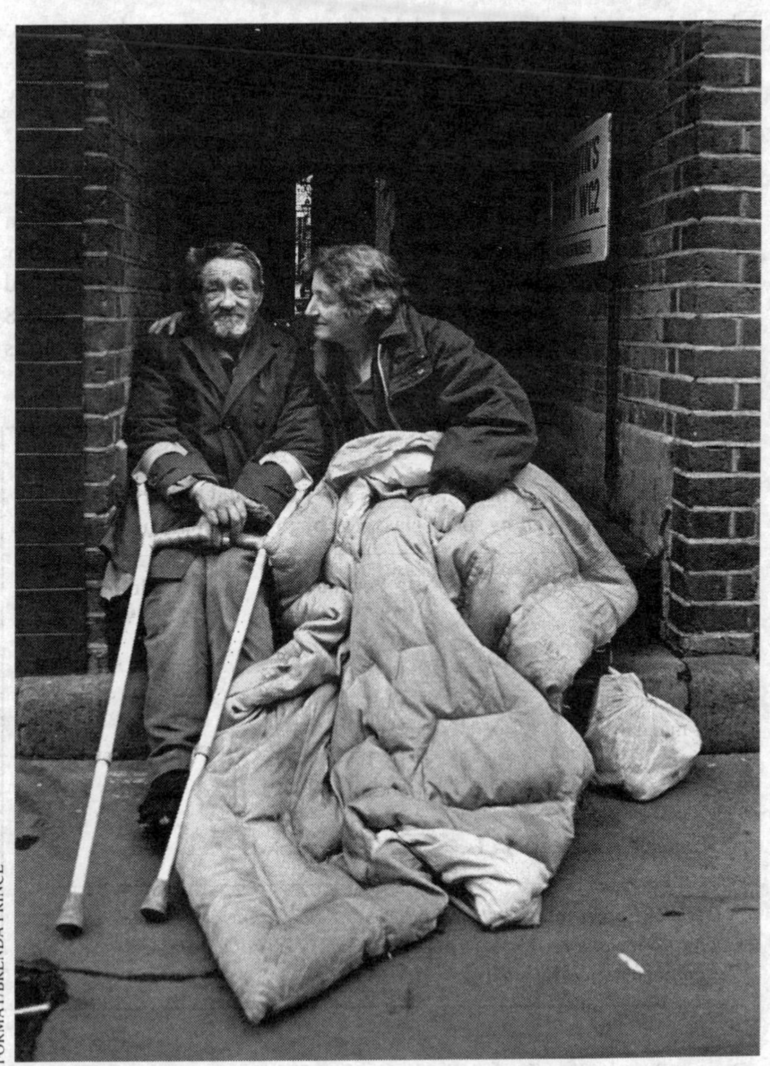

FORMAT/BRENDA PRINCE

***London has a shanty town as large as might be expected in a Latin American city, but it is tucked away.***

showed raised cholesterol and blood pressure in unemployed men. There is also mounting data on the psychological effects of unemployment: redundancy brings on depression and anxiety; economic difficulty increases the risk of such depression.[34]

## Mortality statistics

While society as a whole has witnessed a significant decline in infant mortality, the gap between rich and poor has grown wider. *Mortality Statistics: perinatal and infant: social and biological factors* is published annually by the Office of Population Censuses and Surveys.[35] Table 8 shows the rates of perinatal and infant mortality by social class for births within marriage.

**TABLE 8**

**Perinatal and infant mortality rates per 1,000 total births 1978-79 and 1990 compared by social class (for births within marriage only)**

| | Perinatal | | Infant | |
|---|---|---|---|---|
| **Social Class** | **1978-79** | **1990** | **1978-79** | **1990** |
| I | 11.9 | 6.6 | 9.8 | 5.6 |
| II | 12.3 | 6.0 | 10.1 | 5.3 |
| III non-manual | 13.9 | 7.1 | 11.1 | 6.4 |
| III manual | 15.1 | 7.7 | 12.4 | 6.5 |
| IV | 16.7 | 9.5 | 13.6 | 8.3 |
| V | 20.3 | 9.6 | 17.2 | 11.2 |
| Other | 20.4 | 9.1 | 23.3 | 10.5 |
| **Ratio of social class V: I** | 1.71 | 1.46 | 1.76 | 2.0 |

*SOURCE: Mortality Statistics, Perinatal and Infant: social and biological factors, 1978-79 and 1990, Office of Population Censuses and Surveys, HMSO, 1992*

Perinatal mortality figures show that in 1990, between 9 and 10 out of 1,000 babies born into Social Class V (unskilled workers) were stillborn or died in the first week of birth; this compares to between 6 and 7 out of 1,000 babies born into Social Class I (professional occupations). The figures for infant mortality (deaths occurring in the first year of life) show similar disparities – 11 out of 1,000 babies born into Social Class V died in their first year, compared to between 5 and 6 out of 1,000 for Social Class I. The gap between social classes has fallen for perinatal deaths between 1979 and 1990; for infant deaths it has risen. Inequalities between rich and poor extend throughout the life-span. According to the British Medical Journal:

- unskilled men have 2.5 times and unskilled women nearly double the standard mortality ratios (SMR) of professional men and women;
- 62 of the 66 major causes of death among men were more common among unskilled and semi-skilled men; 64 of the 70 major causes of death in women were more common in the wives of the same groups.[36]

The differential between social classes is underestimated because it includes legitimate births only. In the latest edition of *Mortality Statistics: perinatal and infant* there is an analysis which combines births within marriage and births jointly registered outside marriage. It shows that in 1988-90, 12 out of every 1,000 babies in Social Class V died in their first year compared to 6 out of every 1,000 babies in Social Class I. In more concrete terms, if the babies born to mothers in families with unskilled occupations had the same risk of infant death as those in professional occupations, 508 babies' lives would have been saved in 1988-90.

Peter Townsend's research in the 25 most and least deprived wards in Greater London confirms this pattern. The wards were ranked according to four indicators: unemployment, overcrowding, not having a car and not owning a home. He found that the most deprived wards had an SMR of 136.2 per 1,000 compared to 69.8 in the least deprived wards.[37]

## Illness

> It's cold and damp. We've just got a fire in the children's room which took years to get. I've got bronchitis and so have the children. (Julie)[38]

Poverty not only brings the risk of a shorter life-span, but it also means that the lives of adults and children are more likely to be ground down by illness and disability.

There are well-established links between illness ('morbidity statistics') and social class. The *General Household Survey* examines these patterns, which it breaks down by sex and occupational grouping.[39] The Survey found that self-reported long-standing illness ranged from 27% of professional men and women to 41% of unskilled male manual workers and 47% of unskilled female manual workers. Other research reinforces this finding. A British heart study found that angina was twice as high amongst male manual workers than male non-manual workers in their middle age. The same study found that lung function was also worse in manual groups (this was partly independent of smoking patterns). Other studies have found that self-reported disability is twice as high in Social Class V as Social Class I.[40]

*Hardship Britain* documented the frequent occurrence of health problems among people living on income support: over 65% of the families interviewed by the Family Service Units reported ill-health or disability among parents, and over 70% among children. Almost two-thirds of families interviewed in the Bradford study reported long-term sickness or disability. Asthma, bronchitis and eczema were the most commonly reported conditions in both studies. The studies found that ill health was associated with the stress caused by poverty, with the inability to meet extra expenses caused by certain illnesses and not being able to heat homes sufficiently to be able to relieve certain conditions.[41]

> When you're down your health goes down. When you know you're worried that's the next stress, because stress causes illness. You'll find a lot of people are sick who's poor because they've got a lot of stresses and if you lift them up a few bob it helps, it really does help.
>
> (Lone parent quoted in *Hardship Britain*)[42]

## Growth and development

In *Poverty Can Seriously Damage Your Health*, Issy Cole-Hamilton pinpoints a number of studies which show that children's well-being is closely related to their standard of living.[43] Children in low-income households are more likely to be shorter and to grow up to be smaller adults than people in more affluent households. In 1989, the Department of Social Security found that the height of school children was related to their diet and that boys receiving free school meals were found on average to be shorter than the other boys in the study.[44] Children in social classes IV and V had the poorest dental health of all children.[45] In addition, childhood accidents are related to social class – eg, the death rate from head injuries amongst children was 15 times higher in the local authority wards with the highest overall deprivation index than in those with the lowest deprivation index.[46]

# Homelessness

Homelessness is the most extreme aspect of poor housing conditions.

Living in damp, draughty homes, waiting for repairs, being overcrowded, are all ways in which poverty directly impinges on people's lives.

> London has a shanty town as large as might be expected in a Latin American city, but it is hidden. People live illegally in squats or in cramped, badly equipped hotels and crowded hostels. If they do not fall into a group that the government recognises as having a special need, or they cannot locate one of the very few spare spaces indoors, they find they have no choice but to survive on the streets.[47]

The *Households below Average Income* and the *Low Income Families* statistics cover only private households and therefore do not include people who are living in hostels, bed and breakfast hotels, or out on the streets. It is a perverse irony that the available statistics on poverty exclude the very poorest.

## Numbers of homeless

Shelter's *Homes Cost Less than Homelessness* documents the scale and growth of homelessness. It examines the 'official homeless' figures – ie, those households who are accepted as homeless by local authorities – and the 'unofficial homeless' who do not fall into this category but do not have a home. Below we pick out some key findings:[48]

- In 1991, 146,290 households – about 420,000 adults and children – were accepted as homeless by local authorities in England.
- In the first half of 1992, 73,310 households were accepted as homeless in England.
- Shelter estimates that the number of 'unofficial homeless' could be in the region of 1.7 million. This includes people sleeping rough (8,000), unauthorised tenants/squatters (50,000), single people in hostels (60,000), single people in lodgings (77,000), insecure private tenants (317,000), and 'hidden homeless' people – ie, people who have to share with friends or relatives but need a home of their own (1,200,000).
- Since 1978, official homelessness had nearly tripled.
- Homelessness is particularly acute in London and in urban areas. In the first half of 1992, 15.2 in every 1,000 households were accepted as homeless in Greater London compared to 10.8 in other Metropolitan districts and 5.8 in non-metropolitan districts. However, a recent report by Centrepoint (a shelter for the homeless young people in Central London) has found that the number of

young people who are homeless in the countryside is increasing at a faster rate than in London and the inner cities.[49]

Centrepoint Soho in London conducted a survey of young people who came to stay at their night shelter.[50] They found that in 1991/92:

- a growing proportion were aged 16-17 (nearly half of all admissions compared to 10% in 1979);
- 36% were from black and ethnic minorities;
- 63% had no income at all (the figure was even higher for 16 and 17 year olds – 75% had no income at all); 26% received benefits, 4% were on a Youth Training Schemes and just 6% had paid work;
- 59% had had contact with a social worker, 15% with a probation officer;
- around a fifth had lived in a children's home;
- 56% came from within London; however, the majority left their last home for reasons such as eviction or arguments; only 18% came to look for a job.

## Causes of homelessness

The principal reason for homelessness is a shortage of rented housing at reasonable prices. However, there are a number of immediate reasons for becoming homeless: breakdown of sharing arrangements; dissolution of a marriage or other partnership; loss of private rented tenancy, and other reasons such as mortgage default and rent arrears.[51] More recently, the changes in social security for young people have meant that they are now far more at risk of homelessness than in the past.

The risk of becoming homeless is higher for people living on low incomes and for people from ethnic minorities:[52]

- Around 80% of homeless heads of household are out of work and relying on social security benefits.
- Nearly four in ten households accepted as homeless in London are from an ethnic minority, far above the percentage of these communities in the population as a whole.

## The impact of homelessness

The security of a home is essential for health, a sense of well-being and access to services and employment. These basic needs are beyond the reach of homeless people. A number of studies of living conditions in temporary accommodation graphically illustrate this fact.

- In June 1992, there were 11,080 homeless people in bed and breakfast hotels and 10,160 homeless people in hostels.[53]
- A survey undertaken in London showed that 93% of hotels failed to meet fully the minimum acceptable standards set by the London local authorities; 61% of rooms were overcrowded and one in eight did not have a fire certificate.[54]

*Prescription for Poor Health* documented the conditions for mothers and children living in bed-and-breakfast accommodation.[55] *Prescription for Poor Health* found:

- a high degree of stress among the women – 44% said they were unhappy most of the time, 41% were tired most of the time, 35% often lost their temper, 34% often couldn't sleep at night, 33% said the children got on top of them and 24% said they burst into tears for no reason:

> I'm turning into a cabbage here. Sometimes I think I'm going mad in this box of a room.[56]

- because of inadequate cooking facilities, over 33% of families never prepared a cooked meal for their families or did so less than once a week. In most cases, the women relied on take-aways and cafés. 25% of families had take-aways four times a week;
- babies born to mothers living in bed-and-breakfast accommodation were likely to have a lower birth weight than average;
- children were more likely to get infections and to suffer sickness;
- access to health care was very difficult.

A survey by Her Majesty's Inspectors found that many homeless children were not enrolled at school; others were frequently absent, performed poorly in class and suffered from low self-esteem and expectations.[57]

The Bayswater Hotel Homeless Project's recent report vividly describes the impact of living in bed-and-breakfast accommodation in contrast with having your own home.[58] The women describe:

the cramped conditions

> In B&B there was no getting away from a bed. Everything was done on the bed – eating, sleeping, sitting and there was a baby two feet away. You felt under pressure. My nerves were terrible. Whereas when you're in your own place, baby's upstairs in her room. You've got a kitchen to cook in. You've got a table to sit and eat off. You've got a settee to sit on to watch the TV and

bed to go upstairs to sleep in. It's all completely different. You're more relaxed. (Carol)

the effect on children

In your own flat you can cook, you are healthier, you're more hygienic. You try and keep everything clean in B&B, but it's really hard when you're all in one room. And the children, there's a hell of a lot of difference in the kids. It's taking a long time for my daughter to trust, because she thinks we're going to move. (Clare)

the effect on self-esteem

I am treated differently now. You sometimes came across people who, when you said you were living in B&B, gave you that look. It's difficult to describe but you feel it. They make you feel small and nothing. Now that you have your own place you think, I can start living normally like other people. I can start sorting out my life. You start to think ahead. (Lisa)

## Conclusion

Poverty casts a long shadow. It mars every aspect of life – meeting basic needs, joining in social activities, access to services and the chance of good health. We have looked at just four different aspects of poverty – living on benefits, coping with debts, experiencing poor health and being without a home. Obviously, there are many other facets to the problem – poor housing, inadequate education, an environment that is dirty, noisy or dangerous, patchy transport facilities. Not all of these are experienced by all those in poverty or only by those in poverty; yet there is no doubt that people in poverty are much more likely to suffer each of these forms of deprivation, and often multiple deprivation, than people who are better off. Each of these topics deserves a book in its own right (and many have been written). However, the evidence presented here highlights the hardship and anguish experienced by people living in poverty. It shows how poverty means going short of the basics; it means not being able to turn the heating on, or replace household goods, and not being able to go out. Poverty carries with it the risk of debt and the risk of homelessness. Above all, poverty puts at risk that most precious thing: the chance of a healthy and long life.

## NOTES

1. P Golding (ed), *Excluding the Poor*, CPAG, 1986.
2. B Campbell, 'Poverty Demobilises', Interview in *New Times*, 31 October 1992, and B Holman, 'Poverty is first among crimes', *The Guardian*, 24 June 1992.
3. M Huby and G Dix, *Evaluating the Social Fund*, DSS Research Report No 9, HMSO, 1992.
4. R Cohen, J Coxall, G Craig, A Sadiq-Sangster, *Hardship Britain, being poor in the 1990s*, CPAG Ltd in association with FSU, 1992.
5. *See* note 3.
6. National Children's Home, *Poverty and Nutrition Survey*, 1991.
7. *See* note 4.
8. *See* note 4.
9. S McRae, *Young and Jobless*, Policy Studies Institute, 1987.
10. *See* note 4
11. National Children's Home, *Deep in Debt, A Survey of problems faced by low income families*, 1992.
12. *See* note 4.
13. *See* note 4.
14. Towerwatch, *Shame about the service*, Archway Claimants' Action Group with Islington Council, 1992.
15. *See* note 4
16. J Ford, *Consuming Credit, Debt and poverty in the UK*, CPAG Ltd, 1991.
17. R Berthoud and E Kempson, *Credit and Debt in Britain, The PSI Report*, PSI, 1992.
18. *Housing Finance*, Council of Mortgage Lenders, November 1992.
19. J Ford and S Wilcox, *Reducing Mortgage Arrears and Possessions: An evaluation of the initiatives*, Joseph Rowntree Foundation, 1992.
20. OFWAT, Press Release, 16 November 1992.
21. OFFER, Customer Accounting Statistics ending September 1992; Gas Consumer Council, Debt and Disconnection Figures, 1993; *see* A Hoffland and N Nicol, *Fuel Rights Handbook*, CPAG Ltd, 1992.
22. DSS, *Annual Statistical Enquiry*, Income Support, 1991.
23. *See* note 17.
24. *See* note 17.
25. National Audit Office, *The Social Fund*, House of Commons Paper 190, HMSO, 1991.
26. *See* note 3.
27. *See* note 16.
28. J Ritchie, *Thirty families: their living standards in unemployment*, DSS, HMSO, 1990.
29. *See* note 11.
30. *See* note 16.
31. 'The Nation's Health', King Edward's Hospital Fund for London, 1991 quoted in I Cole-Hamilton, *Poverty Can Seriously Damage Your Health*, CPAG Ltd, 1991.
32. R Smith, 'Poor Britain: Losing Out', *British Medical Journal*, vol 305, 1 August 1992.
33. R Smith, 'Unemployment: here we go again', *British Medical Journal*, vol 302, 16 March 1991.
34. *See* notes 32 and 33 and *The Independent*, 27 January 1993.

35. *Mortality statistics, perinatal and infant: social and biological factors, 1978/79 and 1990*, OPCS, HMSO, 1982 and 1992.
36. *See* notes 32 and 33.
37. P Townsend, 'Living Standards and Health in the Inner City', in eds S MacGregor and B Pimlott, *Tackling the Inner Cities*, Clarendon Paperbacks, 1991.
38. Quoted in G Craig and C Glendinning, 'The impact of social security changes: the views of families living in disadvantaged areas', Barnardos Research and Development, 1990.
39. *General Household Survey 1990*, HMSO, 1992.
40. G Davy Smith, M Bartly, D Blane, 'The Black Report on socioeconomic inequalities in health: 10 years on', *British Medical Journal*, vol 301, 18-25 August 1990.
41. *See* note 4.
42. *See* note 4.
43. *See* note 31.
44. *See* note 31.
45. *See* note 31.
46. *See* note 31.
47. D Canter et al, *The Faces of homelessness in London*, Interim Report to the Salvation Army, January 1990.
48. L Burrows and P Walenkowicz, *Homes Cost Less than Homelessness*, Shelter, 1992.
49. E Button, *Rural Housing for Youth*, Centrepoint Soho, 1992.
50. R Strathdee, *No Way Back, Homeless sixteen and seventeen year olds in the 1990s*, Centrepoint Soho, 1992.
51. J Greve with E Currie, *Homeless in Britain*, Joseph Rowntree Memorial Trust, 1990.
52. *See* note 48.
53. *See* note 48.
54. *See* note 48.
55. J Conway et al, *Prescription for poor health: the crisis for homeless families*, London Food Commission, Maternity Alliance, SHAC, Shelter, 1988.
56. *See* note 55.
57. *The Independent*, 6 August 1990.
58. H Crane, *Speaking from Experience*, Bayswater Hotel Homeless Project, 1990.

CHAPTER FIVE

# Women and poverty

*The simple fact is that throughout the last century women have always been much poorer than men. At the start of this century 61% of adults on all forms of poor relief were women.*

Women and Poverty in Britain[1]

There is nothing new about women's poverty. Today, 62% of adults supported by income support are women.[2]

Focusing on women's poverty raises crucial issues for the examination of poverty as a whole.[3] Caroline Glendinning's and Jane Millar's *Women and Poverty in Britain* brought together many of the central aspects of women's poverty. The authors argue that looking at women's risk of poverty is not simply a question of illuminating the disparate *levels* of income which exist between men and women. It is also about:

- their *access* to incomes and other resources; *and*
- the *time* spent in generating income and resources; *and*
- the *transfer* of these resources from some members of a household to others.

This approach facilitates a much more complete understanding of the nature of poverty which is not captured by straightforward statistics on family or household incomes.

## Indicators of women's poverty

### Low Income

The major sources of data on poverty are not broken down by sex. Income is measured by the household or family unit. The *Low Income Families Statistics* and the Department of Social Security's figures –

*Households below Average Income* – are no exception. However, it is possible to make a rough estimate of how many women are living in poverty by making assumptions about the number of women who are lone parents, pensioners and so forth:[4]

- In 1989, approximately 5.1 million women and 3.4 million men were living in poverty (defined as on and below the income support level).

As the figures show, there are considerably more women in poverty than men – women outnumber men by about 1.7 million and make up around 60% of the adults living in poverty. Research by Peter Esam and Richard Berthoud at the Policy Studies Institute shows that, in 1990/91, over 4.6 million women had independent incomes of less than £25 a week compared to 0.4 million men (see Table 9). Just under a third of married women without children under pension age had an income of less than £25 a week of their own compared to 2% of men. The average income of married men without children was nearly two and a half times that of married women without children.[5]

**TABLE 9**

**Personal weekly incomes of adults, analysed by sex and family status in 1990/1**

| | Pensioners | | Non-pensioners | | |
|---|---|---|---|---|---|
| | Single | Married | Single | Married no children | Married with children |
| **Men** | | | | | |
| Number | 0.9m | 2.6m | 5.1m | 5.5m | 5.8m |
| Average income | £97 | £109 | £123 | £208 | £223 |
| Less than £25 | nil | – | 5% | 2% | 1% |
| **Women** | | | | | |
| Number | 3.5m | 2.6m | 4.5m | 5.5m | 5.8m |
| Average income | £81 | £40 | £106 | £87 | £60 |
| Less than £25 | nil | 24% | 6% | 31% | 35% |

*SOURCE: PSI tax/benefit model, P. Esam and R. Berthoud, Independent Benefits for Men and Women, Policy Studies Institute, 1991*

Although the *Family Expenditure Survey* does not provide data about the incomes of men and women living in families, it does provide useful information about single person households broken down by sex. It shows that in 1991:

- the gross incomes of women under pension age were only 82% of men's; for women over pension age the figure was 77%;
- women were more reliant on social security benefits than men, particularly in retirement, and were less likely to have other income such as annuities, pensions and investments.

The greater reliance on social security in retirement among women is the outcome of lower earnings, intermittent work patterns, and fewer rights to occupational pensions.[6]

## Unemployment

> I have missed working. I've missed the company as much as the money. Before, I loved being at home but I loved being in work too and I miss it, the girls and all. I haven't really settled to it because my nerves have gone all wonky being in the house. It's all right when the children are here but when everybody goes I am back on my own all day.
>
> (Quoted in C Callender, *Redundancy, Unemployment and Poverty*)[7]

The full extent of unemployment amongst women is hidden as the official unemployment statistics are based on the numbers claiming benefit. The *Labour Force Survey* count of unemployment shows much higher rates of unemployment amongst women than the claimant count. In spring 1992:

- 631,000 women were unemployed according to the claimant count – 23% of the total numbers unemployed;
- 900,000 women were unemployed according to the *Labour Force Survey* definition (ie, people who did no paid work in the previous week, had actively looked for work in the last four weeks and were free to start work in two weeks, regardless of whether they were claiming benefits) – 33% of the total numbers unemployed;
- 564,000 women were unemployed according to a slightly less stringent definition of unemployment in the *Labour Force Survey* (ie, people who want work, are available, but have not looked in the last four weeks) – 73% of the total numbers unemployed;
- 1,464,000 women were unemployed if you combine the two previous measures (ie, all wanting and available for work) – 41% of the total numbers unemployed.[8]

In financial terms redundancy is likely to be even worse for women than men. Redundancy payments are based on length of service and pay levels. Part-time workers are disadvantaged in terms of redundancy pay. As Claire Callender writes:

> Women receive lower redundancy payments than men and a larger proportion of them are ineligible for payments altogether. This makes women cheaper to dismiss and makes them more vulnerable to redundancy.[9]

## Low pay

> I was earning roughly £35 to £40 a week. It was piece work, 13p per skirt – you had to sew hundreds to get to £35-£40 . . . I had to work sometimes until midnight, from nine in the morning, just to pay rent, electricity and gas.
>
> (Sevin, mother of three)[10]

- In 1991, 6.53 million women were low paid – ie, 65% of the total number of people on low wages according to the Council of Europe's decency threshold. (This is defined as £193.60 a week or £5.15 an hour in 1991/92).
- There is a strong association between low pay and part-time work. In 1991, 4.46 million women worked part-time and 79% of them were low paid. Only 976,000 men worked part-time with a slightly lower proportion who were low paid (71%).[11]
- Many black women are likely to have even lower earnings and/or do more shift work (see Chapter 6).
- In 1992, women's average gross hourly earnings including overtime were 80% of men's.
- Research by the Equal Opportunities Commission estimated that around three-quarters of employees who are covered by Wages Council agreements are women. On average, women earned 25% more than the Statutory Minimum Requirement which the Wages Councils impose, while men earned 100% more on average. The abolition of the Wages Councils will have a particularly detrimental effect on women's wages.[12]

## Lone Mothers

> It is precisely because lone mothers are women that they have a very high risk of poverty. (J Millar, *Lone Mothers and Poverty*)[13]

In 1990, there were well over one million lone mothers. Nine out of ten lone parents are women. As we have seen, they are much more likely to be in poverty than other groups:

- lone mothers' employment rates have declined in the last ten years: in 1981, 45% of lone mothers with a dependent child aged 15 or under were in employment; in 1990 this had fallen to 39%. By contrast, married mothers' employment rates increased over the same period from 47% to 60%.[14]
- 852,000 lone mothers were reliant on income support in 1991. Over two-fifths of lone parents were on income support for several years; 366,000 had been on supplementary benefit/income support for three years or more.[15] Being on benefit for long periods inevitably brings hardship and often debt.

The combination of coping with bringing up children on their own, the difficulties of managing on a single wage, very often at low levels, with little access to affordable childcare, means that many lone mothers find themselves forced to rely on means-tested benefits for long periods.

## Benefits

> Women are . . . less likely than men to be receiving the superior contributory benefits and more likely to be receiving the inferior non-contributory equivalents. Many women are entitled to neither (leaving aside benefits for children) and are therefore reliant on means-tested income support or on a man for economic support.
>
> (R Lister, *Women's Economic Dependency and Social Security*)[16]

One of the main features of our social security system is the division between national insurance benefits, non-contributory and means-tested benefits. As long as sufficient contributions have been made, national insurance benefits are paid on an individual basis regardless of income. Non-contributory benefits are not means-tested, but they are lower than national insurance benefits. Means-tested benefits are based on a test of income and capital. Because women are more likely to have breaks in employment and to work part time and earn low wages, many fall below the threshold for making national insurance contributions. In 1992, over 2.25 million women fell into this category.[17] The result is that women forfeit their right to national insurance benefits. Women are therefore less likely to have benefits in their own right than men, and as a result are more dependent on non-contributory benefits and the 'Cinderella' part of the social security system – means-tested benefits.

Table 10 below, taken from Ruth Lister's research for the EOC, illustrates this clearly.[18] More men are claiming contributory benefits for people below pension age and more women are claiming means-tested and non-contributory benefits. Retirement pension (a contributory benefit) is an exception to this pattern because of the high proportion of women pensioners. However, a much higher proportion of women over pension age are reliant on income support than men over pension age: 17% of women over pension age (1,140,000) claimed income support compared to 8% of men (270,000).[19]

**TABLE 10**

**Social security claimants by sex, 1991**

Great Britain | Per cent

| Benefit | Men | Women |
|---|---|---|
| Industrial Death Benefit | Nil | 100 |
| Industrial Injury Disablement Benefit | 89 | 11 |
| Invalidity Benefit | 76 | 24 |
| Maternity Benefit | Nil | 100 |
| Retirement Pension | 35 | 65 |
| Sickness Benefit | 74 | 26 |
| Unemployment Benefit | 68 | 32 |
| Widows Benefit | Nil | 100 |
| Reduced Earnings Allowance | 83 | 17 |
| Attendance Allowance | 37 | 63 |
| Child Benefit | 2 | 98 |
| One Parent Benefit | 9 | 91 |
| Invalid Care Allowance | 18 | 82 |
| Mobility Allowance | 52 | 48 |
| Severe Disablement Allowance | 40 | 60 |
| Family Credit | 1 | 99 |
| Income Support | 43 | 57 |

*SOURCE: R Lister, Women's Economic Dependency and Social Security, Equal Opportunities Commission, 1992*

## Exclusion

> Her father's always going on that he hasn't got any money and yet he's got a Cortina. I walk everywhere and I stay within this area.
>
> (Jenny, lone mother)[20]

The indicators of poverty above look at hard facts, like wages and social

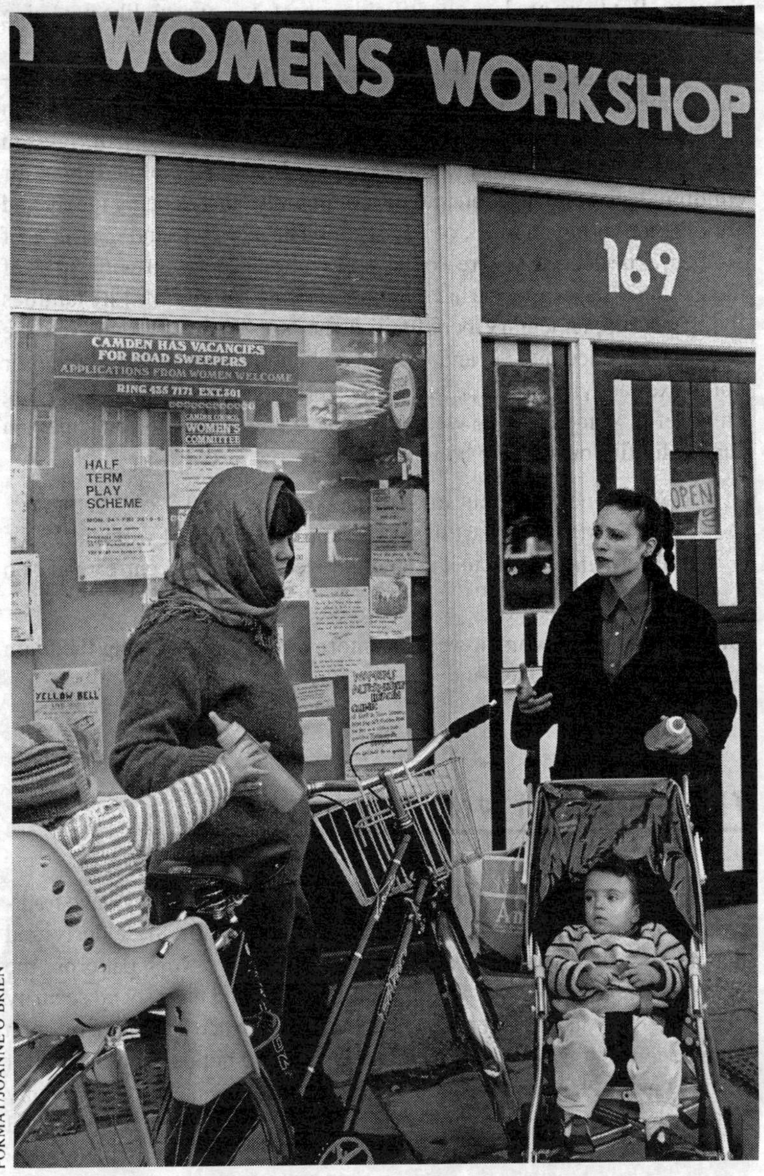


FORMAT/JOANNE O'BRIEN

***Caring for children has a knock-on effect on women's employment and earning capacity. Thus simply being female has a downward pressure on overall earnings.***

security. But there are less quantifiable aspects to poverty, like not being able to go out for a drink or a meal, or missing out on seeing friends. There is some evidence to show that this aspect of poverty is also different for men and women. A local poverty survey undertaken in Islington in 1990 looked at social deprivation. This was defined as lack of rights in employment such as no paid holiday or sick pay, lack of activities for children, lack of integration into the community such as being lonely and cut off, not voting and lack of education. The survey found that 37% of women experienced severe social deprivation compared with 30% of men.[21] This bears out earlier findings from a survey of 140 families living on supplementary benefit in Tyne and Wear. It compared the activities pursued by men and women on benefit. It shows that while for both sexes activities outside the home were severely curtailed by living on benefit, women, on the whole, were even less likely to participate in such activities outside the home than men:

- 18% of men went out for a drink compared to 3% of women;
- 18% of men took part in sport compared to 8% of women;
- 11% of men went to the unemployed workers' centre while no women did.

On the other hand women were far more likely to be cooking the main meal or cleaning and dusting.[22]

## The causes of women's poverty

Women's lives are shaped by the family responsibilities they have traditionally taken on – the tasks of childcare, caring for the elderly and maintaining the home. These tasks shape women's work patterns, the type of occupations they work in, their earnings and their social security benefits. They push women into financial dependence upon men or upon state benefits. It is often assumed that women do not need an income of their own and that money, food and other resources are shared evenly within the family. For many women neither employment nor social security can keep them out of poverty.

## Women's unpaid work

### Domestic labour

Women are responsible for the bulk of domestic work. *British Social Attitudes*, an annual survey, looked at the distribution of household tasks undertaken by men and women.[23] It found that the traditional division of labour is alive and kicking. In 1991:

- 45% of women were mainly responsible for shopping compared to 8% of men (47% share);
- 70% of women were mainly responsible for making the evening meal compared to 9% of men (20% share);
- 68% of women were mainly responsible for cleaning compared to 4% of men (27% share);
- 84% of women were mainly responsible for washing and ironing compared to 3% of men (12% share);
- 60% of women looked after children when sick compared to 1% of men (39% share).

The only task that men were more likely to do than women was repairing household equipment – 82% of men were mainly responsible for this task compared to 6% of women.

Married women are less likely to work full time than those women without a partner. Heather Joshi argues that:

> the lower propensity of married women to take full-time jobs even when they have no young children must . . . partly arise from the extra demands on their time of looking after husband, home and social network.[24]

Catherine Marsh carried out a survey of the hours that men and women work for the Equal Opportunities Commission. She found that British men worked the longest hours in Europe: 23% of men working full-time in Europe worked 46 hours or more compared to 42% of British men. Britain and Denmark are the only two countries with no statutory maximum working week. She also found that the usual pattern was that one partner (usually male) worked very long hours and the other (usually female) worked much shorter hours and thus there was 'very little evidence of domestic job sharing'.[25] She concludes:

> There seems no way in which a style of work which involved such a long commitment to paid employment could be emulated by anyone who had a major responsiblity for children. It might be useful to consider regulation of the hours of work of men as the single most effective means of promoting equality at the workplace.

This domestic division of labour is echoed in the more traditional attitudes that men have to women's responsibilities than women themselves have. Sharon Witherspoon and Gillian Prior found that just over one half of fathers disagreed with the view that the man should be the main breadwinner and the woman should look after the home and children, compared to three-quarters of women. They conclude:

> Whatever talk there is of the 'New Man', he is much rarer than the 'New Woman'. This gap in attitudes has consequences for family life in general, as well as for women's decisions to work outside the home. In the absence of changes in men's attitudes, or in their working hours outside the home, or in their contribution within the family towards childcare and domestic duties, it seems unlikely that even a greater availability of childcare outside the home would alter domestic arrangements greatly. Indeed without these changes, it is conceivable that many useful forms of work flexibility which might be offered to women – such as job-sharing, career-breaks, special sick-leave, or term-time working – might serve to reinforce rather than mitigate the already formidable level of occupational segregation based on gender, to women's longer term disadvantage.[26]

## Caring for children

Looking after children swallows up a large amount of time and is still usually done by women. A 1984 survey estimated that women were responsible for 48 out of 50 hours spent on basic childcare tasks.[27] More recently, the *London Living Standards Survey* found that women with a child under 5 spent 65 hours a week on childcare compared to 20 hours spent by men.[28]

Caring for children has a knock-on effect on women's employment and earning capacity. Heather Joshi compared the average earnings of a woman with two children to that of a childless woman over their lifetimes. She found that a mother with two children would lose an average of £202,500 in foregone earnings over a lifetime.[29] This is the result of 8 years out of the labour market, working part-time and having lower earnings. This takes no account of the loss of pension rights. Joshi estimates that these may amount to as much as the overall loss in earnings. Joshi also compared the lifetime average earnings of a woman without children with a man and found that the difference was nearly as much as the difference between a woman without children and a mother. Thus, simply being female has a downward pressure on overall earnings.[30]

## Caring for elderly or sick or disabled people

> I hadn't anticipated giving up work, I thought I could manage the three hours. But the thing was . . . in the summer days she came out to meet me, her petticoat round her top. She'd got changed during the afternoon. My heart nearly broke when I saw her . . . and then twice she ran after me as I was getting on the bus – didn't want me to go. The time had come to stop work.
>
> (Ms Grey, who gave up her job as a child welfare clinic clerical officer several months after her mother came to live with her, quoted in C Glendinning, *The Costs of Informal Care*)[31]

It is not only caring for children that has a knock-on effect on women's lost earnings, but also caring for adult relatives who are elderly or sick or have a disability. There has been a great deal of discussion about the overall number of carers and what proportion of those are women. The 1985 *General Household Survey* estimated:

- that there were 6 million carers;
- that 3.5 million carers were women (15% of all women) and 2.5 million were men (12% of all men);
- that women tended to care for more hours and were more often sole or main carers than men.[32]

Recent research by Gillian Parker suggests that the numbers *heavily* involved in caring are substantially lower at around 1.3 million, but that the number of women caring may have been underestimated.[33] Obviously, the longer the hours of caring the more likely the carer is to be working part-time or not at all. Therefore, it is *more* likely that women, who have heavier caring duties than men, are *less* likely to have earnings from full-time employment.

The *financial cost* of caring is substantial. Maria Evandrou has shown that female sole carers have a slightly greater risk of having less money than male sole carers: 23% of female sole carers fell into the bottom fifth of the income distribution, compared to 20% of men.[34] Heather Joshi has estimated that in 1990 the annual 'cost' of giving up full-time work in the later stages of life to care for an elderly or sick person was £12,750 for someone without children and £10,500 for a mother. (The losses are lower for women with children because their earnings have already been depressed by having children.)[35]

### Time costs

Work at home, whether caring for the home or children or adults, is often neglected in any discussion of poverty. The amount of *time* spent trying to achieve a given standard of living – eg, cleaning, cooking and other forms of 'home production' – is an important aspect of poverty.[36] Jane Millar and Caroline Glendinning argue:

> The value of time – both in the generation of resources and in their use – has hitherto been largely ignored in poverty studies. If time were included it would almost certainly point out substantial differences between men and women.[37]

In other words, poverty is not just about income but about how income and other resources are generated and used. For example, it may take a woman on low pay 50 hours a week to earn an average wage while a woman on higher earnings might need to work half as many hours to achieve the same income. The amount of *time* trying to earn a living wage is an important aspect of her poverty. Another example is the amount of time it takes to do household tasks. Visits to the launderette, daily trips to the shops because there is never enough money for a big shop, making sandwiches because there isn't enough money for school dinners – all these absorb time. Not having sufficient money, or a washing machine, or a car, all mean that it takes much more time and work for someone in poverty to achieve the same standard of living as someone who is comfortably off.

## Women's paid work

On the whole, women and men work in different parts of the job market. This sexual division of labour is deeply entrenched. Sue Lonsdale estimates that a quarter of jobs are typically female and three-quarters are typically male.[38] The latest *Labour Force Survey* in 1991 shows that more than two-thirds of working women were employed in non-manual work (compared to under half of men) and that 82% worked in service industries (compared with just over half of men).[39]

The division between women and men in the world of paid work reflects the divisions in domestic work. Women tend to work in jobs that are similar to the jobs they do at home. In 1991:

- 18% of women worked in clerical occupations compared to 7% of men;
- 13% of women worked in personal services, such as catering, cleaning and hairdressing, compared to 3% of men;
- 9% of women worked in secretarial occupations compared to 0.3% of men;[40]

- 9% of women worked as sales assistants or check-out operators compared to 2% of men.

Many of these occupations have high proportions of low-paid workers. According to the *New Earnings Survey*, in 1992:

- 29% of women full-timers in clerical and secretarial occupations earned below £170 a week;
- 73% of women full-timers in catering, 75% in cleaning and 86% in hairdressing earned below £170 a week;
- 78% of women full-timers who worked as sales assistants or check-out operators earned below £170 a week.[41]

Women are also far less likely to have access to occupational and fringe benefits at work. A recent study found that a lower proportion of full-time women workers had access to almost all types of benefit (after

**TABLE 11**

**Percentage of jobs where employer provides benefits, by gender**

| | Male full-timers | Female full-timers | Female part-timers |
|---|---|---|---|
| pensions* | 73 | 68 | 31 |
| sick pay* | 66 | 58 | 27 |
| paid time off | 64 | 48 | 30 |
| unpaid time off | 54 | 54 | 57 |
| company car or van | 30 | 10 | 5 |
| free/subsidised transport | 31 | 24 | 17 |
| goods at a discount | 47 | 40 | 31 |
| free or subsidised meals | 39 | 47 | 25 |
| finance/loans | 21 | 20 | 12 |
| accommodation | 14 | 17 | 5 |
| life assurance | 39 | 19 | 5 |
| private health | 31 | 22 | 9 |
| recreation facilities | 40 | 36 | 24 |
| maternity pay | – | 31 | 16 |
| childcare | 1 | 13 | 10 |

* above basic government scheme

*SOURCE: Unequal Jobs, Unequal Pay, ESRC, The Social Change and Economic Life Initiative, Working Paper 6, 1989*

allowing for differences in skill and job content) in comparison with men. For part-time women workers this pattern was even more marked (see Table 11).[42]

Women are far more likely to be working part time than men because of their domestic responsibilities. The 1991 *Labour Force Survey* showed that:

- 76% of male employees worked full time and 4% part time;
- 51% of female employees worked full time and 40% part time;
- 45% of married women employees worked full time and 46% part time.[43]

> I think employers are hesitant to employ you full-time, knowing that you've got two young children. When I had Christopher, I didn't tell them I was a single parent. I did five nights a week, and Christopher went to my friend at nights and then I came home and looked after him in the day. I didn't know what living was about until I stopped doing night duty. I didn't see anybody.
>
> (Valerie, lone mother)[44]

Patterns of part-time work are directly linked to responsibilities for caring for children or others. As the youngest child gets older the mother is more likely to be in paid work. A majority of women with children in the youngest age group are not in paid work (see Table 12).[45]

**TABLE 12**

**Employment rates for women of working age with children in 1991**

| | age of youngest child | | |
|---|---|---|---|
| | **0-4** | **5-10** | **11-15** |
| **% working full time** | 14% | 21% | 32% |
| **part time** | 29% | 45% | 42% |
| **% not in paid work** | 57% | 34% | 26% |

*SOURCE: Department of Employment, Women and the Labour Market: results from the 1991 Labour Force Survey, Employment Gazette, September 1992*

Getting paid work is also intimately linked to the availability of childcare. The United Kingdom has one of the worst records of provision for publicly funded childcare places in the European Community. Only Luxembourg and Ireland have worse provision for under 2-year-olds and only Portugal less for 3- and 4-year-olds. In the United Kingdom, only 2% of 0 to 2-year-olds and only 44% of over 3s were in publicly funded childcare places in 1985-86. Compare this with 44% and 87% in Denmark. Even in poorer countries like Greece and Spain, 62% and 66% respectively of 3-year-olds upwards were in publicly funded childcare.[46]

> Childcare in this country is a joke. For a woman who has got very little resources unless you are lucky enough to get a government subsidised nursery, any private childcare is really expensive . . . that one factor stops a lot of women from coming off social security and getting a job.
>
> (Grace, lone mother)[47]

An important new development is the *decrease* in the number of hours worked by women. According to Catherine Marsh, in 1979, 29.8% of female manual part-time workers and 23% of female non-manual part-time workers worked less than 16 hours a week.[48] By 1992, this had risen to 39.7% and 36.6% respectively.[49] Looking at service industries alone, there is an even higher proportion of women working less than 16 hours a week. This trend is important because it means women are able to earn less money, are less likely to qualify for certain social security benefits and may not be covered by the employment protection legislation.[50] The 1975 Employment Protection Act prevents unfair dismissal, and brings entitlement to maternity benefits, the right to reinstatement after maternity and access to redundancy payments. However, to qualify a person must work for 16 hours or more for two years continuously with the same employer, or for 8 hours or more for five years. The Trade Union Reform and Employment Rights Bill, which is currently going through Parliament, improves the situation somewhat. In order to bring the UK into line with the EC, women have gained a right to protection from dismissal due to pregnancy and 14 weeks of maternity leave without qualifying conditions. However, other aspects of employment protection continue to exclude many employees, largely women who are working very short hours. As Sue Lonsdale writes, this creates two classes of part-time workers: the protected and the unprotected.[51]

Women are also more likely to have temporary, seasonal or casual jobs than men. 7% of women (0.74 million) of working age in employment had such jobs compared to 4% of men. 10% of women with a child under 5 and 10% of women with a child in primary school had temporary jobs. These work patterns are clearly related to women's domestic responsibilities.[52]

The shift in industrial structure to service industries, the increase in part-time work, the decrease in the number of hours worked by women and the expansion of temporary work are all aspects of the 'flexible' labour market. However, such developments do not always serve women well. As Ruth Lister writes:

> The general trends towards a more 'flexible' labour market, offering many women low-paid, insecure jobs without employment rights, mean that, at the very time women's economic activity rates are increasing, the labour market is decreasingly likely to offer them an adequate independent income.[53]

## Whose money?

> I won't touch jumble sales . . . I'll buy the cheapest for myself, or second hand, but not for the kids.
>
> (Molly, mother of six, living with husband who is registered disabled)[54]

> I'll go to jumble sales for my clothes . . . But I'm not seeing me kid and me husband walk to town with secondhand clothes on. I'll make do myself, but I won't make do for them. I wouldn't mind a new coat but I can't have one.
>
> (Emily, mother of three, husband unemployed)[55]

The distribution of money, food, and other goods inside the home is an area which is seen as *private* and is therefore very difficult to research.[56] The quotations above illustrate the ways in which women often put the needs of their families above their own. By impoverishing themselves women help to prevent or reduce poverty for other members of their family.[57] Thus a woman can be in poverty while other members of her family are not or she may be in deeper poverty than they are. Research by Vogler in 1989 looked at 1,200 households. She found that only a fifth used a system of pooling money between husband and wife and that women 'command less of the family income than men'.[58] This confirms earlier research by Jan Pahl. In *Money and Marriage* Pahl looks at how money is handled inside the family.[59] She shows that women in couples are likely to have less income of their own than men: 83% of women in couples had an income of less than £57 a week compared with 6% of men (the result of differential earnings, savings, gifts and child benefit). Pahl also found that in poorer households and in households in the North, North-West and in Wales, women are more likely to be responsible for the family budget. But holding the purse strings does not necessarily confer power:

> Women are responsible for family finances but they have none of the power that goes with possession. Having it in their hands never made money their own.
>
> (Beatrix Campbell)[60]

The bulk of the money a woman brings into the home is spent on household consumption. Pahl also found that, as far as household spending was concerned, men contributed more in absolute terms and women contributed more in relative terms:

> Put simply, if a pound entered the household economy through the mother's hands more of it would be spent on food for the family than would be the case if the pound had been brought into the household by the father.[61]

In addition, Pahl found that husbands were more likely to have money for personal spending and leisure than the women:

- 44% of men compared to 28% of women had personal spending money;
- 86% of men and 67% of women spent money on leisure pursuits.

> He liked cars and drinking and there wasn't the money for it. Me and the kids used to go short on food and clothes because he spent the money.
>
> (Vanessa, lone mother)[62]

> He wanted extra money off me which I couldn't give him, which led to rows and then in the end I were saying there were only the £5 electricity money left and he were taking it and spending it. And then on Monday when I cashed the family allowance, he wanted money out of that as well. So that didn't help.
>
> (Carol, lone mother of three, expecting another)[63]

It is not only the sharing of money and resources that can be unequal within a home, but also the impact of things that a family does not have. For example, living in an overcrowded flat with damp and heating problems has a greater effect on a mother at home with a child than on her husband who is at work, simply because of the amount of time the woman spends at home.

> Not having hot water or a bathroom means different things to the man who uses hot water for washing and shaving in comparison with the woman who is responsible for childcare, the washing of clothes and cleaning the house.
>
> (S Payne, *Women, Health and Poverty*)[64]

## Failures in the social security system

The social security system fails to protect women adequately from poverty because it does not recognise the complexity of most women's lives. Beveridge's social security scheme assumed a traditional family unit with the full-time male breadwinner and woman at home looking after the home and children. The social security system has not kept pace with changes in women's roles and employment patterns. Such a model cannot accommodate the mixture of paid work and unpaid work (such as caring for children and others) and the changes in family patterns which particularly affect women's capacity to provide an adequate income for themselves and their families. Many of the recent changes in social security have had a detrimental effect on women. Here are just a few examples:[65]

- the abolition of the universal maternity grant. This has been replaced by the maternity payment now available only to women on income support and family credit, it has not kept pace with inflation;
- childcare costs cannot be offset against earnings for income support claimants (they could under supplementary benefit);
- the introduction of the social fund with all its weaknesses (such as loans and budget limits) particularly affects women. Lone parents (most of whom are women) have a high reliance on the social fund. The difficulties of repaying loans and the effect of this on managing budgets very often falls on women's shoulders as they are more likely to have overall budgeting responsibility;
- the freezing of child benefit for three years between 1988 and 1990;
- the abolition of free school meals for family credit recipients (although there was some cash compensation);
- the weakening of the State Earnings Related Pension which is now based on a lifetime's earnings and only partially protects women with domestic responsibilities;
- the emphasis on private provision such as private pensions, which tends to reinforce market inequalities between men and women.

There have been some positive changes such as extra help for carers (there is a carers' premium in income support), increased earnings disregards for carers and lone parents and new benefits for people with disabilities. However, as Ruth Lister concludes:

> the dominant trends in social security policy have been to place greater emphasis on means-tested as opposed to non-means-tested provision and on private as opposed to public forms of income maintenance. Whilst certain specific policies have been to women's advantage, the overall impact of these trends is corrosive of women's economic independence.[66]

## Conclusion

Women's poverty is compounded over a lifetime. Their lower rates of pay, work patterns interrupted because of caring for others, the trap of part-time work, and the diminished social security, occupational and private benefits received as a result of their work patterns combine to impoverish women throughout their lives. Women's longer life expectancy and their reduced access to pensions mean that a high proportion are living out their lives on pitiful levels of income.

Many measures which would help people living in poverty would benefit women in particular. CPAG believes that the following policies would begin to deal with the poverty faced by women:

- A statutory minimum wage for full- and part-time workers.
- Pro-rata employment rights for part-time workers.
- Improving the rights of parents in employment (eg, parental leave, paternity and maternity leave etc).
- Developing training schemes which encourage young women to work in occupations which are traditionally male and vice versa.
- The replacement of the national insurance threshold with a tax threshold so that employers and employees (largely women) no longer have an incentive to create, or work in jobs, of very few hours a week.
- Encouraging employers to extend flexible working arrangements such as flexible hours, job-sharing arrangements, working from home and term-time contracts for men as well as for women.
- Tightening up the European Directive on working hours by ensuring that there is a statutory maximum working week.
- Increased availability of subsidised childcare including school holiday care and care for after school hours.
- Steps towards a non-means-tested social security system without contribution conditions so that women with caring responsibilities would not be penalised for spending time out of the labour market.
- Individual entitlement to benefit.

### NOTES

1. J Lewis and D Piachaud, 'Women and Poverty in the twentieth century' in C Glendinning and J Millar (eds), *Women and poverty in Britain, the 1990s*, Wheatsheaf, 1992.
2. This is based on the following assumptions: in 1991, 2,522,000 women and 1,965,000

men received income support, 763,000 partners were provided for, 97% of whom are women. This makes a total of 3,262,000 women and 1,988,000 men provided for by income support. *See* DSS, *Social Security Statistics 1992*, Government Statistical Service, HMSO, 1992.

3. J Millar and C Glendinning, 'Gender and poverty: a survey article', *Journal of Social Policy*, Vol 18, part 3, July 1989.
4. Using income support statistics this figure assumes that 35% of single people (excluding lone parents) under pension age are women; that 88% of single people over pension age are women; and that 96% of lone parents on income support are women. Figures derived from DSS, *Social Security Statistics* (*see* note 2).
5. P Esam and R Berthoud, *Independent Benefits for Men and Women*, An enquiry into options for treating husbands and wives as separate units in the assessment of social security, Policy Studies Institute, 1992.
6. Central Statistical Office, *Family Spending, A Report on the 1991 Family Expenditure Survey*, Government Statistical Service, HMSO, 1992.
7. Claire Callender, 'Redundancy, Unemployment and Poverty', in C Glendinning and J Millar (eds), see note 1.
8. T Lynes, *The wrong side of the tracks*, factsheet on unemployment and benefits, CPAG Ltd, 1992.
9. *See* note 7.
10. Quoted in 'Women and poverty' photographic exhibition, CPAG, 1986.
11. *The New Review, No 13*, Low Pay Unit, December 1991/January 1992.
12. S Lonsdale, 'Patterns of Paid Work', in C Glendinning and J Millar (eds), see note 1.
13. J Millar, 'Lone Mothers and Poverty', in C Glendinning and J Millar (eds), see note 1.
14. R Bartholomew, A Hibbett and J Sidaway, 'Lone Parents and the Labour Market: evidence from the Labour Force Survey', *Employment Gazette*, Department of Employment, November 1992.
15. Department of Social Security, *Social Security Statistics 1992*, HMSO, 1992.
16. R Lister, *Women's Economic Dependency and Social Security*, Equal Opportunities Commission, 1992.
17. *House of Commons Hansard*, 11 January 1993, col 626.
18. *See* note 16.
19. DSS, *Social Security Statistics 1992*, HMSO, 1993.
20. *See* note 10.
21. Islington Council, *Islington: Poverty in the 80s, A Digest*, 1990.
22. J Bradshaw and H Holmes, *Living on the edge: a study of the living standards of families on benefit living in Tyne and Wear*, Tyneside CPAG, 1989.
23. K Kiernan, 'Men and Women at Work and at Home', in R Jowell et al (eds), *British Social Attitudes, 9th Report, 1992/93*, Dartmouth, 1992.
24. H. Joshi, 'The Cost of Caring', in C Glendinning and J Millar (eds), *see* note 1.
25. C Marsh, *Hours of Work of Women and Men in Britain*, Equal Opportunities Commission, HMSO, 1991.
26. S. Witherspoon and G Prior, 'Working Mothers: Free to Choose?', R Jowell et al (eds), *British Social Attitudes, 8th report, 1991/92*, Social and Community Planning Research, Dartmouth, 1991.
27. D Piachaud, *Round about 50 hours a week*, CPAG, 1984.
28. U Kowarzik and J Popay, *London Living Standards Survey*, 'Unpaid Work', unpublished paper, 1988.
29. *See* note 24.

30. *See* note 24.
31. C Glendinning, *The Costs of Informal Care: Looking Inside the Household*, Social Policy Research Unit, HMSO, 1992.
32. H Green, *Informal carers, General Household Survey*, HMSO, 1988.
33. G Parker, 'Counting Care: numbers and types of informal carers', in J Twigg (ed), *Carers, Research & Practice*, HMSO, 1992.
34. M Evandrou, *Challenging the Invisibility of Carers: Mapping Informal Care Nationally*, WSP/49, Suntory Toyota International Centre for Economics and Related Disciplines, 1990.
35. *See* note 24.
36. D Piachaud, 'Problems in the Definition and Measurement of Poverty', *Journal of Social Policy*, Vol 116, part 2, April 1987.
37. *See* note 1.
38. *See* note 12.
39. *Employment Gazette*, 'Women and the labour market: results from the 1991 Labour Force Survey', Department of Employment, September 1992.
40. *See* note 39.
41. Department of Employment, *New Earnings Survey*, Part D, Government Statistical Service, HMSO, 1992. Note that these figures underestimate the extent of low pay in these sectors because they do not take account of part-time workers.
42. S Howell, J Rubery, B Burchell, *Unequal Jobs, Unequal Pay*, Economic and Social Research Council, Working Paper 6, 1989.
43. *Employment Gazette*, 'Results of the 1991 Labour Force Survey', Department of Employment, April 1992.
44. *See* note 10.
45. *See* note 39.
46. P Moss, *Childcare and equality of opportunity*, Commission of the European Communities, 1988.
47. *See* note 10.
48. *See* note 25.
49. Department of Employment, *New Earnings Survey 1992*, Part F, Government Statistical Service, HMSO, 1992.
50. *See* note 16.
51. *See* note 12.
52. *See* note 39.
53. *See* note 16.
54. G Craig and C Glendinning, quoted in *The impact of social security changes: the views of families living in disadvantaged areas*, Barnardos Research and Development, 1990.
55. *See* note 54.
56. J Brannen and G Wilson (eds), *Give and take in families: studies in resource distribution*, Allen and Unwin, 1987.
57. *See* note 1.
58. C Vogler, *Labour Market Change and Patterns of Financial Allocation Within Households*, Working Paper no 12, Oxford: ESRC/Social Change and Economic Life Initiative, 1989, quoted in C. Glendinning and J. Millar (eds), *see* note 1.
59. J Pahl, *Money and Marriage*, Macmillan, 1989.
60. B Campbell, *Wigan Pier Revisited*, Virago, 1984.
61. *See* note 59.

62. *See* note 54.
63. *See* note 54.
64. S Payne, quoted in R Lister, *see* note 16.
65. *See* R Lister (note 16) for greater detail.
66. *See* note 16.

CHAPTER SIX

# Race and poverty

*Blackness and poverty are more correlated than they were some years ago. In spite of government concern with racial disadvantage, and the undoubted limited success of positive action and equal opportunities in helping to create a black middle class, the condition of the black poor is deteriorating.*

K Amin and K Leech[1]

Despite often shocking levels of poverty faced by black people and other members of ethnic minorities, there is still precious little social policy research about race and poverty. *Households below Average Income* – the source of official data about low-income families – contains no breakdown of statistics by ethnic origin. Neither did the *Low Income Families* statistics.[2] However, a welcome new development is that the Department of Social Security's *Family Resources Survey*, available in future years, has a question on ethnic origin and will provide, for the first time, official data which looks at income and ethnic origin. Until then the principal sources of information on racial inequality are the *Labour Force Survey by Ethnic Origin*,[3] the Policy Studies Institute survey of 1982 (now becoming out of date) and many useful local surveys.[4]

Below we look at some of the indicators and causes of poverty broken down by ethnic origin.[5] We draw heavily on a recent report published by CPAG and the Runnymede Trust called *Poverty in Black and White: deprivation and ethnic minorities*.

## Indicators of Poverty

### Unemployment

- Unemployment rates for black and other ethnic minority groups have always been much higher than for white people. Although the gap has narrowed since 1984, it remains substantial. In the period 1989-91, the male unemployment rate for black people and other ethnic minority groups was 13%, nearly double the rate for white people which stood at 7%. The disparity in unemployment rates for women was similar: 12% compared to 7% (see Table 13).[6]

- People from Pakistan and Bangladesh had particularly high rates of unemployment: 21% for men and 24% for women in 1989-91.
- For young people, the unemployment rates are even greater. In the period 1989-91, 22% of young men aged between 16 and 24 from black and other ethnic minority groups were unemployed, compared to 12% of white men. For young women the figures were 19% and 9% respectively.[7]
- Even with qualifications, black people and members of other ethnic minorities are still more likely to experience unemployment due to discrimination. In the period 1989-91, the unemployment rate was 6% for ethnic minorities with higher qualifications, and 3% for white people with the same qualifications. For ethnic minorities with 'other qualifications', the unemployment rate was 13% compared to 6% for white people who were similarly qualified.[8]

If you can't be looked at and be seen as white, then you're going to be disadvantaged in employment. It's as simple and easy as that.

(Winston, young black unemployed adult)[9]

**TABLE 13**

**Unemployment rates by sex, age and ethnic origin; average: spring 1989-1991, Great Britain (%)**

| | Men | | Women | |
|---|---|---|---|---|
| | All aged 16 and over | 16 to 24 | All aged 16 and over | 16 to 24 |
| **White** | 7 | 12 | 7 | 9 |
| **Ethnic Minority Groups:** | | | | |
| All | 13 | 22 | 12 | 19 |
| West Indian/Guyanese | 15 | * | 12 | * |
| Indian | 10 | * | 10 | * |
| Pakistani/Bangladeshi | 21 | * | 24 | * |
| All other origins | 11 | * | 11 | * |

* Sample too small

*SOURCE: House of Commons Hansard, 21 May 1992, cols 247-8*

## Low pay and poor working conditions

> I work 40 hours a week in the factory and my take-home pay is between £55 and £66 per week. Last year I started a homeworking job which I can do most evenings and weekends. For this I get paid £15-£20 per week depending on the number of overalls I manage to complete. This money adds towards the household budget and occasionally for clothes for the children . . . With the domestic duties and two jobs I have very little time to relax. I don't even have time to fall ill or complain about a backache. I know the work has to be done, as the man would soon come to collect the overalls. My only social life is going to local weddings.
>
> (Mrs P, 42 years old, Asian, with three children)[10]

A sizeable proportion of people living in poverty work in low-paid jobs. Black people and other ethnic minority groups are more likely to work for low wages than their white counterparts.

The *New Earnings Survey* – the principal source for statistics on earnings – does not provide a breakdown of earnings by ethnic origin. However, it is clear that black people and other ethnic minorities are clustered in industries which have particularly low wages. In 1989-91, over a quarter (29%) of men from black and other ethnic minorities worked in the distribution, hotels and catering sectors, compared to 16 per cent of white men. Within this category, 9% of men from black and other ethnic minorities worked in hotels and catering compared to 2% of white men.[11] Wages in these sectors are particularly low. In 1991, well over a quarter (28%) of men in distribution, hotels, catering and repairs earned less than £150 a week (the average for all industries is 10% of the male manual workforce earning below £150 a week). In hotels and catering, a sub-sector of this group of industries, nearly half the male workforce (47%) earned below £150 a week in 1991.[12]

The employment patterns for women are not as differentiated between white women and women from black and other ethnic minorities. This is partly because women as a whole are concentrated in particular areas of the labour market. For example, around a quarter of all women – whether white or black – work in distribution, hotels, catering and repairs.[13] But this is also an outcome of the way large industrial categories may hide differences between women from ethnic minorities and white women.

Figures from the Policy Studies Institute (PSI) show that in 1982 West Indian and Asian men earned less than white men (see Table 14).[14] White women earn more than Asian women, but less than West Indian women. Part of the explanation for this is that Afro-Caribbean women are more likely to work full time, to undertake more shift work and to be based in large unionised public sector work places, where wages are somewhat higher. In addition, women as a whole are concentrated in the low-paid sector of the economy, so there is less room for disparities based on race.

'Earnings and Ethnicity', a more recent survey published by Leicester City Council in 1990, provides valuable up-to-date data on the earnings and working conditions of white and Asian workers living in Leicester. The survey found that Asians were far more likely to be low paid and have worse conditions at work. In 1990, Asian men in full-time work had gross median weekly earnings of £160 a week – 82% of white men's which stood at £196, while Asian women in full-time work had gross median weekly earnings of £109 a week – 82% of white women's, which stood at £133 a week.[15]

**TABLE 14**
**Gross earnings of full-time employees, 1982**

| | Median Weekly earnings | |
|---|---|---|
| | **Men** | **Women** |
| **White** | £129.00 | £77.50 |
| **West Indian** | £109.20 | £81.20 |
| **Asian** | £110.70 | £73.00 |

*SOURCE: Black and White Britain, C Brown, Third PSI Survey, Gower, 1984*

As well as suffering low pay, a large percentage of Afro-Caribbean and Asian people find themselves experiencing some of the worst working conditions. The Leicester report shows that Asian men were twice as likely to work shifts as white men (31% compared to 17%) and that 15% of Asian women compared to 10% of white women worked shifts.[16] This confirms earlier findings of the 1982 PSI report which showed that:[17]

- 33% of Asian and 29% of West Indian men worked regular shifts compared to 20% of white men.
- 14% of Asian and 18% of West Indian women worked regular shifts, compared to 11% of white women.
- 7% of Asian men and 4% of West Indian men and women worked nights only, compared to 1% of white men; 4% of West Indian women worked nights only compared to 1% of white women and 1% of Asian women.

> I've worked nights on the wards for years and it really does put a strain on you, there's no question about it. You get a lot of nurses and auxiliaries who suffer from the stress-related illness – hypertension, heart trouble, kidney problems, high blood pressure – you name it, they all come from those broken sleep patterns from the night shift. You can't just go home and go to sleep during the day if you've got kids. When you come in from work, you've got to get them ready for school, do the shopping, do the housework, do the washing, and by the time you've finished it's three o'clock and time to collect them from school again, so you just don't get any rest . . . What happens is you just adjust in time to getting less sleep than everyone else, but over the years that takes its toll. (B Bryan et al, *The Heart of the Race*)[18]

## Benefits

There are no government statistics which give a breakdown of benefit claimants by ethnic origin. However, the PSI report shows that black people and other ethnic minority groups are more likely to receive certain benefits (see Table 15) with the exception of retirement pension.[19] It is difficult to interpret these statistics as there is also some evidence to show that people from ethnic minorities are less likely to claim benefits, so these figures are likely to *underestimate* the extent of their poverty.

A higher proportion of West Indian and Asian people claimed unemployment benefit and family income supplement. West Indian people were also more likely to be dependent on supplementary benefit/pension than white people. (The low figure for Asian people may be due to the underclaiming of benefits.)

**TABLE 15**

| **All households** | **White** | **West Indian** | **Asian** |
|---|---|---|---|
| Per cent in receipt of . . . | | | |
| Child Benefit | 34 | 60 | 75 |
| Unemployment Benefit | 7 | 17 | 16 |
| Family Income Supplement | 1 | 5 | 2 |
| Supplementary Benefit/Pension | 14 | 20 | 11 |
| Retirement/Widow's Pension | 35 | 6 | 6 |

*SOURCE: Black and White Britain, C Brown, Third PSI Survey, Gower, 1984*

## Causes of poverty

The persistence of high levels of poverty for black people and other ethnic minority groups is due to a number of different factors:

- Immigration policy has curtailed access to welfare services, forcing some people from abroad to rely on their own family for support.
- Inequalities in the labour market are founded on deeply embedded discriminatory employment practices. This has left black people highly exposed to the economic restructuring which has taken place through the seventies and eighties.
- Family patterns and the age structure of ethnic minority groups mean that some groups are more likely to be vulnerable to poverty.
- Social security policies have been directly and indirectly discriminatory, often leaving black people without support from the state.
- The racism and discrimination in society as a whole have often excluded black people from employment opportunities and access to welfare.

## Immigration policy and poverty

> The prevailing ideology was that Black people had come 'individually and on their own initiative' and thus there was no need to make welfare provision for them. There was thus *no intention* to provide for them, and when Black immigrants *did* use welfare services they were seen as scroungers.
>
> (Fiona Williams: *Social Policy: A Critical Introduction*)[20]

Black people's experience of poverty in the UK has been fundamentally shaped by immigration policy.[21] Legislation has been geared to placing immigrants in particular jobs – for black people this has meant low-paid work in poor conditions. Immigration policy has also attempted to reduce the 'social costs' of people who come to work in Britain, either by curbing access to welfare services or by restricting the right to bring dependants to this country. After the 1971 Immigration Act, the wives and children of Commonwealth citizens could only enter the United Kingdom if a sponsor could support and accommodate them without recourse to 'public funds'. 'Public funds' – clearly defined for the first time in 1985 – consisted of supplementary benefit (now income support), housing benefit, family income supplement (now family credit) and housing under Part III of the Housing Act 1985 (Housing the

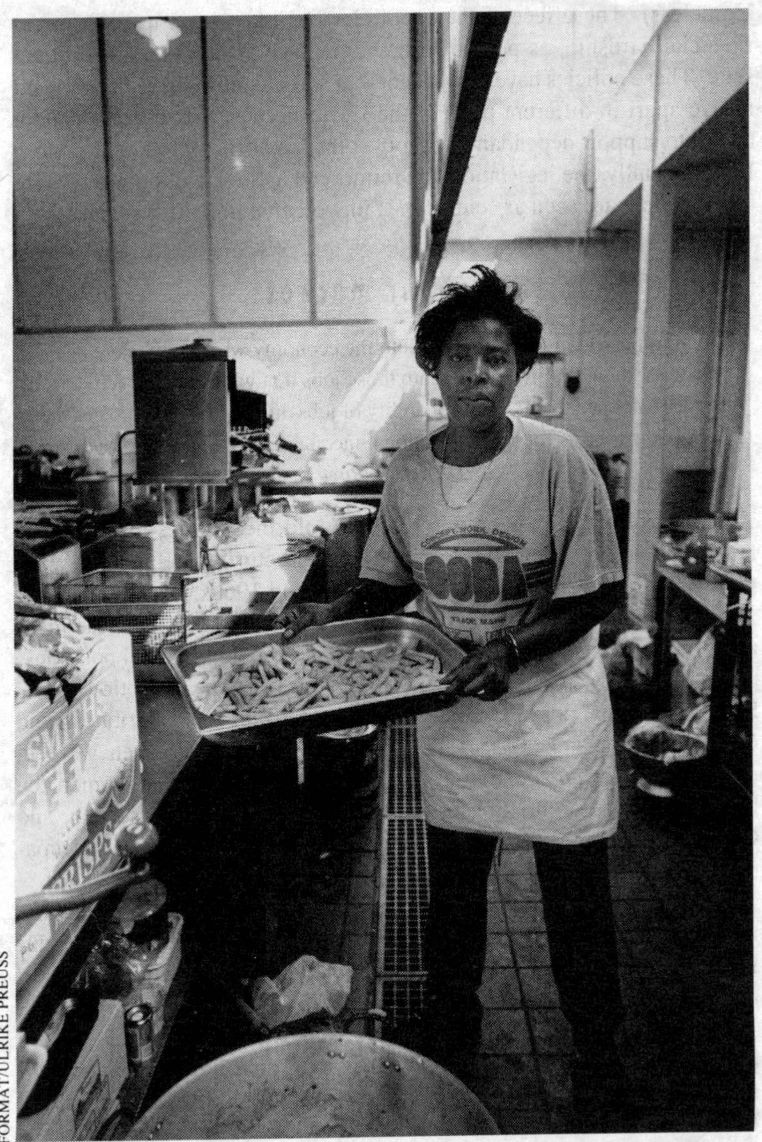

FORMAT/ULRIKE PREUSS

***Every indicator of poverty shows that black people and other ethnic minority groups are more at risk of high unemployment, low pay, poor conditions at work, and diminished social security rights.***

Homeless). The effect of these policies has often been to cause great financial hardship, as people struggle to survive without help from the state. These policies have also meant that some families have been forced to live apart in different parts of the world because UK citizens cannot afford to support dependants without some support from the state. More fundamentally, the legislation has reinforced a climate of opinion where black people are seen as 'outsiders', unwelcome in British society.

## Inequality in the labour market

> Immigrant workers were sucked into the economy where they were needed, whatever their qualifications – into those jobs that white people were becoming less inclined to do. The availability of jobs during labour shortages therefore laid the basis for the occupational inequalities that have persisted since.
>
> (C Brown, *Race Relations and Discrimination*)[22]

The poverty of black people is rooted in old inequalities in the labour market. Black people still work in the manufacturing and manual work for which they were recruited in the 1950s and 1960s.

In the period 1989-91, 32% of Afro-Caribbean and Guyanese men, and 40% of Pakistani and Bangladeshi men, held non-manual positions, compared to 48% of white men. Indian men were the exception – 59% held non-manual posts. On the other hand, 68% of Afro-Caribbean and Guyanese men and 60% of Pakistani and Bangladeshi men were in manual occupations compared to 52% of white men. For women the hierarchical differentiation is not as marked. Afro-Caribbean and Guyanese women were slightly more likely to work in manual occupations than white women.[23]

The segregation of black workers into certain industries and into manual work has particularly exposed them to both the decline of manufacturing industry and the rise in unemployment. Unemployment is a much higher risk for people in manual work.

According to the 1991 census, ethnic minorities made up 5.5% of the population, although they are very unevenly distributed. A quarter of the population in inner London comes from ethnic minority groups.[24] Living in inner city areas has meant that black people have faced the brunt of the exodus of industry from city heartlands. The consequence has been high unemployment for black people.

Broad economic changes are compounded by discrimination. A report on employment in Rochdale found that working in the textile industry increased the chances of becoming unemployed and that this probability increased significantly for Asian people.[25] A quarter of Asian people interviewed thought that being Asian had affected their employment opportunities. The report identifies the causes of unemployment for Asian workers:

> . . . Many firms have closed down their night shifts where traditionally most Asians have worked. Secondly, there has been a major reduction of routine, non-skilled manual work where Asians were traditionally concentrated. Thirdly, many Asians lacked sufficient seniority to have avoided being made redundant in this period. Finally, fewer new textile jobs are advertised formally and recruitment tends to be based upon . . . recommendations from relations and friends.[26]

The evidence of racial inequality in new forms of employment is still tentative. However, such data as exist suggest that new jobs in insurance, banking and finance have tended to reinforce racial inequalities in the labour force. For example, a report on the Asian community's access to employment opportunities generated by computer-related technology in the London Borough of Ealing found that Asians were under-represented in the higher echelons of information technology industry.[27] A similar report examining the barriers facing Caribbeans in the computing industry in the London boroughs of Hammersmith and Fulham concluded:

> Discrimination and stereotyped views held by many people about black people put them at a disadvantaged position when they come to look for jobs in information technology.[28]

## Family patterns

The age profile of black people is younger than white people. In the period 1987-89:[29]

- 24% of West Indian or Guyanese, 30% of Indian, 45% of Pakistani, 47% of Bangladeshi and 19% of white people were aged under 15;
- 32% of West Indian or Guyanese, 26% of Indian, 23% of Pakistani, 25% of Bangladeshi and 22% of white people were aged between 16 and 29;
- 8% of West Indian or Guyanese, 5% of Indian, 2% of Pakistani, 2% of Bangladeshi and 21% of white people were aged 60 and above.

The younger age profile means that black people and other ethnic minorities are disproportionately affected by government policies such as freezing child benefit and cuts in income support for young people. On the other hand, there are fewer black people and ethnic minorities among pensioners. This means that as a whole they are less affected by the poverty which pensioners experience. However, although small in number, black pensioners are in fact more likely than white pensioners to be living on lower incomes because of social security rules which are indirectly discriminatory. As the black and ethnic minority population grows older, they will become more vulnerable to the poverty which afflicts pensioners.

Family patterns also vary considerably between different ethnic groups. Lone parenthood is lower amongst Asian people than white people, but higher amongst Afro-Caribbeans:[30]

- 8% of Bangladeshi and Pakistani families are lone parent families.
- 6% of Indian families are lone parent families.
- 49% of West Indian families are lone parent families.
- 30% of African families are lone parent families.
- 18% of all ethnic minority families are lone parent families.
- 15% of white families are lone parent families.

As we have seen, the risks of poverty are much higher among lone mothers than other groups. This is the result of low wages for women coupled with few and expensive childcare facilities which force many lone parents to stay on benefit. So the risks of poverty which accompany lone parenthood are particularly acute for Afro-Caribbean women.

The 1982 PSI survey found that the average number of children in ethnic minority households was higher than in white households: 12% of West Indian and 31% of Asian households had more than two children compared to 5% of white households.[31] As we have seen, the rise in child poverty over the last decade was steeper than the rise among the whole population. Over the same period, data also show very sharp rises in poverty among children in families composed of couples with three or more children. Yet again, because a greater proportion of ethnic minority households comprise families with children they have been disproportionately exposed to the rise in child poverty.

## Discrimination in social security

Mrs X has lived in the UK for many years and had been receiving supplementary benefit. In October 1980, she went to India for a visit and returned to the

UK in July 1982. By the time she approached the take-up campaign at the end of December 1982, she had not received any benefit. She had received a letter from the DHSS which said: 'Please state below if there is anyone else in this country who can support you (friends or relatives) and also why you cannot return to India. Please also send your passport'.

(P Gordon and A Newnham, *Passport to benefits: Racism in social security*)[32]

The social security system discriminates both directly and indirectly against black people. The result is that in many cases people from ethnic minorities are left exposed to economic and social hardships without the protection of benefits. Established after the Second World War, Beveridge's new welfare scheme assumed a homogeneous society of white, UK-born, full-time male workers. It cannot take account of the changing immigration patterns of the 1950s and 1960s and the effect of these on entitlement to benefits.

## Contributory benefits

Much of our social security system is founded on the contributory principle whereby people receive national insurance benefits such as unemployment benefit and retirement pension in return for contributions made from earnings. In practice, a contributory scheme tends to discriminate against people who are in intermittent and/or low-paid work. Currently, anyone who earns below the national insurance threshold of £56 a week in 1993/94 does not make any contributions, and therefore does not receive any contributory benefits. In addition, because contributions are earnings-related, people in lower paid jobs take longer to satisfy the contribution conditions than people in higher paid jobs. As we have seen, people from ethnic minorities are more likely to be in low-paid work and also have a much higher risk of unemployment. The result is that they often have less access to contributory benefits. For example, many Afro-Caribbean and Asian pensioners are forced to rely on means-tested support in retirement: figures from the PSI show that fewer Asians and Afro-Caribbeans than white people claimed retirement pension and that, as a result, a quarter of Asians and Afro-Caribbeans of pensionable age were dependent on supplementary pension.[33]

In addition, it is important for many people from ethnic minorities to keep close ties with family who are not living in this country. Such visits abroad are often a necessary part of the way of life of certain communities. However, they have important consequences for entitlement to contributory benefits as such visits often mean breaks in contributions which many people cannot make up on a voluntary basis. Thus, the work patterns and ways of life of many people from ethnic minorities inevitably exclude them from contributory benefits. Such benefits have important advantages over other types of social security benefits – in particular, they are not means-tested and they are paid on an individual basis.

## Non-contributory benefits

These benefits have residence and/or presence conditions attached to them. These tests were once very tough indeed. For example, until recently to claim severe disablement allowance a claimant had to prove residence in the UK for 10 out of the preceding 20 years. However, in 1992 the rules were changed and now a person must be 'ordinarily resident' and have been present in Britain for a continuous period of 6 months before claiming.

Other non-contributory benefits such as child benefit were specifically aimed at people present in the UK. (Previously child tax allowances were payable for children supported outside the United Kingdom.) Often families living in this country are still supporting other family members in their countries of origin. Since such obligations are not recognised by our social security system, this often means struggling to survive on much lower incomes:

> Out of my wages of £6 a week I used to send £3 a week back home. My weekly rent was £1.15 and the rest of my money, plus my husband's £6, went towards everything else, such as fares, food, bringing up the baby, raising the deposit on a house and saving for the fares to bring the three children over. (B Bryan et al, *The Heart of the Race*)[34]

## Means-tested benefits

The link between benefits and immigration is explicit in the means-tested part of the social security system in the form of the 'public funds' test and the rules on sponsorship. Under our immigration rules, most people admitted to the UK can enter on condition that they do not rely on 'public funds'.[35] The three main means-tested benefits fall into this category. If receipt of these benefits becomes known to the Home Office it may affect the person's right to stay, to get an extension of leave or a change in conditions of stay or result in leave being curtailed.

Certain groups of people coming to the UK have to be sponsored by a relative or friend. The introduction of 'sponsors' had a crucial impact on ethnic minority groups' access and entitlement to welfare support. It is, in fact, only in a minority of cases that such sponsorship is legally binding, although many people mistakenly believe it to be so. If a sponsor is legally liable but fails to maintain the sponsee the Benefits Agency has the power to recover any benefits paid to the sponsee. However, if the sponsor cannot afford to pay then the Benefits Agency should not pursue the matter. The immigration legislation which introduced the concept of a sponsor has meant that many ethnic minority families have been and are divided across continents. There is now a considerable body of evidence documenting the contact between the DSS and the Home Office. Passport checks on black claimants – regardless of whether they were born in the UK – have become a frequent occurrence at Benefits Agency offices.

## Administration of social security

The administration of social security often discriminates either directly or indirectly against people from ethnic minorities.

> There is no doubt that they don't look well on us people and that is why it takes so long to get an answer from them, or when it's late they take even longer. It's more difficult if you don't know the language or can't read or write English.
>
> (R Cohen et al, *Hardship Britain: being poor in the 1990s*)[36]

A report by the National Association of Citizens Advice Bureaux (NACAB) identified a number of key difficulties with how social security is administered: communication, delays in benefit payments, late claims, wrongful refusal of benefit and underclaiming of benefits.[37]

The NACAB survey identified low take-up as an important problem for people from ethnic minorities. There is growing evidence of low take-up.[38] Fear of creating problems, concern that any fuss might affect the chance to stay and the lack of translated material have created a climate in which ethnic minority groups are unlikely to assert their rights, often doubting their entitlement to benefits.

The National Audit Office recently commissioned National Opinion Polls to undertake a survey of family credit recipients (a means-tested benefit which goes to people in paid work, which replaced family income supplement in 1988). It found that only 69% of ethnic minorities claimants received help with free prescriptions and only 44% received help with free dental care, compared to 74% and 62% of white claimants respectively.[39]

In a recent survey, the Family Service Units interviewed 32 Asian families living on income support in Bradford.[40] They found that 26 of them had made no application to the social fund (the social fund provides some community care grants, but mainly loans, for people on income support). Azra Sadiq-Sangster writes:

> Most of the Asians did not want to take on social fund loans, especially as payments would be deducted from their benefits. Many were not aware of the social fund but, when told about it, they said they would not consider taking it up because they feared having less money on a weekly basis for the sake of a lump sum.[41]

## The 1988 social security changes

The overhaul of social security in 1988 accentuated the emphasis on means-testing and has meant greater hardship for black claimants:

- Under income support the removal of 16- and 17-year-olds' right to benefit except in cases of severe hardship and the lower rate of benefit for under 25s is indirectly discriminatory because black and other ethnic minority groups have a higher proportion of people who fall into this age-group.
- The social fund brings in discretion and no independent right of appeal and greater scope for racism.[42]
- Questions on the date of arrival in this country have been added to the income support form.
- People from ethnic minorities may well be underclaiming family credit because it relies on claimants providing a great deal of evidence about their employment. Many people from ethnic minorities work in low-paying sectors of the economy; some of these employers may not pay tax and national insurance and thus may be reluctant to provide information for their employees.
- The State Earnings Related Pension Scheme (SERPS) was weakened and is to be based on a lifetime's earnings instead of the best 20 years rule. This will indirectly discriminate against ethnic minorities: people who have come to this country in their thirties and forties will have a shorter working life and thus a lower retirement pension.
- The inducements to take up private pensions will merely reinforce existing inequalities in the labour market and thus not benefit the majority of people from ethnic minorities.

These are only some of the difficulties that are caused by the new benefits system. In addition, the extension of means-testing exacerbates all the problems associated with the link between immigration status and entitlement to benefit. The further social security intrudes into the minutiae of individual circumstances the more room there is for racism. Some black people, excluded from all help under the new system, find themselves placed firmly in the category of the 'undeserving poor'.

## Discrimination and racism

> Racial discrimination remains widespread and 'pernicious' to use the Prime Minister's term, and so far from being redundant the Race Relations Act as at present formulated does not provide a strong enough basis for dealing with it.
> (Sir Michael Day OBE, Commission for Racial Equality)[43]

The legal framework for dealing with racism – beginning with the 1965 and 1968 Race Relations Acts and strengthened by the 1976 Act – has had little impact on the levels of discrimination in employment.

Research carried out by the Commission for Racial Equality and PSI suggests that discrimination has not been fundamentally reduced in the 1980s. In 1984/85, the PSI looked at one hundred employers offering a wide range of manual and non-manual jobs in London, Birmingham and Manchester and found that a white applicant was over a third more likely to receive a positive response than an ethnic minority applicant. The research found that at least a third of employers discriminated against Asian and Afro-Caribbean applicants.[44] The levels of discrimination found in this study were similar to those found in research carried out in the 1970s.[45] This research only measured direct discrimination. It gives no indication of the level of indirect discrimination which may affect people from ethnic minorities. Thus, despite legislation, the prevalence of discrimination had not declined. Colin Brown explains:

> We are constantly driven back to the ugly fact of direct racial discrimination, which persists and acts on people's lives whenever it has the chance. It may be that the more subtle aspects of racial inequality have been stressed too much, or too soon. While the main problem of British race relations is, plainly and simply, discrimination based on racial hostility.[46]

*British Social Attitudes* attempts to document the extent of racism today. It reveals a strong feeling that racism is widespread, but that it is in decline. It found that in 1991:

- around half of the people surveyed think that there is a lot of prejudice against Afro-Caribbeans and slightly more against Asians;
- at the same time there has been a sharp decline in the proportion of respondents thinking that prejudice is more widespread than five years ago;

- there was a small decrease in reported prejudice; however, a third of the sample still admitted to being either 'very prejudiced' or 'a little prejudiced' against people of other races;
- there was an increase in the support for anti-discrimination law with 76% supporting it.[47]

## Conclusion

Every indicator of poverty shows that black people and other ethnic minority groups are more at risk of high unemployment, low pay, poor conditions at work, and diminished social security rights. Their poverty is caused by immigration policies which have often excluded people from abroad from access to welfare, employment patterns which have marginalised black people and other ethnic minority groups into low-paid manual work, direct and indirect discrimination in social security and the broader experience of racism in society as a whole.

Tackling poverty among black and ethnic minority groups is both about general policies for reducing poverty – such as reducing unemployment or introducing a minimum wage – and about specific policies. CPAG believes that the following specific policies would begin to reduce racial inequality:

- New employment opportunities and training programmes aimed at black and ethnic minority groups.
- The strengthening of anti-discrimination laws in line with the Commission for Racial Equality's recommendations which include: extending legal aid to industrial tribunals; providing clearer definitions of indirect discrimination; introduction of contract compliance as in the Fair Employment legislation in Northern Ireland; and extending the scope of the 1976 Race Relations Act to cover all areas of government activity.
- The abolition of discriminatory aspects of the social security system.
- The translation of a wide variety of leaflets into minority languages, an obligation on the part of the Benefits Agency to provide interpreters, and take-up campaigns that specifically cater for the black and ethnic minority communities.
- A draft directive in Europe which forbids discrimination in social security (both in social assistance and insurance-based schemes) against people from ethnic minorities.

- The European Community Charter of Fundamental Human Rights should contain a commitment to ending racial inequality.

## NOTES

1. K Amin and K Leech, 'A new "Underclass": race and poverty in the inner city', *Poverty 70*, CPAG Ltd, 1988.
2. *Households below Average Income, A statistical analysis, 1979-1988/89*, Government Statistical Service, HMSO, 1992 and *Low Income Families statistics 1985*, DSS, 1988.
3. *Labour Force Surveys*, Department of Employment, published annually with a summary in the *Employment Gazette*.
4. C Brown, *Black and White Britain, the third PSI survey*, Policy Studies Institute, Gower, 1984.
5. K Amin with C Oppenheim, *Poverty in Black and White, deprivation and ethnic minorities*, CPAG Ltd and Runnymede Trust, 1992.
6. House of Commons, *Hansard*, 21 May 1992, cols 247-8.
7. *See* note 6.
8. 'Ethnic origins and the labour market', *Employment Gazette*, Department of Employment, HMSO, February 1993.
9. S McRae, *Young and jobless*, Policy Studies Institute, 1987.
10. *Last among equals*, West Midlands Low Pay Unit, 1988.
11. *See* note 6.
12. *New Earnings Survey* 1991, Department of Employment, HMSO, 1991.
13. *See* note 6.
14. *See* note 4.
15. K B Duffy, I C Lincoln, *Earnings and Ethnicity*, Principal Report on Research Commissioned by Leicester City Council, 1990.
16. *See* note 15.
17. *See* note 4.
18. B Bryan, S Dadzie, S Scafe, *The Heart of the Race*, Virago, 1985.
19. *See* note 4.
20. F Williams: *Social Policy: a critical introduction*, Polity Press, 1989 quoted in N. Ginsburg, *Divisions of Welfare: a critical introduction to comparative social policy*, Sage Publications Ltd, 1992.
21. For full details on immigration policy, *see* P Gordon and F Klug, *British Immigration control: a brief guide*, Runnymede Trust, 1985.
22. C Brown, 'Race Relations and Discrimination' in *Policy Studies*, 11.2, PSI, Summer 1990.
23. *See* note 8.
24. *The 1991 Census County Monitor: Great Britain*, OPCS, 1992.
25. R Penn, A Martin, and H Scattergood, *Employment Trajectories of Asian migrants in Rochdale: an integrated analysis*, Economic and Social Research Council, Working Paper 14, 1990.
26. *See* note 25.
27. T Ahmed and J Beliappa, *Computer access for Asians in the borough of Ealing: a focus on business and employment*, Confederation of Indian Organisations, London Voluntary Services Council, 1989.

28. C Benson, *An investigation of the access the black community has to employment and training in information technology*, London Voluntary Services Council, 1989.
29. J Haskey, 'The ethnic minority populations of Great Britain: estimates by ethnic group and country of birth', *Population Trends, No 60*, Summer 1990, OPCS, HMSO, 1990.
30. J Haskey, 'Estimated numbers and demographic characteristics of one-parent families in Great Britain', *Population Trends, No 65*, Autumn 1991, OPCS, HMSO, 1991.
31. *See* note 4.
32. P Gordon and A Newnham, *Passport to Benefits?: Racism in social security*, CPAG Ltd and Runnymede Trust, 1985.
33. *See* note 4.
34. *See* note 18.
35. *National Welfare Benefits Handbook 1992/3*, CPAG Ltd, 1992.
36. R Cohen et al, *Hardship Britain: being poor in the 1990s*, CPAG Ltd in association with FSU, 1992.
37. NACAB, *Barriers to Benefit: black claimants and social security*, NACAB, 1991.
38. *See* R Cohen and Mary Rose Tarpey in *Take-up: a review*, Islington People's Rights, 1985.
39. National Opinion Polls. A survey of family credit recipients for the National Audit Office, *Support for Low Income Families*, HMSO, 1991.
40. *See* note 36.
41. A Sadiq-Sangster, *Surviving on Income Support, The Asian experience*, Family Service Units, 1991.
42. S Conlan, 'Without recourse to public funds: immigration and social security since the Second World War', unpublished dissertation, Leicester University, 1989.
43. Commission for Racial Equality, *The Second Review of the Race Relations Act 1976*, CRE, 1992.
44. C Brown and P Gray, *Racial Discrimination: 17 Years after the Act*, Policy Studies Institute, 1985.
45. *See* note 22.
46. *See* note 22.
47. K Young, 'Class, Race and Opportunity', in eds R Jowell et al, *British Social Attitudes, the 9th report*, 1992/93 edition, Dartmouth, 1992.

CHAPTER SEVEN

# The geography of poverty

*The impact of lasting recession has knocked the stuffing out of the South-East. The enduring, if over-simplified, images of a 'depressed north' and 'prosperous south' may not have been overturned in the past two years, but conventional notions about the distribution of prosperity across the nation are under scrutiny. The 1980s saw the South-East economy overheat, fanned principally by the rapid expansion in service industries and aided by a revival in manufacturing activity. The 1990s have ushered in the big freeze. Southerners, already saddled with high rates of personal indebtedness, exploited what proved to be an unsustainable rise in house prices to borrow more. The party ended with a cocktail of collapsing asset values and mounting job insecurity.*

Michael Cassell, 'Long Recession Knocks Stuffing Out of South-East', *Financial Times*, 7 December 1992

The scale and nature of poverty depend partly on where you live. The rapid changes in our economic structure – in particular the decline of the old industrial heartlands – have created distinctive regional and national patterns of unemployment and poverty. The North-South divide has dominated discussion of unemployment in the UK. However, as the quotation above illustrates, there is some initial evidence to suggest that this divide is changing.

In addition, there are, of course, large differences *within* regions – eg, inner London suffers some of the worst levels of deprivation, but is within the largely affluent South-East. The figures we present below shed some light on the differences between nations and regions in the United Kingdom.

# The regional economy

The South-East remains dominant in our national economy. Edward Balls argues in the *Financial Times* that: 'Britain's regional income divide is too stable and deep-seated to be reversed by one recession.'[1] The pie chart below illustrates the share each region had of the national gross domestic product (GDP) in the UK in 1991.[2] The South-East has well over a third of GDP; Northern Ireland a paltry 2%. Making a crude division between 'North' and 'South', the South has 54% of the GDP compared to 46% in the North (the North includes the following regions/countries: North, Yorkshire and Humberside, West Midlands, North West, Wales, Scotland and Northern Ireland; the South includes the remaining regions). Moreover, the 'North' has seen its share of the GDP fall by 2.4% between 1979 and 1991.

**FIGURE 8:**
**Regional Gross Domestic Product (GDP) as a percentage of the UK GDP in 1991.**

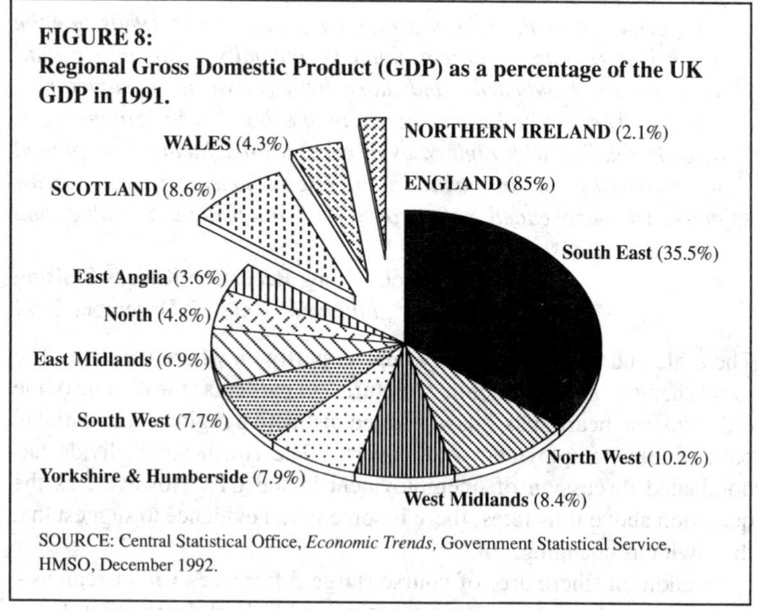


SOURCE: Central Statistical Office, *Economic Trends*, Government Statistical Service, HMSO, December 1992.

There are no up-to-date poverty statistics broken down by region. The latest statistics, produced by the Institute for Fiscal Studies, relate to 1983-1985.[3] The government has refused to provide an analysis of *Households below Average Income* (see Chapter 2) by region. Instead, we look at a number of deprivation indicators: income support statistics, the number of children receiving free school meals and average incomes in each region.

## Income support

Again, the government does not collect the numbers and proportion of people on income support broken down by the standard regions. The only data available are for England, Scotland, Wales and Northern Ireland. As expected, in 1991 the proportion of people who are reliant on income support is slightly higher in Scotland (16%), Wales (15%) and particularly so in Northern Ireland (17%) than in England (14%).[4] These figures underestimate the extent of poverty because they take no account of people who do not take up their entitlement to income support – 1 in 4 of those entitled – or of other people on an equivalent income level.

**TABLE 16**

**Numbers and proportion of the population receiving supplementary benefit (SB)/income support (IS) by nation in the UK**

| | SB 1979 | | IS 1991 | |
|---|---|---|---|---|
| England | 3,652,000 | 8% | 6,500,000 | 14% |
| Wales | 267,000 | 10% | 441,000 | 15% |
| Scotland | 451,000 | 9% | 805,000 | 16% |
| Northern Ireland | 115,359 | 11% | 201,265 | 17% |

*SOURCE: House of Commons Hansard, 26 October 1992, cols 495-496, 11 January 1993, cols 673-4 and cols 540-1*

## Free school meals

One way of finding a window on child poverty in the regions is to look at the number and proportion of children receiving a free school meal. Children in families living on income support are entitled to free school meals. Table 17 below shows which regions have the highest proportion of primary school children getting free meals.[5] Northern Ireland had the highest rates with well over a quarter of primary school children receiving free school meals. Scotland, Wales and the North followed with 21%, 20% and 20% respectively. The regions with the lowest proportions of primary school children eating free school meals were: East Anglia (9%), the South-West (10%) and the East Midlands (11%).

Yet again, these figures underestimate the extent of childhood deprivation because of non-take up of benefits. Some families with children do not take up their entitlement to income support and some families with children who *are* receiving income support do not take up their entitlement to free school meals. In 1988 it was estimated that 1 in 5 children eligible for free meals did not eat them.[6]

There are, of course, important differences within regions. Urban areas have higher rates of children on free meals than non-urban areas. For example, 32% of children in primary schools in Newcastle upon Tyne were receiving free school meals compared to 10% in Cumbria.[7]

**TABLE 17**

**The number and proportion of children on the school roll receiving free school meals in 1991 in primary schools**

| | 1991 | |
|---|---|---|
| | **Numbers** | **%** |
| North | 56,821 | 20 |
| Yorks & Humberside | 66,061 | 15 |
| North West | 115,887 | 19 |
| East Midlands | 38,391 | 11 |
| West Midlands | 76,074 | 16 |
| East Anglia | 14,401 | 9 |
| South-East | 160,236 | 12 |
| South-West | 35,118 | 10 |
| England | 562,993 | 14 |
| Wales | 48,708 | 20 |
| Scotland | 228,172 | 21 |
| Northern Ireland | 50,198 | 27 |

*SOURCE: CPAG, calculations derived from Department for Education, Statistics of Education – Schools 1991, 1992, data from Welsh, Scottish and Northern Ireland Offices.*
*Note: 'primary' includes nursery schools.*

## Income

The *Family Expenditure Survey* for 1991 contains useful data for the regions.[8] Table 18 shows that in Northern Ireland, Scotland, the North and Wales, close to a third of households lived on incomes below £125 a week in 1990-91 (these figures are not adjusted for family size). Around a quarter of households lived below this level in the West Midlands and the North-West. The South-East and the South-West have rather lower proportions of households living on low incomes.

**TABLE 18**

**Proportion of households in each region with gross normal weekly income under £125 per week in 1990-91**

| | % |
|---|---|
| North | 31 |
| Yorkshire & Humberside | 27 |
| North West | 24 |
| East Midlands | 21 |
| West Midlands | 27 |
| East Anglia | 20 |
| South East | 18 |
| South West | 17 |
| Wales | 30 |
| Scotland | 32 |
| Northern Ireland | 32 |
| United Kingdom | 24 |

*SOURCE: Central Statistical Office, Family Spending, A report on the 1991 Family Expenditure Survey, Government Statistical Service, HMSO, 1992*

These regional patterns are borne out by the average household income in each region and how it compares to the average for the UK (see Table 19).[9] Household income in the North and in Northern Ireland is over a fifth less than the average for the UK. Meanwhile, household income in the South-East is a quarter higher than the UK average.

**TABLE 19**

**Average gross normal weekly household income by region in 1990-1991**

| | £ per week | as a % of UK income |
|---|---|---|
| North | 275.70 | 79% |
| Yorkshire & Humberside | 295.17 | 85% |
| North West | 319.65 | 92% |
| East Midlands | 339.93 | 98% |
| West Midlands | 319.28 | 92% |
| East Anglia | 338.95 | 98% |
| South-East | 432.60 | 125% |
| South-West | 355.15 | 102% |
| Wales | 283.25 | 82% |
| Scotland | 305.53 | 88% |
| Northern Ireland | 273.95 | 79% |
| UK | 347.17 | 100% |

*SOURCE: Central Statistical Office, Family Spending, A report on the 1991 Family Expenditure Survey, Government Statistical Service, HMSO, 1992.*

## Employment and unemployment

The structure of employment has changed radically in recent years with a major shift away from traditional manufacturing industry. This explains the persistence of higher rates of unemployment in regions and countries which were centres of manufacturing industry.[10]

- In the United Kingdom, manufacturing accounted for 21% of all employment in 1992, down from 32% in 1976.
- The Midlands and the North, North-West, Yorkshire and Humberside had the highest concentration of employment in manufacturing in 1976 (between a third and nearly half of those in employment were in manufacturing).
- Service industries have increased from 57% to 72% of total employment over the same period. The rise of the new industries has been much more pronounced in the South-East and South-West than in the traditional manufacturing strongholds.

**TABLE 20**
**Unemployment rates in 1966, 1976, 1986 and 1991, by region**

| | Unemployment rate | | | |
|---|---|---|---|---|
| | **1966** | **1976** | **1986** | **1992*** |
| North | 2.4 | 5.3 | 15.4 | 11.6 |
| Yorkshire & Humberside | 1.1 | 3.9 | 12.6 | 10.1 |
| North-West | 1.4 | 5.1 | 13.8 | 10.7 |
| East Midlands | 1.0 | 3.5 | 9.9 | 9.1 |
| West Midlands | 0.8 | 4.3 | 12.6 | 11.0 |
| East Anglia | 1.4 | 3.5 | 8.1 | 8.0 |
| South-East | 0.9 | 3.1 | 8.3 | 9.9 |
| South-West | 1.7 | 4.7 | 9.5 | 9.5 |
| England | – | 3.9 | 11.3 | |
| Wales | 2.7 | 5.3 | 13.9 | 10.0 |
| Scotland | 2.7 | 5.1 | 13.4 | 9.7 |
| Northern Ireland | – | 7.1 | 17.4 | 14.7 |
| United Kingdom | – | 4.2 | 11.2 | 10.1 |

*SOURCE: Central Statistical Office, Regional Trends, Table 10.19, HMSO, 1990 Edition, and Employment Gazette, Department of Employment, December 1992*

* *Note: 1992 figures are for October; the other dates are based on an annual average*

Overall, dividing the country into the 'North' and 'South', the 'North' lost 62% of all the manufacturing jobs that have disappeared since 1976 (1,660,000 jobs) while the South lost 38% (1,032,000). The South gained 55% of all the new service jobs that were gained since 1976 (1,510,000) while the North gained 45% (1,224,000). Figure 9 illustrates the gains and losses in manufacturing and service jobs for each region between 1976 and 1992.

In other words, those areas that have been most impoverished by the dismantling of manufacturing industries have also gained least from the development of new forms of employment.

Not surprisingly, regional and national inequalities are reflected in patterns of unemployment. In 1991, Northern Ireland had the worst

**FIGURE 9: Gains and losses in service and manufacturing jobs by region between 1976 and 1992.**

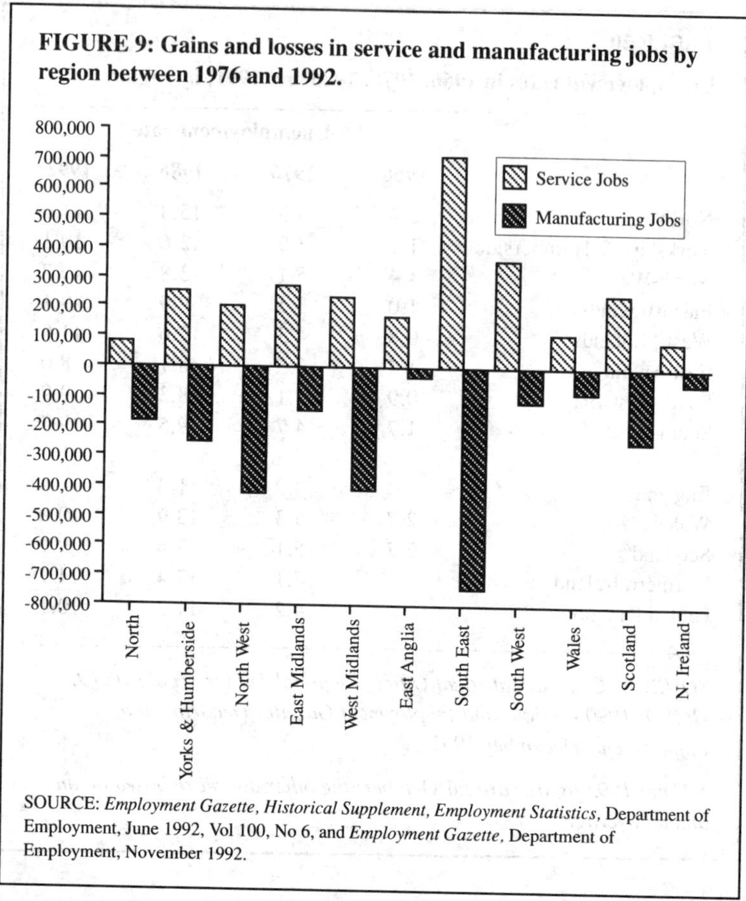


SOURCE: *Employment Gazette, Historical Supplement, Employment Statistics*, Department of Employment, June 1992, Vol 100, No 6, and *Employment Gazette*, Department of Employment, November 1992.

unemployment rate at 14.7%, and was followed by the North with 11.6% (see Figure 10 and Table 20).[11] The pattern of unemployment between the regions has changed. The recession of the early 1980s which brought unemployment to its highest levels in 1986 increased the disparity between the regions. The dramatic fall in manufacturing employment hit the 'North' most severely. The recession of the early 1990s has hit the South-East with a heavier blow; the result is a narrowing of the unemployment rates between regions.[12] For example, in 1986 the gap between the lowest rate of unemployment in East Anglia and the highest in the North (we are leaving out Northern Ireland as it has had persistently high unemployment) was 7.3%; today that gap is just 3.6%. The unemployment rate in the South-East is just below the

**FIGURE 10:**
**Unemployment rates in 1992 – by country and region.**

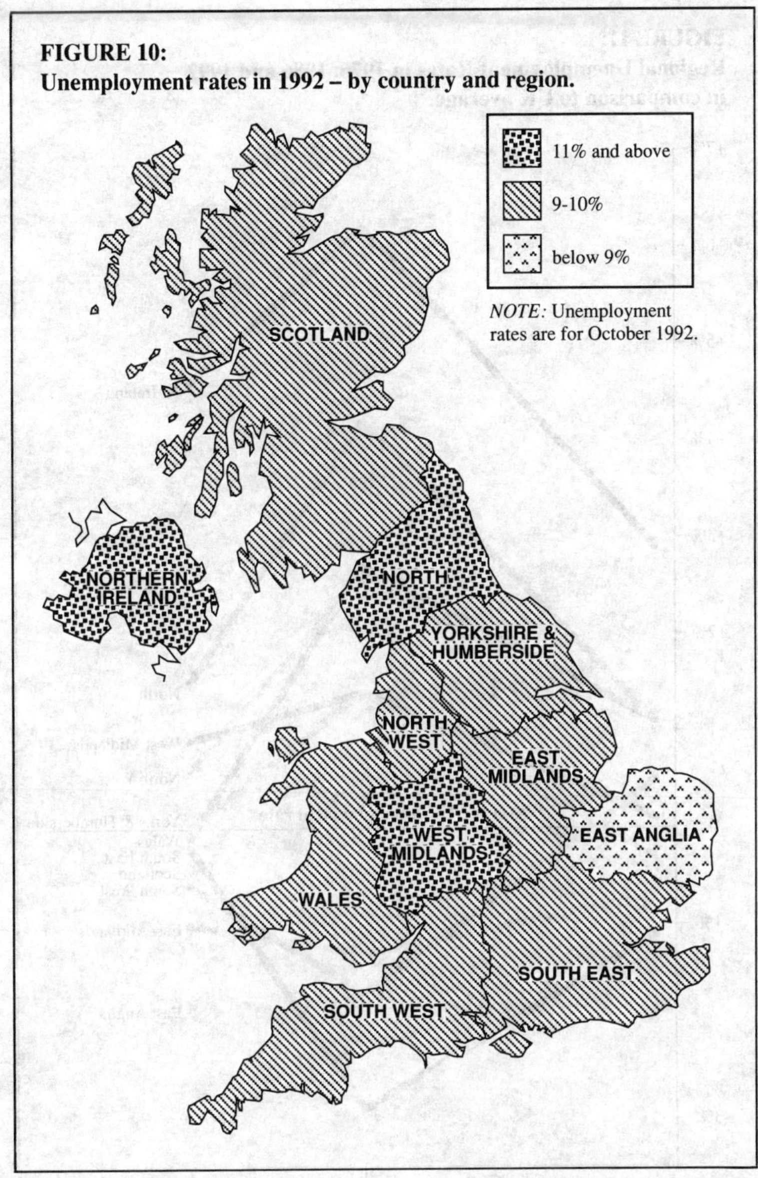


*NOTE:* Unemployment rates are for October 1992.

average for the UK. Figure 11 shows the merging of unemployment rates which has marked this recession.

Rates of redundancies in the different regions also illustrate the changing regional pattern. In spring 1992, surprisingly, the highest

**FIGURE 11:**
**Regional Unemployment Rates in 1976, 1986 and 1992 in comparison to UK average.**

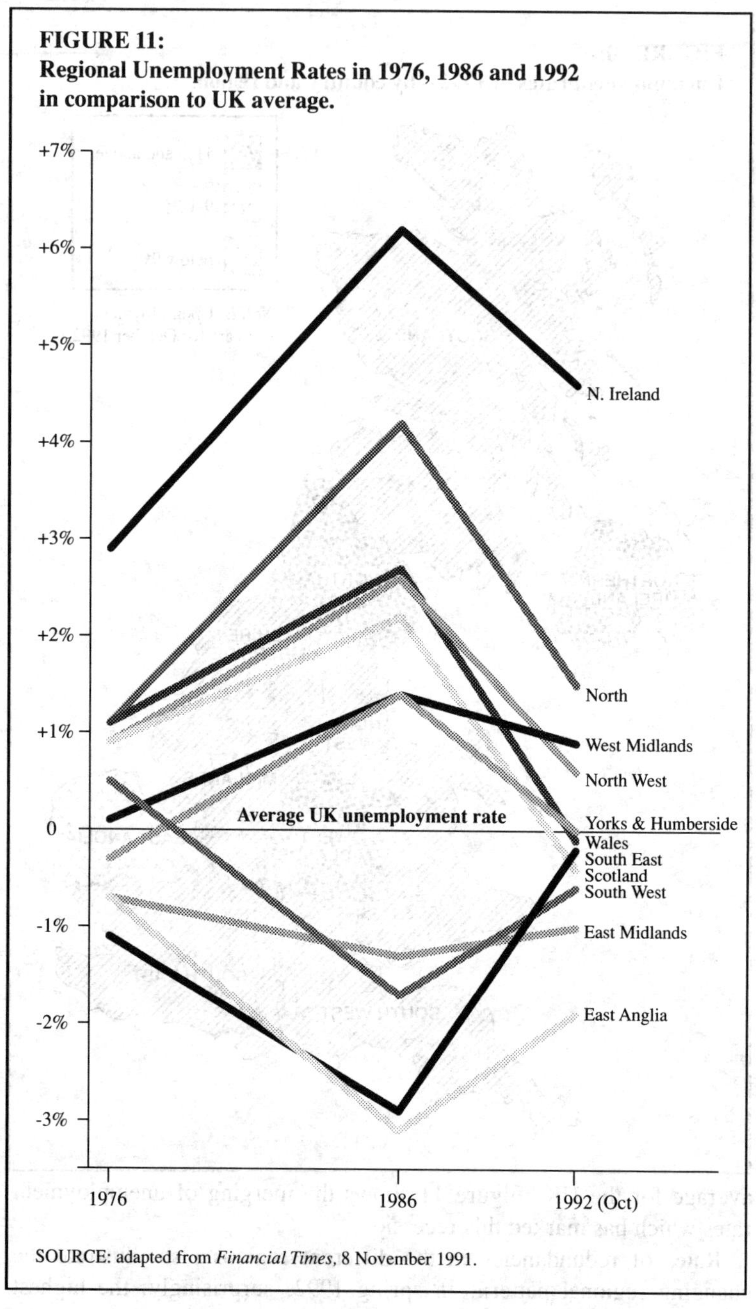


SOURCE: adapted from *Financial Times*, 8 November 1991.

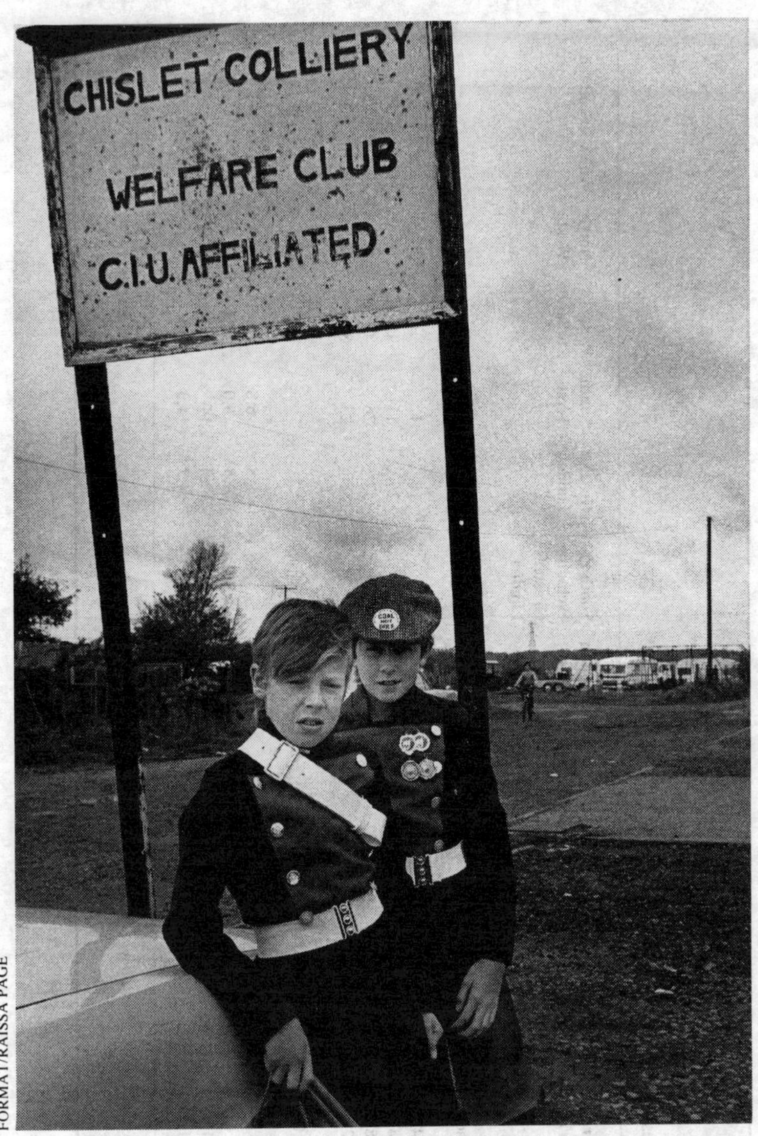


FORMAT/RAISSA PAGE

***Whole towns have and will continue to be devastated by the closure of a steel foundry, a textile factory or a coal mine.***

**TABLE 21**

**Redundancies by region**

| | Great Britain | Northern | Yorkshire and Humberside | East Midlands | East Anglia | South East | South East excluding Greater London | Greater London | South West | West Midlands | North West | Wales | Scotland |
|---|---|---|---|---|---|---|---|---|---|---|---|---|---|
| Redundancies (Thousands) | | | | | | | | | | | | | |
| All | | | | | | | | | | | | | |
| Spring 1989 | 142 | 10 | 14 | 12 | . . . | 40 | 25 | 16 | 12 | . . . | 20 | . . . | 14 |
| Spring 1990 | 181 | . . . | 20 | 17 | . . . | 61 | 35 | 26 | 11 | 17 | 18 | 11 | 12 |
| Spring 1991 | 388 | 21 | 30 | 32 | 12 | 126 | 74 | 53 | 26 | 44 | 43 | 27 | 28 |
| Spring 1992 | 322 | 19 | 31 | 32 | 15 | 101 | 64 | 37 | 25 | 32 | 32 | 17 | 19 |
| Redundancy rates (Redundancies per 1,000 employees) | | | | | | | | | | | | | |
| All | | | | | | | | | | | | | |
| Spring 1989 | 6.4 | 8.3 | 7.5 | 7.0 | . . . | 5.6 | 5.4 | 5.8 | 6.8 | . . . | 8.2 | . . . | 7.2 |
| Spring 1990 | 8.1 | . . . | 10.1 | 10.3 | . . . | 8.5 | 7.9 | 9.5 | 6.0 | 8.1 | 7.4 | 10.4 | 6.1 |
| Spring 1991 | 17.8 | 18.4 | 15.5 | 19.4 | 14.1 | 17.8 | 16.5 | 20.0 | 14.7 | 21.2 | 17.7 | 26.3 | 14.4 |
| Spring 1992 | 15.1 | 16.6 | 16.6 | 19.9 | 17.8 | 14.8 | 14.8 | 14.7 | 14.3 | 16.1 | 13.6 | 16.6 | 9.7 |

*SOURCE: Employment Gazette, Department of Employment, December 1992*

redundancy rate is in the East Midlands. Although the South-East and the South-West have lower rates of redundancy than the Northern regions, the rate of increase over the last three years has been much faster (see Table 21):

- In spring 1989, the redundancy rate (redundancies per 1,000 employees) was 8.3 in the North; three years later it had doubled to 16.6.
- In spring 1989, the redundancy rate was 5.6 in the South-East; by spring 1992 it had nearly tripled to 14.8.[13]

## Repossessions

One of the features of the recession has been the increase in the number of home owners who are in arrears with their mortgages and the number of repossessions. It is the South East which has the most dramatic figures. This is the outcome of higher rates of home ownership and indebtedness and the impact of job losses in this part of the country. There are no regional figures for repossessions; but there are for possession orders. While not all possession orders result in repossession they are a good indicator of the level of housing debt. Greater London and the South East have witnessed the highest number of possession orders in the first six months of 1992 at 13,268 and 17,111 respectively (see Figure 12, p147). East Anglia and the North have had the lowest levels at 1,950 and 3,030.[14]

## The Inner City

> In the ancient world, during the Middle Ages and Renaissance, even in the twentieth century, the word 'city' was frequently associated with wealth, success, culture and opportunity. The word 'civilisation' itself – and the word 'citizen' – derives from it. It is a bitter indictment of our own time that the phrase 'inner city' should today universally conjure up images of disorder, poverty, fear, vandalism and alienation.
>
> Susanne MacGregor and Ben Pimlott, 'Action and Inaction in the Cities'[15]

**TABLE 22**

**Claimants receiving income support/supplementary benefit in deprived areas, people of all ages**

| England | Percentages of estimated adult population | | |
|---|---|---|---|
| | **1983-85** | **1986-88** | **1989-91** |
| Brent | 15.4 | 21.5 | 18.5 |
| Greenwich | 19.4 | 22.2 | 18.8 |
| Hackney | 29.5 | 39.7 | 32.4 |
| Hammersmith & Fulham | 20.8 | 24.8 | 20.0 |
| Haringey | 23.1 | 25.8 | 27.2 |
| Islington | 28.4 | 32.3 | 26.5 |
| Kensington & Chelsea | 17.5 | 22.1 | 15.9 |
| Lambeth | 27.4 | 32.3 | 28.9 |
| Lewisham | 21.5 | 24.9 | 22.1 |
| Newham | 24.4 | 27.4 | 27.3 |
| Southwark | 29.0 | 34.1 | 27.6 |
| Tower Hamlets | 34.7 | 38.3 | 32.6 |
| Wandsworth | 20.8 | 19.4 | 18.1 |
| Greater London deprived areas | 23.5 | 27.6 | 24.4 |
| Knowsley | 32.9 | 34.7 | 33.8 |
| Liverpool | 34.4 | 38.0 | 36.2 |
| Manchester | 22.2 | 34.2 | 32.0 |
| Rochdale | 22.0 | 20.3 | 16.2 |
| Salford | 25.0 | 25.7 | 22.3 |
| North West Region five deprived areas | 27.0 | 32.3 | 29.8 |
| Birmingham | 22.2 | 27.9 | 23.9 |
| Coventry | 23.1 | 24.3 | 19.3 |
| Sandwell | 25.6 | 26.0 | 20.2 |
| Wolverhampton | 24.7 | 27.4 | 21.9 |
| West Midlands Region deprived areas | 23.3 | 26.9 | 22.4 |
| Bradford | 21.3 | 21.2 | 18.5 |
| All 23 deprived areas | 24.2 | 28.1 | 24.6 |
| England | 15.9 | 16.5 | 13.9 |

*SOURCE: Supplementary Benefit/Income Support Quarterly Statistical Enquiries, reproduced from eds. P. Willmott & R. Hutchison, Urban Trends 1, A Report on Britain's Deprived Areas, Policy Studies Institute, 1992*

In recent years, the plight of the inner city has rarely been out of the headlines. Yet very often inner cities lie close to areas of affluence. So far we have looked at inequalities between regions, but very often inequalities *within* regions are far greater.

The inner city has been the melting pot of a number of economic and social changes: the exodus of manufacturing employment, the impoverishment of the housing stock, public services which have borne the brunt of cuts and restructuring, rising crime rates and social division. There

**FIGURE 12:**
**The number and proportion of total possession orders issued by region in England and Wales in the first six months of 1992.**

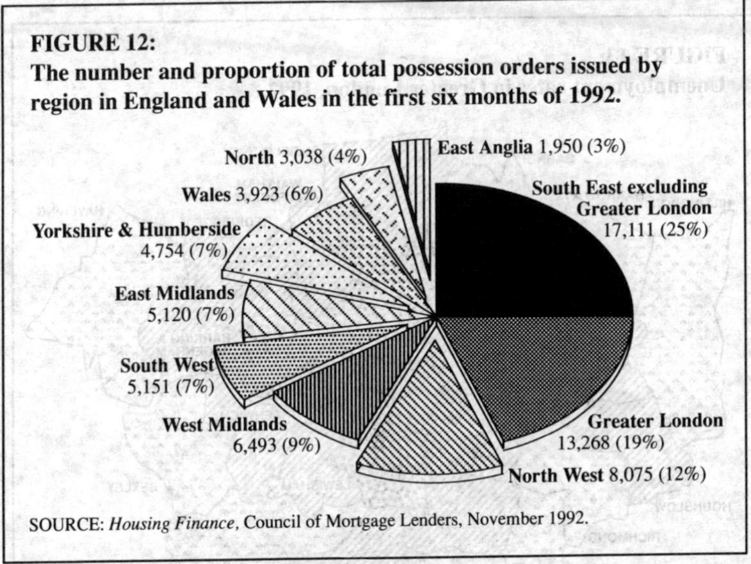


SOURCE: *Housing Finance,* Council of Mortgage Lenders, November 1992.

have been a number of studies which show that conditions in inner city areas have worsened despite government initiatives. Most recent among these is *Urban Trends: A Report on Britain's Deprived Urban Areas*,[16] which looked at a number of deprived urban areas in Britain. Table 22 shows the proportion of people receiving supplementary benefit/income support in deprived areas – an important indicator of poverty. In all parts of the country poverty increased between 1983-85 and 1986-88 and then fell again in 1989-91. The last period does not fully take into account the latest recession. However, the proportion of people receiving supplementary benefit/income support in the deprived areas was higher in each of three periods than in England as a whole. In addition, the gap between the deprived areas and England has widened since 1983-85. The North-West fared particularly badly with close to a third of people on supplementary benefit at the height of unemployment in the mid-1980s. In London, some boroughs had close to two-fifths of people in poverty in the mid-1980s – Hackney had 39.7% and Tower Hamlets had 38.3%.

The report found that the general state of economic activity was the major determinant of prosperity in these areas, rather than regional and urban policies. They also found that:

> . . . in general the gap between conditions and opportunities in deprived areas and other kinds of places – the gap that the government's 1977 White Paper sought to narrow – remains as wide as it was a decade and a half ago. In some respects the gap has widened.[17]

**FIGURE 13:**
**Unemployment rates in Greater London, 1992.**

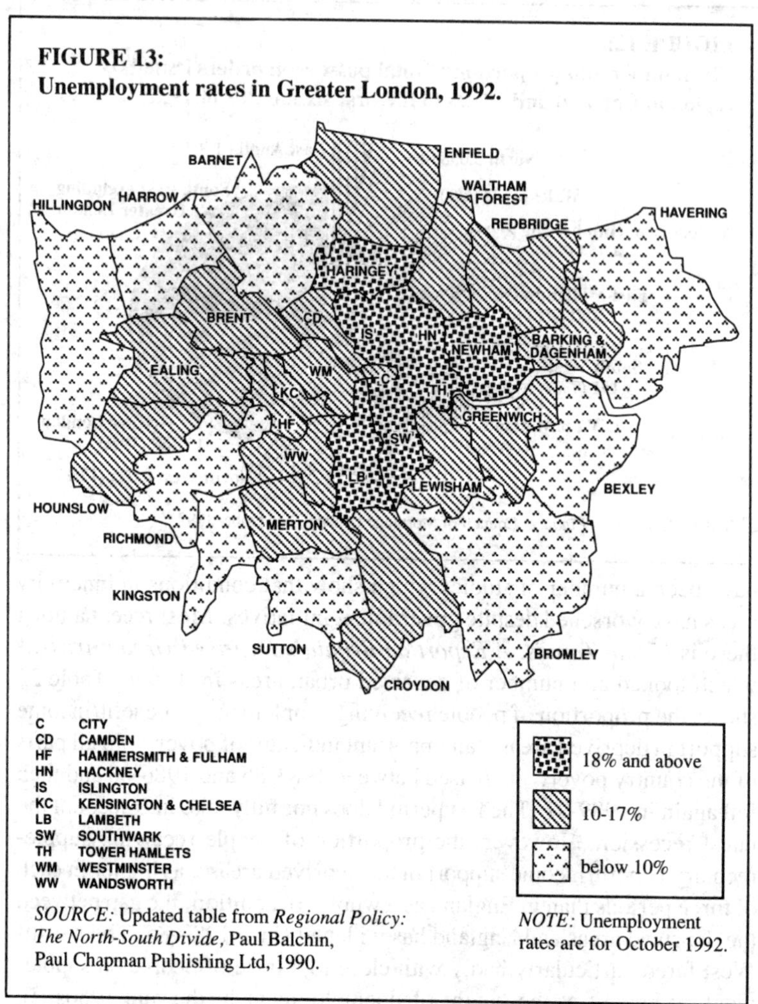


*SOURCE:* Updated table from *Regional Policy: The North-South Divide,* Paul Balchin, Paul Chapman Publishing Ltd, 1990.

*NOTE:* Unemployment rates are for October 1992.

## London

As well as a great deal of wealth, London has many of the features of inner city poverty. As a capital city it attracts both the high salaries of the City and the poverty of the homeless.

In a study of deprivation in London, Peter Townsend found substantial differences between dimensions of poverty in poor and rich areas of London.[18] He ranked 30 representative wards according to levels of deprivation measured by unemployment, overcrowding and the absence of ownership of a car or home. The most deprived wards experienced substantially more material and social deprivation than the least deprived wards (see Table 23). Material deprivation includes: diet, clothing, housing, home facilities, environment, location and work. Social deprivation includes lack of employment rights, lack of integration into the community, lack of participation in social institutions, recreational and educational deprivation. For example, 44% of those interviewed in the poorest group had no play facilities nearby for the under-fives compared to 4% in the least deprived areas; 38% had no central heating compared to 22% in the least deprived group; 21% had inadequate protection against the rain compared to 9% among the least poor group. Patterns of social deprivation were similar – 50% of the children in the poorest group had no summer holiday; 15% had less than 10 years of education; 29% had moved house three or more times in the last five years compared to 22%, 5% and 16% respectively in the least poor areas.

Interestingly, there was also greater political disenfranchisement in the poorer areas – 28% had not voted in the last election compared to 19% in the least deprived areas.

Different parts of London have very different rates of unemployment (see Table 24 and Figure 13).[19] Inner city Hackney and Tower Hamlets had the highest unemployment rates in October 1992 – at around 23% according to the official figures (over 30% using the Unemployment Unit index). On the whole, the outer London constituencies had much lower rates of unemployment: the lowest rates were in Richmond and Bromley at between 7% and 8% (around 10% using the Unemployment Unit index). However, the gap between rich and poor constituencies in London has narrowed because of the sharp rise in unemployment which has hit the South-East particularly hard in the latest recession. In 1990, Hackney had an unemployment rate of nearly six times that of Kingston; in 1992, it was three times that of Kingston.

London also has larger inequalities in pay.[20] Although earnings in the capital are considerably higher on average than in the UK as a whole, the inequalities for male workers within London between the poorest and richest are far greater:

- The average wage for the poorest tenth of full-time male workers

**TABLE 23**

**Experience of different forms of deprivation in different groups of London wards (1985-1986)**

| | Wards | | |
|---|---|---|---|
| | **Most deprived (%)** | **Middle group (%)** | **Least deprived (%)** |
| *Form of material deprivation* | | | |
| Inadequate footwear | 10.6 | 8.0 | 3.9 |
| Inadequate protection against rain | 20.8 | 12.7 | 9.0 |
| Housing overcrowded | 13.4 | 9.1 | 3.8 |
| Some rooms not heated in winter | 37.1 | 36.4 | 26.5 |
| External structural defects | 31.5 | 26.6 | 13.9 |
| Internal structural defects | 15.0 | 14.1 | 6.9 |
| Housing infested | 11.2 | 8.6 | 5.1 |
| No car | 50.9 | 40.3 | 20.8 |
| No washing machine | 32.6 | 28.5 | 10.5 |
| No central heating | 37.8 | 36.6 | 22.0 |
| No telephone | 18.3 | 11.9 | 3.2 |
| No radio | 6.2 | 3.0 | 1.5 |
| No television | 2.6 | 3.0 | 1.4 |
| No garden | 29.8 | 26.4 | 4.4 |
| No play facilities nearby for under-fives | 43.9 | 44.4 | 26.0 |
| No play facilities nearby for children 5-10 | 37.9 | 40.9 | 28.1 |
| Industrial and air pollution | 7.3 | 7.7 | 4.5 |
| Other forms of pollution | 13.4 | 13.4 | 7.2 |
| No surgery/hospital 10 mins. | 11.3 | 7.3 | 6.8 |
| Risk of road accidents | 36.5 | 33.1 | 25.1 |
| Street litter problem | 44.4 | 39.0 | 24.9 |
| 3+ poor conditions at work | 50.2 | 47.1 | 40.9 |
| Works unsocial hours | 56.8 | 54.0 | 47.1 |
| Stands ¾ of day | 45.8 | 32.7 | 37.6 |
| *Forms of social deprivation* | | | |
| No summer holiday | 37.7 | 27.4 | 21.7 |
| Child no holiday 12 months | 52.4 | 34.5 | 21.5 |
| Child no outing last month | 34.4 | 27.1 | 29.6 |
| Moved house 3+ times in 5 years | 29.1 | 27.6 | 16.1 |
| Health problem in family | 47.0 | 41.6 | 40.2 |
| Alone and reports isolation | 10.9 | 8.6 | 6.9 |
| Unsafe in surrounding streets | 15.2 | 7.8 | 4.6 |
| Not voted last election | 27.6 | 24.2 | 19.0 |
| Less than 10 years' education | 14.9 | 6.7 | 5.4 |
| No educational qualifications | 40.1 | 28.5 | 26.7 |

*Note: Total numbers are around 2,700 except in the case of employment-related questions, when the number is approximately 1,550, and children-related questions, when the number is approximately 820.*

*SOURCE: P Townsend, 'Living Standards and Health in the Inner Cities', in eds. S MacGregor and B Pimlott, Tackling the Inner Cities, The 1980s Reviewed, Prospects for the 1990s, OUP, 1990*

**TABLE 24**

**Unemployment rates of London boroughs in October 1992 (percentages)**

| | Dept of Employment Index | Unemployment Unit Index |
|---|---|---|
| Barking & Dagenham | 12.7 | 17.6 |
| Barnet | 9.4 | 13.0 |
| Bexley | 9.4 | 13.2 |
| Brent | 16.7 | 23.4 |
| Bromley | 7.8 | 10.9 |
| Camden | 14.6 | 19.4 |
| Croydon | 10.3 | 14.3 |
| Ealing | 11.1 | 15.3 |
| Enfield | 11.2 | 15.5 |
| Greenwich | 14.1 | 19.7 |
| Hackney | 22.9 | 32.1 |
| Hammersmith & Fulham | 14.6 | 19.7 |
| Haringey | 20.6 | 28.9 |
| Harrow | 8.3 | 11.5 |
| Havering | 8.7 | 12.3 |
| Hillingdon | 8.1 | 11.4 |
| Hounslow | 10.8 | 15.0 |
| Islington | 18.7 | 25.6 |
| Kensington & Chelsea | 11.5 | 15.5 |
| Kingston | 8.0 | 10.7 |
| Lambeth | 19.2 | 26.9 |
| Lewisham | 17.1 | 24.2 |
| Merton | 10.8 | 14.7 |
| Newham | 19.2 | 26.7 |
| Redbridge | 10.0 | 13.8 |
| Richmond | 7.7 | 10.4 |
| Southwark | 19.6 | 27.4 |
| Sutton | 8.3 | 11.3 |
| Tower Hamlets | 22.7 | 31.4 |
| Waltham Forest | 15.1 | 20.6 |
| Wandsworth | 13.8 | 19.1 |
| Westminster & City of London | 12.0 | 16.1 |
| UK | 10.1 | 13.7 |

*SOURCE: Unemployment Unit Briefing: Unemployment: Totals & Rates in Parliamentary Constituencies, October 1992.*

was 56% of the median wage (£360.10 per week) in Greater London and for the richest tenth it was 201% of the median.

- The average wage for the poorest tenth of full-time male workers was 58% of the median (£295.90 per week) in Britain and for the richest it was 184% of the median.

For women there is little difference in wages because they tend to work in the low-paid sector of the economy.

As Doreen Massey writes, despite the public attention focused on inner cities, many of the problems which these areas face are national problems:

> 'the inner city problem' is *not* a problem of place. What the term refers to, or should refer to, are problems of poverty, unemployment, and deprivation, of a declining industrial base, or increasing inequality.[21]

## Rural poverty

> The rural poor are the invisible poor. They endure an inconspicuous poverty, obscured by the popular image of life in the country – peaceful, caring communities living in rose-bedecked cottages. Yet they exist, the victims of low incomes, bad transport, poor housing and lack of ready access to services or community support. (*Sunday Times*, 14 May 1989)

It is estimated that in the mid-1980s, a quarter of rural households lived in or on the margins of poverty.[22] But because poverty in rural areas is more dispersed, it is more hidden. Rural areas are undergoing substantial structural changes and poverty is rising. The mainstays of employment such as farming and fishing have been shrinking and will shrink further. Low wages persist; it is rural areas which have the lowest rates of pay in Britain: Dyfed in Wales comes at the bottom of the league with male manual average weekly earnings at £215.10 a week; the Borders in Scotland follows with £220, and then Cornwall with an average of £223.80.[23] Employment in agriculture has been decimated over decades. For example, in June 1971 employment in agriculture, forestry and fishing stood at 421,000; by June 1992 this had fallen by 37% to 264,000.[24] Wages in this sector are notoriously low. In April 1992:[25]

- the average gross weekly wage for full-time manual males in agriculture, forestry and fishing was £203.10 a week (including overtime); 55% earned below £200 a week compared to an average of 26% in all industries;
- the average gross weekly wage for full-time manual females in agriculture, forestry and fishing was £152.60 a week; 60% earned below £150 a week compared to an average of 45% in all industries.

The latest recession has added grist to the mill. Tourism, once the hope of many of these areas, has been sharply hit by the drop in consumer demand. Cornwall is a good example: the key industries – fishing, farming, tourism and china clay – are under threat. Hotel bookings are at only 30% of overall capacity.[26]

Two reports published in 1990 highlighted the extent of poverty in rural England – the Church of England's 'Faith in the Countryside'[27] and 'Tackling Deprivation in Rural Areas' by Action for Communities in Rural England.[28] They draw attention to particular problems in rural areas: a lack of inexpensive housing to rent or buy; migration from the countryside caused by few employment opportunities and low wages; the lack of public transport facilities resulting in some groups of people without a car being 'effectively housebound'; and the closure of local schools and local services.

## Conclusion

The geography of poverty is difficult to delineate. We have seen that Northern Ireland ranks as one of the poorest areas in terms of unemployment, income and reliance on income support. By contrast, the South-East and East Anglia have fared rather better. Indeed, there is a 'North'-'South' divide that has grown over the 1980s and appears to be remarkably stable. However, the latest recession has started to bring the chill of redundancy, factory closures, shops to let and home repossessions to the once affluent South-East. The rates of unemployment by region have started to converge in the 1990s. But the broad brush approach to regional inequality masks vast differences within regions. For example, the lower unemployment and higher incomes in East Anglia hide the rural poverty of very low-paid agricultural workers; the high average income in the South-East ignores the acute pockets of poverty in inner London. Inner cities, cheek by jowl with comfortable suburbia, have been at the meeting-point of a number of different factors that have impoverished many of them: unemployment, the decline of the housing stock, a reduction in public services and social polarisation.

## NOTES

1. E Balls, 'Recessions Cannot Close the Divide', *Financial Times*, 8 November 1991.
2. Central Statistical Office, 'Regional Accounts 1991', *Economic Trends*, Government Statistical Service, HMSO, December 1992.
3. *See* previous edition of *Poverty the Facts* (1990) and Social Services Committee, *Households below Average Income 1980-1985*, HMSO, 1990, 378-I.
4. House of Commons *Hansard*, 26 October 1992, cols 495-496; and 11 January 1993, cols 673-4 and cols 540-1.
5. CPAG calculations derived from Department for Education, *Statistics of Education – Schools 1991*, 1992 and data from Welsh, Scottish and N. Ireland offices.
6. I Cole-Hamilton with S Dibb and J O'Rourke, *Factsheet: School Meals*, CPAG Ltd and the Food Commission, 1991.
7. *See* note 5.
8. Central Statistical Office, *Family Spending, A report on the 1991 Family Expenditure Survey*, Government Statistical Service, HMSO, 1992.
9. *See* note 8.
10. *Employment Gazette*, Department of Employment, November 1992 and *Employment Gazette, Historical Supplement*, Employment Statistics, June 1992, volume 100, No 6.
11. *Employment Gazette*, Department of Employment, December 1992.
12. *See* note 1.
13. *See* note 11.
14. *Housing Finance*, Council of Mortgage Lenders, 1992.
15. Ed S MacGregor and B Pimlott, *Tackling the Inner Cities: The 1980s Reviewed, Prospects for the 1990s*, Clarendon Press, 1991.
16. P Willmott and R Hutchison, *Urban Trends 1: A Report on Britain's Deprived Urban Areas*, Policy Studies Institute, 1992.
17. *See* note 16.
18. P Townsend, 'Living Standards and Health in the Inner Cities', in ed, S MacGregor and B Pimlott (*see* note 15).
19. *See* note 11 and Unemployment Unit Briefing, *Unemployment Totals and Rates in Parliamentary Constituencies*, November 1992.
20. Department of Employment, *New Earnings Survey 1992*, Part E, Government Statistical Service, HMSO, 1992.
21. D Massey, 'Local Economic Strategies', in ed, S MacGregor and B Pimlott (*See* note 15).
22. B McLaughlin, 'Rural Rides', *Poverty No 63*, CPAG, Spring 1986.
23. Department of Employment, *New Earnings Survey 1992, Part E*, Government Statistical Service, HSMO, 1992.
24. *See* note 10.
25. Department of Employment, *New Earnings Survey 1992, Part A*, Government Statistical Service, HMSO, 1992.
26. *The Guardian*, 29 December 1992.
27. 'Faith in the Countryside', Churchman Publishing, 1990.
28. 'Tackling Deprivation in Rural Areas', ACRE, 1990.

CHAPTER EIGHT

# Poverty in Europe

*The prospect of the single internal market will generate a higher rate of economic growth, but unless the Community takes appropriate action and mobilises its resources more effectively, poverty will continue to exist.*

Interim Report, Commission of the European Communities[1]

In 1985 nearly 52 million people – 16% of the population – in the European Community (EC) were living in poverty.[2] How does the United Kingdom compare with its European partners? This is not just an academic question. The development of the single European market will bring significant economic and social changes which will reshape patterns of poverty and inequality within the Community. In the light of such an upheaval, it becomes even more important to look at poverty in relation to our neighbours in order to assess how far we are experiencing common or differing trends, and to gauge the impact of a free market in Europe on our societies.

The countries of the EC are very different, ranging from highly industrialised Germany to countries like Greece, Ireland, Portugal and Spain which have large agricultural sectors. There are also considerable disparities in wealth: Luxembourg has the highest per capita gross domestic product, and Portugal and Greece the lowest, in relation to the European average (see Table 25). These characteristics shape the nature of poverty in the different countries. There are also large differences within countries. For example, in 1989 in the Southern region of Italy the proportion of the workforce in agricultural work was 18.4%, in comparison with 9.2% in Italy as a whole. The gross domestic product per capita in this region is 68% of the average for the EC, while Italy as a whole has 104% of the average for the EC.[3]

**TABLE 25**

**European Community Comparisons: Gross Domestic Product (per head) in 1988**

| Country | |
|---|---|
| European Community | 100 |
| Belgium | 101 |
| Denmark | 109 |
| France | 108 |
| Germany | 113 |
| Greece | 54 |
| Ireland | 65 |
| Italy | 104 |
| Luxembourg | 121 |
| Netherlands | 103 |
| Portugal | 54 |
| Spain | 75 |
| United Kingdom | 107 |

*Note: GDP per head is compared to the European Community average.*
*SOURCE: Central Statistical Office, Regional Trends 27, 1992, Table 2.1, HMSO, 1992*

## Patterns of poverty in the European Community

### Overall poverty rates

The latest survey by Eurostat shows comparative rates of poverty in the EC in 1985.[4] It adopts two approaches to measuring poverty; the first uses a poverty line which varies from country to country – ie, poverty is measured in relation to the prevailing living standards of the member country. The second uses a Community-wide poverty line. In the context of the development of a single market and the attempt to bring greater convergence between member states, it is appropriate to begin to look at poverty using a Community-wide definition.

### Using country-specific poverty lines

The poor shall be taken to mean persons, families and groups of persons

**FIGURE 14:**
**Poverty rates in the European Community in 1985**
**(numbers living below 50% of average national expenditure)**

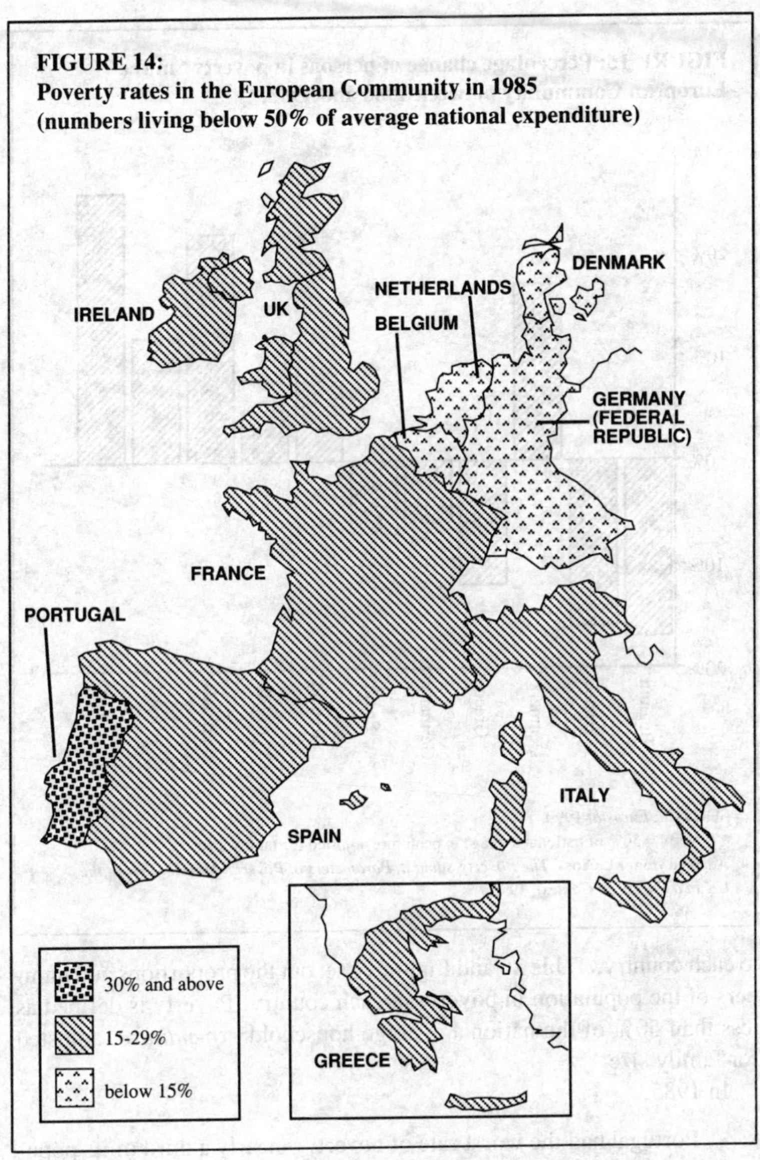


whose resources (material, cultural, social) are so limited as to exclude them from the minimum acceptable way of life in the Member State in which they live.

(Definition of poverty adopted in the Council Decision of 19 December 1984)

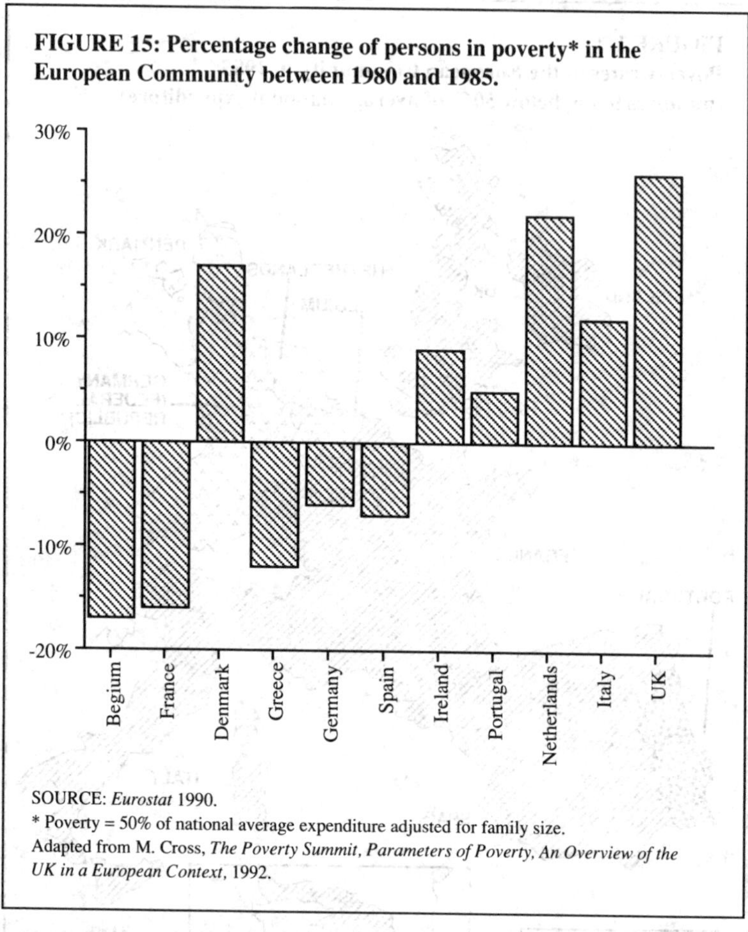


**FIGURE 15: Percentage change of persons in poverty* in the European Community between 1980 and 1985.**

SOURCE: *Eurostat* 1990.
* Poverty = 50% of national average expenditure adjusted for family size.
Adapted from M. Cross, *The Poverty Summit, Parameters of Poverty, An Overview of the UK in a European Context*, 1992.

to each country. Table 26 and Figure 14 set out the proportions and numbers of the population in poverty in each country. Poverty is defined as less than 50% of the national average household *expenditure*, adjusted for family size.[5]

In 1985:

- Portugal had the worst rate of poverty – nearly a third of its population was living in poverty;
- Ireland, Spain and Greece followed with between 18.4% and 19.5% of their population in poverty;
- of the more prosperous countries, the UK had the highest poverty rate at 18.2%;

**TABLE 26**

**National Poverty Rates and Numbers in the European Community in 1980 and 1985 (Persons and Children)**

| Country | Persons | | | | Children | | | |
|---|---|---|---|---|---|---|---|---|
| | 1980 | | 1985 | | 1980 | | 1985 | |
| | % | Nos (000) | % | Nos (000) | % | Nos (000) | % | Nos (000) |
| Belgium | 7.1 | 701 | 5.9 | 583 | 8.0 | 158 | 6.7 | 126 |
| Denmark | 7.9 | 407 | 8.0 | 409 | 8.7 | 92 | 9.1 | 87 |
| Germany | 10.5 | 6,448 | 9.9 | 6,074 | 11.5 | 1,244 | 13.7 | 1,287 |
| Greece | 21.5 | 2,073 | 18.4 | 1,817 | 20.7 | 473 | 18.9 | 395 |
| Spain | 20.9 | 7,829 | 18.9 | 7,257 | 22.1 | 2,124 | 20.2 | 1,817 |
| France | 19.1 | 10,313 | 15.7 | 8,681 | 20.7 | 2,453 | 19.5 | 2,290 |
| Ireland | 18.4 | 625 | 19.5 | 684 | 22.4 | 231 | 27.9 | 286 |
| Italy | 14.1 | 7,941 | 15.5 | 8,880 | 16.1 | 1.972 | 15.1 | 1,688 |
| Netherlands | 9.6 | 1,363 | 11.4 | 1,661 | 13.1 | 403 | 17.7 | 506 |
| Portugal | 32.4 | 3,167 | 32.7 | 3,310 | 36.2 | 901 | 36.6 | 880 |
| United Kingdom | 14.6 | 8,226 | 18.2 | 10,324 | 20.1 | 2,354 | 24.0 | 2,642 |

*Notes: The poverty line used is 50% of* national *average household expenditure adjusted for family size. Luxembourg is not included in the Eurostat figures.*

*SOURCE: Eurostat, Poverty in Figures: Europe in the Early 1980s, Luxembourg: Office for Official Publications of the EC, 1990.*

- in France and Italy around 15% of the population were living in poverty;
- Belgium, Denmark, Germany and the Netherlands had the lowest rates of poverty – between about 6% and 11% of the population.

The patterns of increases and decreases in poverty between 1980 and 1985 are illustrated in Figure 15. *One very striking change is the sharp increase in poverty in the United Kingdom between 1980 and 1985.* During this period, the UK had the sharpest rise in poverty in the EC – from 14.6% to 18.2%. Ireland, Italy and the Netherlands also experienced rises in poverty rates, but not as substantial as in the UK. Meanwhile, in Denmark and Portugal, poverty rates stayed relatively constant over the period. In France, Greece, Belgium, Germany and Spain, the levels of poverty declined. (However, the extent of poverty in Germany may have worsened since unification.)

In 1985, over 12 million children in the European community – 19% of all children – were living in poverty.[6] Thus the rate of poverty for children in the EC was higher than for the population as a whole. As Table 26 shows, countries with high rates of poverty for the population as a whole tended to have even higher rates of child poverty. Portugal again fared worst, with 37% of children living in poverty, followed by Ireland and the UK which had around a quarter of children living in poverty. Four countries experienced sharp rises in child poverty between 1980 and 1985: Germany, the UK, the Netherlands and Ireland.

Malcolm Cross, writing in a paper for the Edinburgh Poverty Summit, suggests that:

> Unpublished data for the end of the decade tends not to alter these trends to any significant extent. The fact that the recession has been considerably worse in the UK than elsewhere makes it very probable that the contribution the UK makes to the ranks of Europe's poor is now significantly greater.[7]

## Using a Community-wide poverty line

We now turn to look at poverty rates using a Community-wide definition of poverty based on 50% of European Community average household expenditure, adjusted for family size (see Table 27). This approach obviously yields different results.[8] In 1985 the countries on the periphery of the EC had the highest rates of poverty, using a common definition: 69.5% of people were in poverty in Portugal, 32.4% in Spain, 25.6% in Ireland and 20.9% in Greece. Countries at the centre

**TABLE 27**

**Poverty Rates and Numbers in the EC using a Community-wide definition of poverty (persons and children)**

| Country | Persons | | | | Children | | | |
|---|---|---|---|---|---|---|---|---|
| | 1980 | | 1985 | | 1980 | | 1985 | |
| | % | Nos (000) | % | Nos (000) | % | Nos (000) | % | Nos (000) |
| Belgium | 2.7 | 268 | 1.8 | 182 | 3.1 | 61 | 2.1 | 39 |
| Denmark | 3.9 | 201 | 2.7 | 136 | 4.3 | 45 | 3.1 | 29 |
| Germany | 7.2 | 4,416 | 7.1 | 4,335 | 7.9 | 852 | 9.8 | 919 |
| Greece | 28.9 | 2,784 | 20.9 | 2,062 | 28.1 | 642 | 21.6 | 450 |
| Spain | 30.8 | 11,512 | 32.4 | 12.453 | 32.1 | 3,088 | 33.6 | 3,022 |
| France | 16.7 | 8,997 | 12.1 | 6,685 | 17.8 | 2,110 | 15.0 | 1,761 |
| Ireland | 21.4 | 729 | 25.6 | 898 | 25.9 | 266 | 35.0 | 359 |
| Italy | 15.0 | 8,437 | 13.9 | 7,912 | 17.1 | 2,092 | 13.4 | 1,504 |
| Netherlands | 3.7 | 517 | 4.6 | 664 | 5.0 | 153 | 7.1 | 202 |
| Portugal | 68.6 | 6,701 | 69.5 | 7,023 | 70.3 | 1,751 | 71.2 | 1,713 |
| United Kingdom | 14.9 | 8,368 | 15.8 | 8,944 | 20.4 | 2,392 | 21.0 | 2,309 |
| Community | 16.8 | 52,930 | 15.9 | 51,924 | 19.7 | 13,452 | 19.4 | 12,307 |

*Notes: The poverty line used is 50% of* Community *average household expenditure adjusted for family size. Luxembourg is not included in the Eurostat figures.*

*SOURCE: Eurostat, Poverty in Figures: Europe in the early '80s, Luxembourg: Office of Official Publications of the EC, 1990.*

and in the North had the lowest rates: between 1% and 7% in Belgium, Denmark, the Netherlands and Germany.

The UK, despite its relative affluence, has shockingly high rates of poverty in comparison with its European partners. It has the fifth highest rate of poverty in the EC, closely following the countries which are seen as traditionally poor (15.8%). It has also experienced one of the steepest increases in poverty over the period. After Ireland and Spain, the UK had the highest rate of increase in poverty between 1980 and 1985 in the EC, together with Portugal and the Netherlands. (Using household figures rather than persons, poverty increased by more than in any other country in the EC.) Meanwhile poverty has been decreasing in the rest of the EC, most dramatically in Greece and France.

The patterns for children are remarkably similar. Yet again there was a divide between the periphery and the core of Europe; and a similar ranking of countries.[9] What is particularly noticeable is that the rate of child poverty in the UK nearly matches the rate in Greece – 21.0% in the UK compared to 21.6% in Greece.

Adopting the Community-wide definition throws new light on how member countries compare with one another; in particular it reveals that the UK is uncomfortably close to being categorised as one of the 'poor' nations of Europe. Malcolm Cross sums up the UK position:

> The UK is unlike the wealthier countries of Europe in having higher rates of poverty, and unlike the poorer ones in seeing this position becoming more entrenched.[10]

## 'New' poverty

As is the case in the UK, patterns of poverty in the EC as a whole are changing. In *'New Poverty' in the European Community* Graham Room points to five aspects of 'new poverty': the rise in the numbers on social assistance; the growth of unemployment and insecure employment; the rise in bad debts and arrears; and the increase in lone parents and homeless people.[11] While many of these factors are not new, Room argues that:

> what *is* new about the 1980s is the widening range of the population which is subject to this economic insecurity. Added to this are insecurities which result from the transformation of the family . . . our social security systems seem to be incapable of coping with these two sources of increasing insecurity in the systems of production and reproduction.[12]

These changes pose the challenge for European policy makers in the future, and one which must be met in the context of a sharp increase in the number of elderly people between 1975 and 1985; a change which has created its own demands.

## Attitudes to poverty in the European Community

Attitudes to poverty in Europe have changed over the last 13 years.[13] A 1989 survey conducted by the European Commission found that people were more likely to explain poverty as the result of society's injustice than as the result of laziness and lack of will-power. This is a substantial change compared with a similar survey conducted in 1976. The transformation is especially marked in countries where there was a stronger belief that poverty was due to laziness:

- In the UK in 1976, 43% of those surveyed thought that poverty was due to laziness, but in 1989 only 18% thought so.
- In Ireland and Luxembourg, in 1976, 30% and 31% respectively thought that poverty was due to laziness; in 1989, only 14% and 25% thought so.
- Denmark is the only exception to this trend, with a rise from 11% to 18% between 1976 and 1989.

However, as Peter Golding points out in an analysis of attitudes to poverty, the data are not as conclusive as it first appears.[14] The same survey asks the most common reasons for people being poor. People in the UK are still more likely than those in any other country in the EC to offer laziness as an explanation of poverty. Another interesting finding is that poverty is far more invisible in the UK than in the rest of the EC (with the exception of Luxembourg) despite our rapidly rising rate of poverty. Fewer people in the UK believe that people in their locality are poor.

The same survey of attitudes found that a very large majority of Europeans did not think that the measures taken by public authorities against poverty were sufficient. This was particularly high in Spain (77%), in Italy (84%), in Portugal (76%) and in the UK (70%).

## A social Europe?

The future of the EC, its structure and goals, is very much an open question. The changes in Eastern Europe, the reunification of Germany and the doubts about ratifying the Maastricht Treaty on European union all pose large question marks over the sort of Europe that can be envisaged. These issues lie beyond the scope of this book.[15] However, the scale of poverty identified above and the possible impact of an internal market make it essential to look briefly at the future of the social dimension of Europe.

In 1991 the European Commission pinpointed two adverse effects of the Single European Market on tackling poverty:

> The first of these is the limitation of margins for manoeuvre traditionally employed by the Member States in their social policies . . . There is in the second place . . . an increased risk, at least in the short term, of insecurity and marginalisation affecting certain categories.
>
> (quoted in AB Atkinson, *Towards a European Safety Net?*)[16]

Thus, the creation of an internal market may bring increased poverty and inequality, while at the same time diminishing individual nations' powers to rectify those changes. Tony Atkinson describes how relocation and concentration of production, increased unemployment and downward pressure on wages for the low-skilled will, at least in the short term, increase poverty in certain parts of Europe.[17] There are a number of different views on whether a single market will result in employment centralising in the more affluent countries or dispersing to low-income countries on the periphery. Either scenario will bring increased insecurity and poverty for some sections of society. Meanwhile, the 'convergence' conditions for monetary union impose strict rules on national governments' economic and fiscal powers. Governments have to achieve a high degree of price stability – ie, low inflation – and limit budget deficits to 3% of GDP. So, for example, a government could not borrow heavily in order to increase social protection.[18] It is this conundrum – increased poverty, but decreased powers to tackle it – which makes the social dimension of Europe crucially important.

The social dimension has been grafted on to a European Community which was conceived as primarily an economic union.

But as David Piachaud suggests, if poverty and inequality are not to increase it is essential that the social dimension is taken seriously:

> The European Community is pursuing the conception of the Single Market without countering the costs this may impose, not least in terms of greater marginalisation and exclusion – and more poverty. Yet there cannot be genuine economic integration without social integration – which does not mean harmonization of the inadequate social policies of the member states but rather social policies that allow all citizens of Europe to be integrated in the economy and society.[19]

The Community Charter of the Fundamental Social Rights of Workers, known as the Social Charter, is a serious attempt to elaborate the social dimension of the EC more clearly. The Charter set out the social rights of workers including freedom of movement, fair remuneration for employment, improved living and working conditions, adequate social protection, freedom of association and collective bargaining, vocational training, equal treatment, participation of the workforce in decision-making, health and safety, the protection of children and adolescents, decent living standards for the elderly and the social integration of people with disabilities. The Charter itself as yet has no legal status, but provided the basis for an Action Programme which initiated legislation which covered social issues.

The UK has strongly opposed the extension of the social dimension of the European Community. The Social Charter was adopted in December 1989 by each member of the EC with the exception of the UK. The UK has maintained its opposition to the social dimension in the latest negotiations on the Maastricht Treaty. As a result of the UK's opposition, the Social Chapter, which extends the EC's right to legislate on social policy, was excluded from the Maastricht Treaty itself and is attached to the Treaty in the form of a Social Protocol. Moreover, the UK excluded itself from agreements embodied in the Social Protocol, again adopted by all the other members of the EC.

The final report of the Second EC Poverty Programme expressed concern about the high (though declining) incidence of poverty among the elderly, about the increasing number of lone-parent families – a group with a high risk of poverty – and, above all, about the rise in unemployment, which it saw as the main cause of poverty in the EC.[20] It went on to say of the unemployed, in particular:

> There is considerable risk of two different societies developing within Member States, one of them active, well-paid, well-protected and with an employment-conditioned structure; the other poor, deprived of rights and devalued by inactivity.[21]

The UK is far from being exempt from these problems, but its continued intransigence over the Social Chapter and related initiatives to strengthen the social dimension deprives UK workers and poor people of the benefit of progressive measures implemented elsewhere in the EC. The danger is that the living standards and employment rights of people in the UK will increasingly fall behind those of our European partners.

## Conclusion

The United Kingdom experienced an unparalleled rise in poverty over the eighties in comparison with its neighbours in the European Community. Even using a Community-wide definition, the UK experienced one of the steepest rises in poverty in the EC and is slipping closer to the traditionally poor countries. It now has the third highest unemployment rate in the EC. The creation of the single market and the upheavals in Eastern Europe herald important changes within this region of the world – shifting industry, employment, wealth and poverty both between and within countries.

CPAG believes that the 'social dimension' of the 1992 European single market should be strengthened, and that in particular the UK should:

- sign the Agreement contained in the Social Protocol attached to the Maastricht Treaty with the result that the UK would also be covered by EC decisions on social policy;
- call for a renegotiation of the 'convergence conditions' for monetary union to emphasise the reduction of unemployment;
- endorse European draft directives on parental leave and leave for family reasons, and on pro-rata rights for part-time workers and temporary workers;
- propose draft directives on: the requirement on member states to establish a national minimum wage and a guaranteed national minimum income, minimum standards of provision for childcare services, and moves to combat discrimination in social security against ethnic minorities and against unemployed people;
- support a systematic and published analysis of poverty country by country;

- support the creation of an all-party anti-poverty group in the European Parliament to monitor changes in poverty.

## NOTES

1. *Interim report on a specific community action programme to combat poverty*, Commission of the European Comunities, 1989.
2. Eurostat, *Poverty in Figures: Europe in the Early 1980s*, Luxembourg: Office for Official Publications of the European Communities, 1990.
3. Central Statistical Office, *Regional Trends 27, 1992*, Table 2.1, HMSO, 1992.
4. *See* note 2.
5. Previous studies have used 50% of average *income* (adjusted for family size) as a poverty line. *See* M O'Higgins and Dr S Jenkins, 'Poverty in Europe: estimates for 1975, 1980 and 1985', unpublished paper, August 1989. *See* note 2 for a discussion on the relative merits of using expenditure or income as a measure of poverty on a comparative basis.
6. *See* note 2.
7. M Cross, *Parameters of Poverty, An Overview of the UK in a European Context*, Briefing Paper for Edinburgh Poverty Summit, December 1992.
8. *See* note 2.
9. *See* note 2.
10. *See* note 7.
11. G Room, *New poverty in the European Community*, Macmillan, 1990 and G Room, 'A time for change', in ed. S. Becker, *Windows of Opportunity: Public policy and the poor*, CPAG Ltd, 1991.
12. Quoted in D Piachaud, Book Reviews, *Journal of European Social Policy*, Volume 2, Number 2, 1992.
13. *The perception of poverty in Europe*, Poverty 3, Eurobarometer, Commission of the European Communities, 1990.
14. P Golding, 'Poor Attitudes', in (ed) S Becker, *Windows of opportunity: Public policy and the poor*, CPAG Ltd, 1991.
15. *See* R Dahrendorf, 'The New Europe', in *Journal of European Social Policy*, Volume 2, Number 2, 1992.
16. AB Atkinson, *Towards a European Social Safety Net?*, Number WSP/78, Suntory-Toyota International Centre for Economics and Related Disciplines, 1992.
17. *See* note 16.
18. J Grieve Smith, *Full Employment in the 1990s*, Institute for Public Policy Research, 1992.
19. *See* note 12.
20. *Final Report on the Second Poverty Programme 1985-1991*, (Com 91), Brussels, 1991.
21. *See* note 20.

CHAPTER NINE

# Growing divisions

For the first time since the Second World War the share of income of the poor is shrinking. The eighties witnessed a widening gulf between rich and poor.

Some believe that such a divide is irrelevant as long as overall standards of living improve. But for CPAG, along with many other organisations and individuals, such divisions scar our society. As former Conservative Minister Sir Ian Gilmour writes:

> Not only did the poor not share in the limited economic growth that did take place between 1979 and 1990, the poor were relatively poorer than they had been in 1979 and probably many were absolutely poorer as well. Thatcherites, of course, were not merely not 'One-nation Tories'; they were strongly opposed both to the idea and its advocacy. Rather than be One-nation Tories, they preferred to be two-nation Liberals. In consequence, their policies were unrelentingly divisive and discriminatory against the poor, whose human dignity was relentlessly ignored.
>
> 'That policy is violent,' David Hume wrote 250 years ago, 'which aggrandizes the public by the poverty of individuals'. Still worse is one which aggrandizes the rich by the poverty of the poor. Whether or not Thatcherite social policy added to national violence by provoking riots and increasing crime, it was, in the sense used by Hume, undoubtedly 'violent'.
>
> (Sir Ian Gilmour, *Dancing with Dogma: Britain Under Thatcherism*)[1]

## Indicators of divisions between rich and poor

### Income inequality

Governments have three fundamental responsibilities: to defend the security

**FIGURE 16: Change in Income Distribution 1979 to 1988/89.**

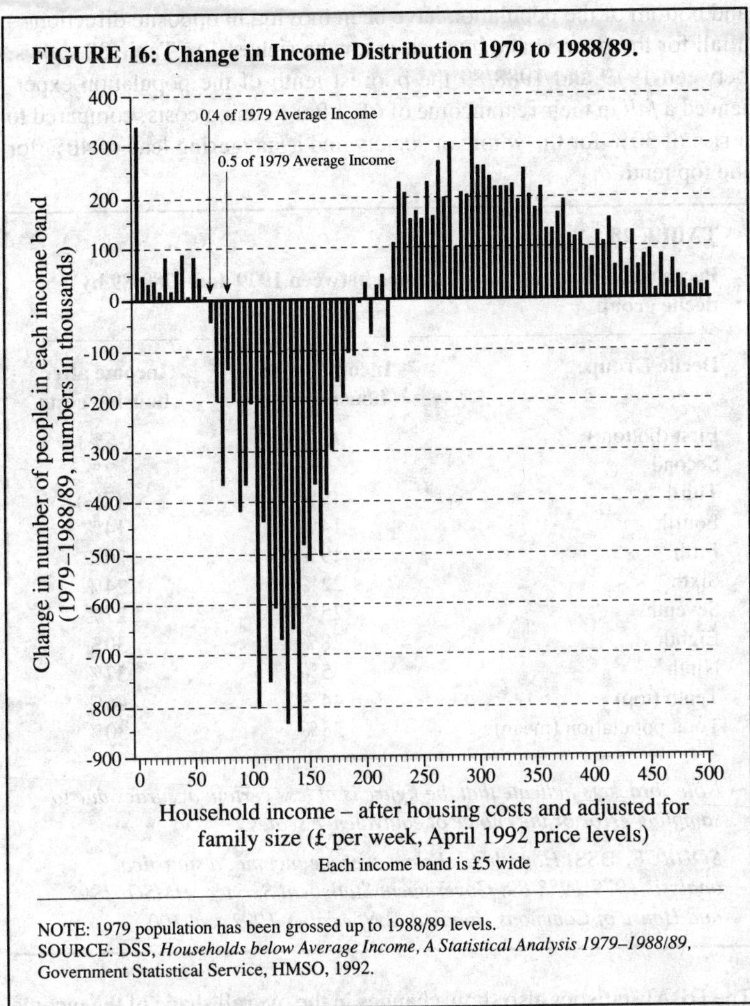


NOTE: 1979 population has been grossed up to 1988/89 levels.
SOURCE: DSS, *Households below Average Income, A Statistical Analysis 1979–1988/89*, Government Statistical Service, HMSO, 1992.

of the realm, to protect the value of the currency and to raise the living standards of the people.

(Rt Hon J Major, the Prime Minister,
Speech to the Conservative Central Council, 23 March 1991)

The gulf that has opened between poor and rich is clearly demonstrated by analysis of the data in the government's *Households below Average Income* statistics.[2] Over the last decade, the living standards at the top and bottom of the population have been moving in opposite directions – a fall for the poorest and huge rises for the richest. As Table 28 shows, between 1979 and 1988/89 the poorest tenth of the population experienced a *fall* in their real income of 6% after housing costs, compared to a rise of 30% for the whole of society and a staggering leap of 46% for the top tenth.

**TABLE 28**

**Percentage changes in real income between 1979 and 1988/89 by decile group**

| **Decile Group** | **Income before housing costs** | **Income after housing costs** |
|---|---|---|
| First (bottom) | (2%) | (-6%) |
| Second | 5% | 2% |
| Third | (9%) | (7%) |
| Fourth | 14% | 14% |
| Fifth | 19% | 20% |
| Sixth | 22% | 24% |
| Seventh | 25% | 27% |
| Eighth | 28% | 30% |
| Ninth | 35% | 37% |
| Tenth (top) | 44% | 46% |
| Total population (mean) | 28% | 30% |

*Note: brackets indicate that the figure is of less certain accuracy due to sampling error or the choice of equivalence scales.*

*SOURCE:* DSS, *Households below average income, a statistical analysis 1979-1988/89, Government Statistical Service, HMSO, 1992 and House of Commons Hansard, 2 November 1992, col 100.*

The HBAI statistics also show changes in the overall shape of the income distribution between 1979 and 1988/89 (see Figure 16). Incomes have become more dispersed and increased overall with the exception of the poorest. There has been a rise in the numbers in the lowest bands of equivalent income (below £60 a week), a fall in the numbers with equivalent incomes between £75 and £200 a week, and a rise in the numbers with incomes above £250 a week. The official data show how the poor became detached from the rest of society, excluded from the short-lived prosperity of the 1980s.[3]

Not surprisingly, HBAI shows how between 1979 and 1988/89 the poorest half of the income distribution have seen their share of total income after housing costs drop from 32% to 27%, while the richest half increased their share from 68% to 73%. As Tony Atkinson explains:

> The Report No 7 of the Royal Commission on the Distribution of Income and Wealth found that the income share of the bottom half of the population was little different in 1976-77 from that in 1949, concluding that 'the income distribution shows remarkable stability from year to year.'[4]

We are witnessing the reversal of a long-term pattern. The share of income of the poorer sections of society is shrinking for the first time since the Second World War. It is no longer possible for the government to claim, as Mrs Thatcher did so confidently in 1988, that 'everyone in the nation has benefited from increased prosperity – everyone'.[5]

This trend is supported by rather different figures in *Economic Trends*, which examine shares of total income.[6] These show that the earlier distribution from rich to poor has been put into reverse. The statistics reveal that in recent years household income has not trickled down but filtered up from the poorer sections of society to the richer ones.

**TABLE 29**

**Percentage distribution of total original and post-tax income of households, adjusted for family size, broken down into quintile groups (fifths)**

| **Original Income** | **1977** % | **1979** % | **1990** % |
|---|---|---|---|
| **Quintile group** | | | |
| Bottom | 3.6 | 2.4 | 2.0 |
| 2nd | 10 | 10 | 7 |
| 3rd | 18 | 18 | 15 |
| 4th | 26 | 27 | 25 |
| Top | 43 | 43 | 51 |
| **Post-tax income** | | | |
| **Quintile group** | | | |
| Bottom | 9.4 | 9.5 | 6.3 |
| 2nd | 14 | 13 | 10 |
| 3rd | 17 | 18 | 15 |
| 4th | 23 | 23 | 23 |
| Top | 37 | 37 | 45 |

*SOURCE: Economic Trends*, January 1993, *HMSO, 1993*

Table 29 shows how the total amount of income held by households is distributed between the richest and poorest fifths of society. Two measures of income are used: 'original income' (ie, income before any taxes and benefits have been paid) and 'post-tax income' (ie, income after direct and indirect taxes and cash benefits). Both measures of income are adjusted for family size. Households are divided into fifths from bottom to top; these are known as *quintile* groups.

On both definitions of income, inequality has risen substantially between 1977 and 1990:

- the poorest fifth's share of total original income fell from 3.6% to 2.0%;
- the richest fifth's share of original income went up by 8 percentage points from 43% to 51%;
- the poorest fifth's share of all post-tax income has gone down from 9.4% to 6.3%;
- the richest fifth's share of all post-tax income has grown by 8 percentage points from 37% to 45%.

**FIGURE 17:**
**Percentage shares of total household income (adjusted for family size) in 1990.**

NOTE: Percentages do not add up to 100% due to rounding.

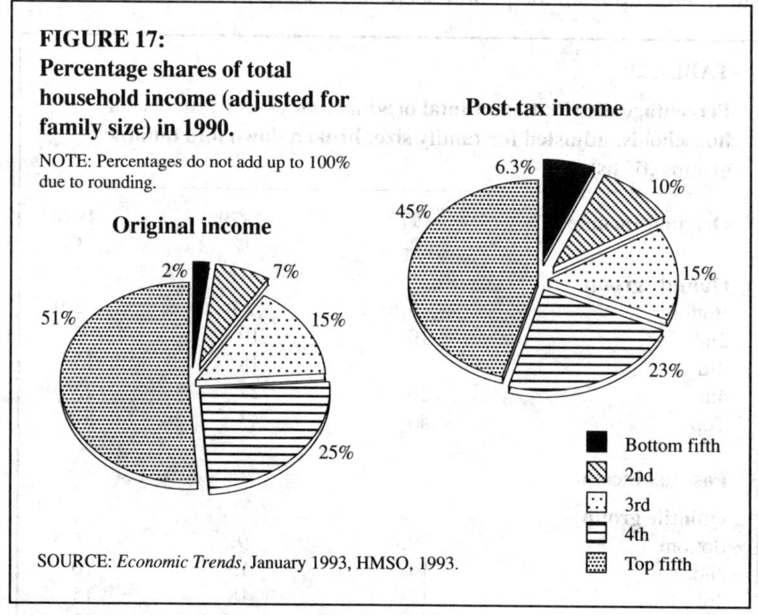


SOURCE: *Economic Trends*, January 1993, HMSO, 1993.

In fact, most of this shift from poor to rich occurred after 1979. The share of the top fifth in 1990 *after* taxes and cash benefits (45%) is now higher than it was in 1979 *before* any taxes and cash benefits had been paid.

Official data from a number of sources confirm the picture of

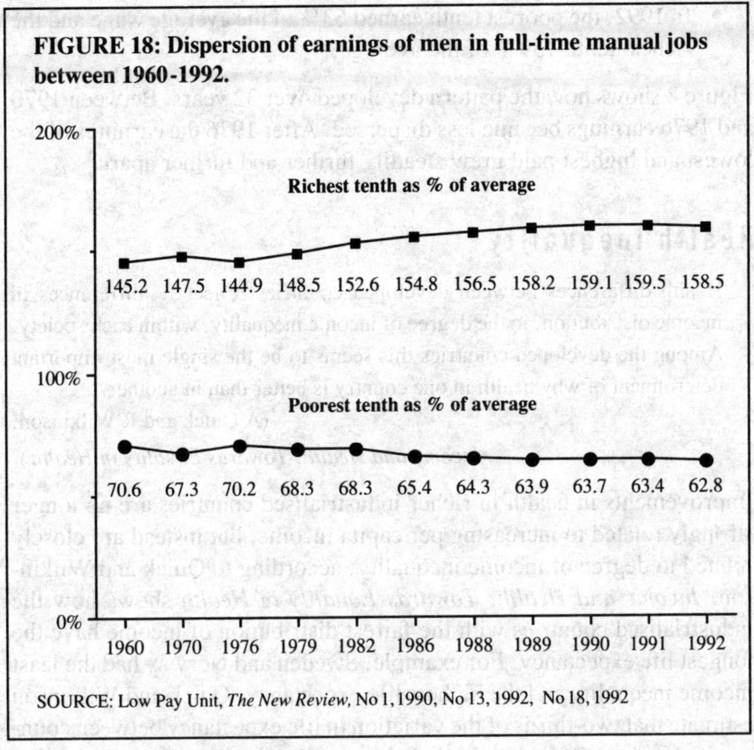


growing inequality. In an analysis of the *Family Expenditure Survey*, Stephen Jenkins summarises the trends:

> The income distribution was more unequal in the mid- to late 1980s than in the early 1980s, and than in the early 1970s, whatever inequality measure is used. But while inequality has increased, so too have average real incomes, with the gains most marked in the 1980s and amongst the rich; the poorest have gained little.
>
> (Stephen P Jenkins, *Income Inequality and Living Standards*)[7]

## Pay inequality

The last decade has been characterised by a substantial rise in earnings. However, the improvement of living standards for the average person masks a growing gap between the highest and lowest paid.[8]

- In 1979, the poorest tenth of men in full-time manual work earned 68% of the average wage and the richest tenth earned 149%.

- In 1992, the poorest tenth earned 63% of the average wage and the richest tenth 159% of the average.

Figure 8 shows how the pattern developed over 32 years. Between 1970 and 1976 earnings became less dispersed. After 1976 the earnings of the lowest and highest paid grew steadily further and further apart.

## Health inequality

> Health differences between developed countries reflect . . . differences in income distribution, in the degree of income inequality, within each society. Among the developed countries this seems to be the single most important determinant of why health in one country is better than in another.
>
> (A Quick and R Wilkinson, *Income and Health: Towards Equality in Health*)[9]

Improvements in health in richer industrialised countries are no longer strongly related to increasing per capita income, but instead are closely related to degree of income inequality, according to Quick and Wilkinson. *Income and Health: Towards Equality in Health* shows how the industrialised countries with the fairest distribution of income have the longest life expectancy. For example, Sweden and Norway had the least income inequality and the highest life expectancy. Quick and Wilkinson estimate that two-thirds of the variation in life expectancy between countries related to differences in their income distribution. They found that in Britain the largest increases in life expectancy were in periods of rapid income redistribution. As we have seen in Chapter 4, health inequalities remain entrenched. If inequalities in income continue to rise, the fear is that the health chances for rich and poor will continue to diverge. Quick and Wilkinson suggest a possible explanation for the link between income inequality and health inequality:

> Economic inequality probably has its main effect on health through psychological and social processes such as the damage it does to people's self-confidence, to social relations and to the quality of the social fabric.[10]

## Wealth inequality

Wealth has to be distinguished from income. But shares of wealth are rarely discussed. Although inequalities in wealth have been reduced since the mid-sixties, the gulf between the poorest half of society and the top is still vast. In 1990, the most wealthy 10% of the population owned

51% of the nation's marketable wealth, while the poorest half of the population owned a mere 7%.[11] As Table 30 illustrates, patterns of wealth have not changed markedly since 1976:

- There has been a slight shift of wealth from the very rich to the fairly rich.
- The poorest half of society have seen a small fall in their share of the nation's wealth – by 1% since 1976, but by 3% since 1986.

**TABLE 30**

**Distribution of marketable wealth**

| | 1976 | 1979 | 1986 | 1990 |
|---|---|---|---|---|
| Most wealthy 1% | 21 | 20 | 18 | 18 |
| Most wealthy 10% | 50 | 50 | 50 | 51 |
| Least wealthy 50% | 8 | 8 | 10 | 7 |

*SOURCE: Inland Revenue Statistics, 1992, Table 11.5, HMSO, 1992*

One of the mainstays of government policy has been the creation of a 'share-owning' democracy and a society of home-owners.

As part of this policy, a number of public assets have been privatised, such as telephones, gas, electricity and water; British Rail and the Post Office are to follow suit. However, a 'capital-owning' democracy is hard to maintain; *Social Trends* shows that the proportion of the population owning shares declined from 25% to 22% between 1990 and 1991. However, this is still a much higher proportion than in 1981, when the figure stood at 7%.[12] But share-ownership does not in fact spread wealth very widely. In 1987 the *General Household Survey* found that:

- 13% of all share-owners were in professional occupations; 30% in managerial occupations; 23% in skilled manual occupations; 8% in semi-skilled occupations; and just 2% in unskilled occupations;
- share-ownership increases with rising income: only 10% of people with a gross weekly income of £50 or less (mainly pensioners) owned shares, and 15% of people with a gross weekly income of £50-£100 while 67% of people with a weekly income of £450 or more owned shares.[13]

As the figures show, inequalities of share ownership simply mirror inequalities of income.

Owning your own home has become an increasingly important source of personal wealth. In 1971 housing was one-fifth of all personal wealth, but by 1988 it was a third.[14]

> The growth in home ownership has been at the cost of an alarming rise in housing insecurity . . . Most people [are faced] with a stark choice between owner-occupation and the serfdom of council housing, often badly managed, in poor condition and rationed by queueing. It is hardly surprising that, faced with this choice, so many have become owner-occupiers.
>
> (*Financial Times* leader, 23 November 1992)

In 1990 two-thirds of people owned their own homes, compared to just over half (52%) in 1979.[15] This striking change in patterns of tenure has had and will have far-reaching effects. Inheritance patterns will have a significant impact on some households in years to come as they will have no housing costs to speak of and thus a greater disposable income. For others on lower incomes or who have experienced insecurity in their jobs home ownership has proved to be an intolerable burden, leading to the sharp rise in repossessions. The expansion of owner-occupation has also had crucial consequences for the third of society who cannot afford to buy their own homes. Table 31 shows how in 1990 nearly two-thirds of heads of households renting from the local authority or a New Town are economically inactive, a very large rise since 1981 when it stood at 42%. The table also reveals the growing gap between local authority/ New Town housing and other sectors: a much lower proportion of all households – some 38% – were economically inactive in 1990.[16]

**Table 31**

**Proportion of Heads of Households who were economically inactive renting from a local authority/New Town compared with all households in 1981 and 1990**

| | **1981** | **1990** |
|---|---|---|
| Local Authority/New Town | 42% | 61% |
| All Households | 32% | 38% |

*SOURCE: M Smyth and F Browne, OPCS, General Household Survey, Government Statistical Service, HMSO, 1992, Table 3.7.*

Peter Willmott and Alan Murie sum up the polarisation of housing in Britain today:

> In the last decade or so the picture has changed. Council housing as a whole has become more and more the preserve of poor people. And within the council sector the poorest and most disadvantaged have more and more had to live on the worst estates. Britain is splitting into two nations: a majority living in decent houses which they own themselves and a minority condemned to the worst of the stock. This process of splitting up is called 'polarisation'. It matters because poor people are living on housing estates that are so decrepit, vandalised and unsafe as to be below acceptable standards. It matters, too, because people living there feel helpless, looked down on by others as inferior.[17]

The third of society who are excluded from owning a home and thereby holding this form of wealth are forced to rely on a shrinking and impoverished public and privately rented sector.

The government's commitment to extending 'choice' is, in Fran Bennett's words:

> prejudiced from the start by an allegiance to the inherently circumscribed principle of ownership. 'No principle is more crucial than what I call the "right to own",' said John Major – referring, in particular, to a home, shares and pensions. Those who can benefit from the 'opportunities' offered by tax relief on mortgage interest and private pension provision will, it appears, continue to do so – thus effectively blocking off one major route for the government to create a fairer distribution of resources and hence wider opportunities for all.[18]

## The causes of growing inequality

There is no doubt that inequality has increased substantially in recent years. The data have shown that this is because market incomes before taxes and benefits have become more unequal as a result of the rise in unemployment, the deregulation of the labour market, higher pay awards at the top end and an increase in owner-occupation, among other factors. These are the main causes of growing inequality. But inequality is also the result of a widening disparity of incomes after taxes and benefits have been paid, as a result of changes in tax and social security policy. In this section we concentrate on tax and benefits (see Chapter 3 for data on unemployment and the labour market).

> Although social security is the principal instrument for reducing inequality taxation can play an important and independent role.
>
> (D Mitchell, *Income Transfers in Ten Welfare States)*[19]

As the quotation above illustrates, social security and tax policies are crucial determinants of the scale of inequality.

There have been substantial reductions in income tax for people living on higher incomes, particularly in the 1980 and 1988 Budgets – the top rate of income tax has fallen from 83% to 40%. If the 1978/79 tax system were in place today, £31.4 billion more tax revenue would be raised. Who has benefited from this £31.4 billion?

- the bottom 50% of tax-payers have gained an average of £400 a year or £4.8 billion in total – 15% of the total tax cuts.
- the top 10% of tax-payers have gained an average of £6,000 a year, or £15.2 billion – nearly half (48%) of the total tax cuts.
- the top 1% of tax-payers at the very top end of the income distribution have gained an average of £33,300 a year, or £8.7 billion in total – over a quarter (27%) of the total tax cuts.[20]

In *Changing Tax*, John Hills analyses the effect of changes in taxation and social security between 1978/79 and 1988/89.[21] He shows the differences between the 1988/89 tax and social security system and those that would have resulted if the 1978/89 system had been uprated with the subsequent rise in national income. He reveals the way in which government policies have sharply increased the division between rich and poor:

- the bottom 50% lost nearly £8.50 a week;
- the top 10% gained nearly £40 a week;
- 57% of families lost and 40% gained.

As John Hills concludes:

> Remarkably, what has happened has been a virtually zero net cost reform: the cuts in direct taxes have been entirely paid for by the cuts in the generosity of benefits . . . the overwhelming majority of the bottom half . . . have lost; the overwhelming majority of the top 30% have gained.[22]

The Institute for Fiscal Studies (IFS) has done a more recent analysis of the effects of changes to the tax and benefit system between 1979 and 1992.[23] Unlike *Changing Tax* the IFS updates the 1979 tax and benefit

FORMAT/ULRIKE PREUSS

***Britain is splitting into two nations: a majority living in decent houses which they own themselves and a minority condemned to the worst of the stock.***

system in line with prices rather than national income. The analysis takes no account of the change from single payments to the social fund (which particularly affected families with children) and the loss of free school meals for certain groups and so may overestimate some of the gains for the poorest and for families with children.

The IFS found losses for the poorest and large gains for the more affluent, but on a less dramatic scale than in *Changing Tax* (see Table 32). They found that between 1979 and 1992:

- the poorest tenth lost an average of £1 a week: 48% gained and 40% lost, 2% had no change;

**TABLE 32**

**Distributional Effects of Tax and Benefit Changes 1979-92, by Income Decile**

| Decile | Average gain/loss (£ per week) | % gaining | % losing |
|---|---|---|---|
| First (poorest) | -1 | 48 | 40 |
| Second | 2 | 66 | 24 |
| Third | 2 | 65 | 27 |
| Fourth | 4 | 69 | 24 |
| Fifth | 9 | 81 | 13 |
| Sixth | 13 | 84 | 10 |
| Seventh | 15 | 85 | 10 |
| Eighth | 21 | 89 | 7 |
| Ninth | 25 | 90 | 7 |
| Tenth (richest) | 87 | 92 | 6 |
| All | 18 | 77 | 17 |

*SOURCE: E Davis et al, Alternative Proposals on Tax and Social Security, Commentary No 29, Institute for Fiscal Studies, 1992*

- the richest tenth gained an average of £87 a week: 92% gained and 6% lost, 2% had no change ;
- the average gained an average of £18, 77% gained: 17% lost and 6% had no change.

The IFS explains the reasons for the changes:

> Clearly the most important reasons for the large gains among the richest have been the cuts in income tax rates, particularly in the higher rates of income tax. Some on the very highest incomes have gained several hundred pounds a

week as a direct result of these cuts . . . Others on moderate to high incomes have also gained from the basic rate cuts.[24]

The IFS also looked at the patterns of gains and losses for different family types (see Table 33) between 1979 and 1992. They found that single people without children who were not in work were the only group to lose – an average loss of £2 a week (58% of this group lost from the changes compared to 31% who gained). There were only very small gains for couples who were not working, both with and without children. Naturally, groups who had been in work fared much better. The IFS concludes:

**TABLE 33**

**Distributional Effects of Tax and Benefit Changes 1979-92, by Family Type**

| Family Type | Average gain/loss (£ per week) | % gaining | % losing |
|---|---|---|---|
| Single, not working | –2 | 31 | 58 |
| Single, employed | 15 | 84 | 12 |
| Single-parent family | 14 | 64 | 17 |
| Couple, not working, no children | 4 | 58 | 36 |
| Couple, not working, children | 2 | 70 | 22 |
| Couple, one working, no children | 15 | 69 | 27 |
| Couple, one working, children | 18 | 74 | 18 |
| Couple, two working, no children | 31 | 91 | 6 |
| Couple, two working, with children | 37 | 88 | 8 |
| Single pensioner | 6 | 78 | 15 |
| Couple pensioner | 12 | 72 | 20 |
| Multiple family unit, no children | 20 | 81 | 14 |
| Multiple family unit, with children | 20 | 75 | 19 |
| All | 18 | 77 | 17 |

*SOURCE: E Davis et al, Alternative Proposals on Tax and Social Security, Commentary No 29, Institute for Fiscal Studies, 1992*

> poor single people have done worst from benefit reforms since 1979 . . . all the poorer non-working groups have also lost out from the rule change which means they can no longer get 100% rebates on their local tax bills. And of course VAT increases have hit the poor, who have not been compensated by cuts in direct taxes because they do not pay them . . . Of the three non-working categories there have been fewest losers among those with children. This reflects the aims of the 1988 reforms which were specifically designed to direct more help towards poorer families with children.[25]

It is interesting to look at our social security and tax policies in a broader context. The Luxembourg Income Study looks at poverty and inequality in a number of countries inside and outside Europe. Using the latest data from 1989, Deborah Mitchell examines the effectiveness of social security benefits and tax in different industrialised countries in reducing inequalities.[26] She found that the UK falls into a middle band. Table 34 shows how the countries were ranked.

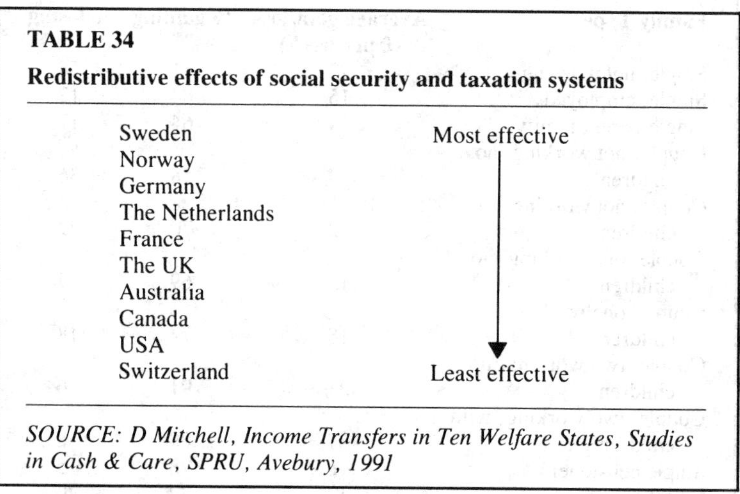

**TABLE 34**

**Redistributive effects of social security and taxation systems**

|  | |
|---|---|
| Sweden | Most effective |
| Norway | |
| Germany | |
| The Netherlands | |
| France | |
| The UK | |
| Australia | |
| Canada | |
| USA | |
| Switzerland | Least effective |

*SOURCE: D Mitchell, Income Transfers in Ten Welfare States, Studies in Cash & Care, SPRU, Avebury, 1991*

## Conclusion

> For Conservatism is grounded in fairmindedness, a sense of what is right; in shared aspirations and mutual respect. It builds on self-respect, not envy. It seeks to unite, and not to divide. To create . . . a Britain without barriers.
>
> (Rt Hon J Major, Speech to the Conservative Women's Conference, 27 June 1991)

Despite John Major's appeal to a united nation, rich and poor are more sharply divided than ever. Even after tax and benefits and family size are taken into account, in 1990 the poorest fifth held just 6.3% of all household income; the richest fifth held over seven times as much – 45%. Changes in taxation and social security policies have brought a *declining* share of the national income to the poor and a *rising* share to the affluent. Inequality matters because the lifestyle of the rich and the array of goods they consume create a culture of affluence which locks out the poor. Social policies are reinforcing divisions and the exclusion experienced by the people who are living in and on the margins of poverty.

The task of tackling inequality lies in many different areas of policy. A more progressive tax system, an employment and training strategy which puts tackling unemployment at the forefront, a statutory minimum wage and more generous benefits, would begin to tackle the inequalities that beset our society.

## NOTES

1. I Gilmour, *Dancing with Dogma, Britain under Thatcherism*, Simon and Schuster, 1992.
2. DSS, *Households below Average Income, a statistical analysis 1979-1988/89*, Government Statistical Service, HMSO, 1992.
3. *See* note 2.
4. A B Atkinson, *DSS Report on Households below Average Income 1981-1987*, paper for the Social Services Select Committee, 1990.
5. House of Commons, *Hansard*, 17 May 1988, col 796.
6. *Economic Trends*, January 1993, HMSO, 1993.
7. S P Jenkins, 'Income Inequality and Living Standards: Changes in the 1970s and 1980s', *Fiscal Studies*, Vol 12, No 1, February 1991.
8. *The new review*, No 1, Low Pay Unit, December/January 1990 and *The new review*, No 18, Low Pay Unit, October/November 1992.
9. A Quick and R Wilkinson, *Income and Health, Towards Equality in Health* Socialist Health Association, 1991.
10. *See* note 9.
11. *Inland Revenue Statistics 1993*, HMSO, 1992.
12. *Social Trends 23*, Government Statistical Service, HMSO, 1993.
13. *General Household Survey 1987*, tables 8C and 8D, HMSO, 1990.
14. P Ormerod and M Wilmott, 'Willpower: homeownership, inheritance & the next century', *Poverty 73*, CPAG Ltd, 1989.
15. M Smyth and F Browne, OPCS, *General Household Survey 1990*, Government Statistical Service, HMSO, 1992.
16. *See* note 15.

17. P Willmott and A Murie, *Polarisation and social housing*, Policy Studies Institute, 1988.
18. F Bennett, 'A Window of Opportunity', in eds S Becker, *Windows of Opportunity, public policy and the poor*, CPAG Ltd, 1991.
19. D Mitchell, *Income Transfers in Ten Welfare States*, Studies in Cash & Care, SPRU, Avebury, 1991.
20. House of Commons, *Hansard*, 19 June 1992, cols 688-9.
21. J Hills, *Changing tax: how the tax system works and how to change it*, CPAG Ltd, 1990.
22. *See* note 21.
23. E Davis et al, Alternative proposals on tax and social security, *Commentary No 29*, Institute for Fiscal Studies, 1992
24. *See* note 23.
25. *See* note 23.
26. *See* note 19.

# Conclusion

Poverty blights the lives of a fifth of the United Kingdom's population and around a quarter of its children. The evidence amassed in these pages shows how poverty multiplied more rapidly in the UK between 1975 and 1985 than in any other country in the European Community. It shows how the 'North' and some inner cities have been ravaged by unemployment but also how recession has eaten into the heartlands of the more affluent regions. It shows how unemployment and lone parenthood bring high risks of poverty. It shows how poverty seeps into people's lives – endangering their homes and their health. It shows how the UK has become more unequal than at any time since the Second World War and how the poorest have not shared in the rising prosperity of the 1980s. It shows how our society excludes millions from full participation in society. It exposes the way in which the dice are loaded against millions of children, denying them the chance to fulfil their potential.

Poverty is often created when the tie to the labour market is severed – because of unemployment, or caring for another person at home, or disability. But access to the labour market does not in itself guarantee escape from poverty. Often employment provides only low, insecure or sporadic earnings. Poverty is also intensified when the extra costs of having a child, coping with a disability or caring for an elderly relative are not met adequately by earnings or social security benefits. Such poverty is not random but shaped by class, by gender and by race.

Policies to tackle poverty have to respond to several challenges:

- **demographic pressures** – the greater numbers of elderly, and especially very old people with greater disabilities;
- **economic changes** – higher unemployment, changing work patterns, low wages, growing inequality, and the concentration of poverty among black and other ethnic minority communities;
- **social changes** – shifting patterns of family life, especially the increase in the proportion of women with children in paid work and the rise in the number of lone parents;

- a **crisis of confidence** in the capacity of the welfare state to deal with poverty.

Grappling with these challenges has to take place against the background of a social security system which seems to have lost its way. It also takes place in a new context in which the focus is increasingly widened to include the European Community.

Beveridge's post-war vision of social security to meet people's needs from cradle to grave has been severely undermined both by changes in society and by specific policies. The mainstay of Beveridge's social security scheme was national insurance: those in full-time paid work (largely men and single women) were to be catered for during interruptions to their work (unemployment, sickness etc) and after retirement. Others (women and children) were to be provided for as 'dependants' of the male breadwinner. But such a model no longer fits reality. Recent policies have weakened or abolished some key benefits (such as the freeze in child benefit between 1988 and 1990 and the abolition of the maternity grant) and have withdrawn certain rights. Over the last ten years, the marked shift towards means-testing in conjunction with the rise in unemployment has brought staggering numbers into the maze of means-testing, with its complexity, discretion, and delays. The ability of some parts of the social security system to function adequately has been called into question.

The social and economic consequences of the single market in the European Community are as yet unrevealed and yet potentially more far-reaching than other economic changes experienced up to now. They bring the threat of increased inequalities not only between countries in Europe, but also *within* countries themselves. The 'social dimension' of Europe is at present but a pale counterpart of the economic dimension. The protocol of the Maastricht Treaty, which embodies the 'social dimension', is being side-lined; and the UK refuses to sign it.

In the light of all these changes, what kind of strategy should we be pursuing in the United Kingdom to prevent poverty?

First, it must be a comprehensive strategy. The task of tackling poverty lies in many different areas of government responsibility, in policies for industry and the regions, for housing, education, social services and transport, and for the environment and energy, as well as in the traditional areas of employment, social security and taxation. We only touch briefly on the broader areas here. We focus on three principal tools for tackling poverty and redistributing resources:

- improving access to the labour market and conditions within it;

- improving the benefits which support those who are either not in paid work or who work part time;
- making the tax system fairer.

Employment, social security and taxation policies are the central tools for sharing out resources more fairly between rich and poor, healthy and sick, white people and black people, employed and unemployed, able-bodied and disabled and between men and women.

> The wages, social security and tax system should, together, ensure that all members of society have sufficient income to enable them to meet their public and private obligations as citizens and exercise effectively their legal, political and social rights as citizens.
>
> (Charter for Social Citizenship)[1]

As the pages of *Poverty: the Facts* reveal, poverty denies people the chance of achieving their potential. Thus, the framework for any anti-poverty policy must be to give people the bricks with which to build their future and the future for their children. These bricks include: a decent home, a comprehensive and free health system, free education, subsidised childcare, cheap public transport, an insulation and energy saving programme, and a healthy environment.

More specifically, CPAG urges active steps towards the following policies.[2]

## Employment

> Of course the creation of wealth is important . . . but the question remains for what is that wealth to be used? The well-being of all members of that society cannot just be an incidental consequence of an economic policy but must be an integral part of the overall policy which decides in which direction our society should be heading. Only in this way can a proper relationship be reached between economic and social policy. (*Not Just for the Poor*)[3]

Formulating a strategy for employment lies at the heart of policies to reduce poverty. Employment policies should be about access to employment, about ensuring both flexibility and security for the workforce, about promoting anti-discrimination in employment and about preventing poverty at work. Such policies should include:

- Employment rights which apply equally to full- and part-time workers, including a statutory minimum wage.
- Provisions to enable women and men to combine paid work with

caring responsibilities at home – increased access to childcare facilities for both under school age and school-aged children which provide a stimulating environment for children; equal pay for women and men.

- Access to decent jobs and training for all, especially groups who experience discrimination in employment – women, black people and other ethnic minorities, unskilled workers, people with disabilities and long-term unemployed people.
- Endorsement of the European draft directives which improve the rights of parents and women at work – parental leave and leave for family reasons and pro rata rights for part-time and temporary workers.

## Social Security

> As we see it, social security has wider aims than the prevention or relief of poverty. It is the response to an aspiration for security in its widest sense. Its fundamental purpose is to give individuals and families the confidence that their level of living and quality of life will not, in so far as is possible, be greatly eroded by any social or economic eventuality. This involves not just meeting needs as and when they arise but also preventing risks from arising in the first place, and helping individuals and families to make the best possible adjustment when faced with disabilities and disadvantages which have not been or could not be prevented. (*Into the 21st Century*)[4]

The principles which should underpin social security are:

- Solidarity – collective security against risks, such as unemployment or sickness.
- The sharing by society as a whole of the responsibility for caring for children, elderly people and people with disabilities.
- Preventing poverty, rather than patching over it.

These principles mean a social security system which would provide:

- Adequate benefits to meet people's needs – physical, social and cultural – to enable people to participate fully in society. Benefits should be paid as far as possible without means tests and contribution tests.
- Individual autonomy – benefits paid on an individual basis so that women as well as men can claim benefits in their own right.
- Equal access and treatment regardless of sex, race, marital status or sexual orientation.

- Clear rights to benefits, which should be administered efficiently and humanely by sufficient staff.
- Simplicity – benefits should be easy to understand and administer.
- Flexibility – benefits should be paid in a way which includes those working part time within the social security system and in a way which takes account of cultural differences.

Above all, it is essential that the social security system caters for everyone rather than just people in poverty. This means moving away from the means test, rather than further strengthening its role. This is the only way to guarantee that social security does not become a second-class service for the most vulnerable.

> We are only likely to be able to meet the needs of the weak and vulnerable – which may include all of us at different points of our lives – if services recognise their special needs and do not push them to the margins of society. In justifying this conclusion, we must return once again to the basic truths which we believe must underlie any system of welfare. It must be concerned with the well-being of all members of society: the notion of interdependence and concern for the poor and oppressed demands no less. Any model which splits off the least fortunate members of society and treats them in a way which is fundamentally different from the rest is unacceptable.
>
> (*Not only for the Poor*)[5]

## Taxation

> Income, wealth and social welfare are unequally distributed in all OECD countries, and redistribution is an objective of society and the State . . . There is a well-established role for the welfare state which is firmly rooted in the idea of market failure and the desire for redistributional justice.
>
> (*Social Expenditure 1960-90*)[6]

Taxation policies determine how much income people can keep out of their earnings or benefits and they are one of the principal means of redistributing income and wealth from rich to poor. Fairer policies on taxation should include:

- Creating a more progressive tax structure.
- Fully independent taxation for men and women, which does not depend on marital status.
- A local tax system which reflects ability to pay.

As well as these broad policies CPAG believes that it is essential for governments to commit themselves to:

- Research into people's basic physical and social needs in order to provide a rationale for adequate benefits.
- The publication of annual statistics on low incomes which include a breakdown by region, gender and ethnic origin.

Only then will all governments be compelled publicly to recognise the existence of poverty and develop policies to combat it.

As inequalities have grown and poverty has become more pressing and more intense, there has been strong public support for policies which tackle these injustices. The 1992/93 *British Social Attitudes Survey* revealed that in 1991:

- 79% of people believed that income differences in Britain are too large.
- 65% thought taxes should be increased to pay for more social spending.
- 58% thought that government should spend more on benefits for the poor even if this meant higher taxes.[7]

An earlier *British Social Attitudes Survey* shows that nearly two-thirds support action to reduce income differences.[8] Such surveys reveal that the welfare state retains enduring popularity despite cuts and changes. It has become fashionable to argue that the problems of poverty, low pay and unemployment can only be tackled after the development of a strong and stable economy – that to put concerns about poverty before economic development is to put the cart before the horse. However, CPAG is convinced that long-term economic growth must go hand in hand with social justice: that only a society which is not wracked by social division and the exclusion of the poor can provide the foundations for stability and growth.

It has recently become equally fashionable to argue that redistribution has reached its limits; that taxation cannot be increased and that benefits will have to be means-tested or hived off to the private sector to reduce the bill to a level acceptable to the better-off. Yet this approach ignores the increase in unemployment that has created in large part the increase in social security expenditure – however inadequate it is. Prevention is better than picking up the pieces. Failure even to pick up the pieces – which is what limiting redistribution in reality means – is an abnegation of responsibility.

We need to build on the attitudes expressed in opinion surveys above.

We need to point out that the 'modern' recipe of privatising provision where possible and means-testing the rest would result in a general reluctance to finance social welfare, the blunting of individual aspirations by increasing the numbers in poverty trap and the paring back of provision for the poor. We would indeed be left with a 'residual' welfare state.

Each step upwards in the unemployment figures means an ever larger pool of long-term unemployed and yet more young people facing a jobless and poverty-stricken future. It is this divide between those in well-paid, secure jobs and those who are marginalised – either without work or in intermittent low-paid jobs – which poses the challenge for policy makers, political parties, the general public and above all for government.

> It is only so far as poverty is abolished that freedom is increased.
>
> Harold Macmillan, *The Middle Way*[9]

## NOTES

1. R Lister, *The exclusive society: Citizenship and the poor*, CPAG Ltd, 1990.
2. These policies come from a variety of sources, in particular from R Lister, *There is an alternative*, CPAG Ltd, 1987; and the 'Charter for Social Citizenship' in R Lister, *Exclusive Society: Citizenship and the poor*, CPAG Ltd, 1990.
3. *Not just for the poor: Christian perspectives on the welfare state*, Church House Publishing, 1986.
4. *Into the 21st Century*, International Labour Office, 1984.
5. *See* note 3.
6. *Social expenditure 1960-1990*, OECD, 1985.
7. Eds R Jowell et al, *British Social Attitudes, the 9th report*, 1992/3 Edition, Dartmouth, 1992.
8. Ed R Jowell et al, *British Social Attitudes special international report, 6th Report*, Social and Community Planning Research, Gower, 1990.
9. H Macmillan, *The Middle Way*, 1962.

# Appendix 1: Poverty lines

We have looked at two sources of information to estimate the numbers living in poverty and the changes in their incomes: *Low Income Families* statistics (LIF) and *Households below Average Income* (HBAI). However, neither measure of poverty is entirely satisfactory.

## The limitations of the statistics

Both sets of statistics have strengths and weaknesses. They have three weaknesses in particular. Firstly, they can only provide a snapshot of poverty. They do not show how long people have been living in poverty for; it could be a month, or several years. Different groups might be more or less likely to experience long-term poverty. Such material can only be provided by longitudinal data. Secondly, they underestimate poverty because they are based on the *Family Expenditure Survey* (which excludes the homeless and those in residential care) and they disregard the costs of being poor (eg, having to buy poor quality goods which do not last long or having to use local shops which are more expensive). Thirdly, they are based on income rather than expenditure and thus do not reveal much about people's actual living standards.

## Using income support as a poverty line derived from Low Income Families statistics

**Advantages:**

- Income support is a minimum level of income set by Parliament for people not in 'full-time' work who meet certain conditions. It allows us to measure incomes in relation to this minimum level and thus judge how effective the goverment is in ensuring that people do not fall below it and that they are given the resources to rise above it.

- LIF uses the 'benefit assessment unit' (see Definitions and Terms) as the unit of measurement rather than the 'household' (as is used by HBAI). More than one benefit unit may live in a single household. For example, if a lone-parent family on income support shares with a relative or friend who is on an average income, the lone-parent family is still counted as having a low income despite the higher income of the relative or friend. This reflects the assumption that income is not always shared fairly within households. CPAG believes that the best unit of measurement is the individual; but the 'benefit unit' is closer to the 'individual' than the 'household' is. Thus, on the whole the 'benefit unit' is a more appropriate unit of measurement than the 'household'.

**Disadvantages:**

- These are not official figures, but have been produced by the independent Institute for Fiscal Studies for the House of Commons Social Security Committee.
- The difficulty of using income support both as a measure of poverty and as the tool to relieve poverty. Each time it is raised in real terms (ie, above inflation) to improve the living standards of the poorest, the number of people defined as poor is automatically increased. If income support was reduced by half, the numbers living in poverty would also be halved (see p35).
- Income support's level and coverage are determined by overall government priorities, rather than being related to people's needs. Thus, by using a benefit level as a poverty line, the anomalies in the benefit itself are mirrored in the way poverty is measured – eg, young people aged 18-24, who are single and childless, receive a lower rate of income support than those aged 25 and over. This is not necessarily a reflection of need. This means that the poverty line is higher for those aged 25 and over than those below 25.

## Using 50% of average income as a poverty line derived from Households below Average Income

**Advantages:**

- These are official figures published by the government.
- They provide the only set of continuous data since 1979.
- It is an unapologetically 'relative' poverty line (see Chapter 1)

which looks at low incomes in relation to the incomes of the rest of society. 50% of average income rises and falls as average income rises and falls.

- The definition of poverty used in the European Community is 50% of average national income/expenditure, so using 50% as a benchmark in the UK is a similar approach.

## Disadvantages:

- 50% of average income does not relate incomes to the minimum rates of benefit specified by Parliament – income support. This means we can no longer judge the government by its own standards.
- The figures are based on the *household* unit rather than the benefit unit, as was used in the LIF figures. Using the *household* unit leads to a substantial *underestimate* of the number of people living on a low income. The DSS estimates that the numbers falling below 50% of average income after housing costs would be *1.8 million higher* (some 13.8 million people) using the *benefit unit* as the unit of measurement rather than *households*.
- Some people would argue that 50% of average income measures inequality rather than poverty.
- The 'average' may fluctuate from year to year for either statistical reasons or economic ones. For example, if average income fell drastically, say as a result of an oil-shock induced recession, the number of people below 50% average income (and thus in 'poverty') would also fall, even though many of those on low incomes may actually be worse off.
- The equivalence scales (which are used to adjust income for family size) used in HBAI, known as the McClements scales, have lower weights for children than the equivalence scales used in LIF. This affects both the overall total and the composition of those in poverty. Research by the IFS has shown:

> The choice of scale makes a substantial difference to the recorded extent and make-up of poverty and inequality. In recent years, increasing the weight given to children increases the numbers recorded as living 'in poverty' (living on below half average income). Decreasing the weight given to them reduces recorded poverty numbers. Using the income support scales in constructing poverty statistics would therefore show greater recorded poverty than is found using the McClements scales.[1]

The list of advantages and disadvantages makes it abundantly clear that there is no straightforward answer to finding an uncontroversial poverty line. We have chosen to use both the LIF and HBAI, drawing out the strengths of each analysis.

## NOTES

1. J Banks and P Johnson, *Children and Household Living Standards*, Institute for Fiscal Studies, 1993.

# Appendix 2: Definitions and terms

**Average:** is a single number that is intended to be representative of a set of numbers. There are different kinds of averages – mean, median and mode. In *Poverty: the facts* only the mean and median are used. The **mean** is when all the numbers are added up and then the total is divided by the number of numbers. The **median** is the mid-point of any range of numbers. The mean is less stable than the median as it tends to be dragged up by higher incomes. In the government figures – *Households below Average Income* – people's incomes are measured as a proportion of the mean income.

**Benefit Assessment Unit:** individual or couple, with or without children, on which entitlement to supplementary benefit or income support is based (*see* Low Income Families).

**Child:** In the government figures – *Households below Average Income* and *Low Income Families* – a child is defined as anyone aged under 16, or 16-19 if s/he is in full-time non-advanced education.

**Community charge benefit:** also known as poll tax rebate. This replaced the rate rebate which was payable under housing benefit. It covers a maximum of 80% of the community charge/poll tax.

**Council tax benefit:** This replaces community charge benefit from April 1993. It covers 100% of the council tax for those living on income support or an equivalent level of income.

**Decile groups:** successive tenths of all households arranged by income from bottom to top.

**Equivalence scales:** are used to adjust income to take account of different family or household sizes. This is done in order to reflect the extent to which families or households require different incomes to achieve the same standard of living. The scales give different weights to adults and children. For example: a two-parent family with two children has an income of £200 a week. Assuming that a couple has a weight of 1.00 and each child 0.5, when income is **equivalised**, it is £100 a week (£200 divided by 2.00). There is a great deal of controversy about which equivalence scales are appropriate – eg, how much weight to place on children's needs at different ages. The government's *Households below Average Income* statistics use different equivalence scales from those used in *Low Income Families*.

**Family credit:** is a means-tested social security benefit for families with children in low-paid work (for 16 hours a week or more). It replaced family income supplement as part of the 1986 Social Security Act (fully implemented in 1988).

**Family Expenditure Survey:** is conducted annually by the Central Statistical Office. The *Family Expenditure Survey* is a survey of people's expenditure and income in the United Kingdom.

**Households below average income (HBAI):** was produced by the Department of Social Security for the first time in 1988 and has replaced the *Low Income Families* statistics. HBAI is based on an analysis of the *Family Expenditure Survey*. HBAI measures the numbers of people living on incomes below the average (the mean). The HBAI figures are for the United Kingdom. HBAI uses **household** income which is adjusted for household size (equivalised) and then divided by the numbers of individuals in the household. Income is **current** (ie, the income stated at the time of the **Family Expenditure Survey** interview). Income is defined as: net earnings after income tax, national insurance and occupational pension contributions, gross profit from self-employment, all social security benefits including housing benefit, maintenance, investment income, and some income in kind, such as luncheon vouchers and free school meals. Income is net of the following items: income tax payments, national insurance contributions, contributions to occupational pensions, domestic rates, community charge and repayments of social fund loans. The statistics show income before and after housing costs. Housing costs are defined as: rent and rates, water rates, ground rent and service charges, mortgage interest and structural insurance for home owners. CPAG argues that one possible poverty line is 50% of average income after housing costs.

**Housing benefit:** is a means-tested social security benefit which helps people on low incomes in and out of work with their housing costs.

**Income:** can be measured in a number of different ways. See *Households below Average Income* and *Low Income Families* for definitions used in these series. In Chapter 9, figures are used from the government's Central Statistical Office publication *Economic Trends*. We have picked out two measures of income: original income (ie, income before taxes and benefits) and post-tax income (ie, income after direct (eg, income tax and national insurance) and indirect taxes (ie, VAT) and cash benefits).

**Income support:** is a social security benefit which is supposed to provide a minimum income for people who are not in 'full-time' work (ie, work less than 16 hours a week) who meet certain conditions. It is means-tested. It replaced supplementary benefit as part of the 1986 Social Security Act (implemented in 1988) – *see* Social Security Act 1986. Income support and its predecessor supplementary benefit are often regarded as the 'safety net' of the social security system; they were intended to provide a kind of minimum income guarantee. However, the government has deliberately excluded some groups from income support through rules on full-time work, or capital, or age. Thus, increasingly income support is becoming a far less effective safety net.

**Institute for Fiscal Studies:** is an educational charity which promotes research and discussion of tax and finance matters. It has undertaken a great deal of work on behalf of the House of Commons Social Security Committee in looking at the distribution of low income.

**Low income families (LIF):** was produced by the Department of Health and Social Security for the last time in 1988. These were based on the *Family Expenditure Survey*. LIF showed the numbers of people living on a low income – below 140% of supplementary benefit. The Social Security Committee has commissioned the Institute for Fiscal Studies to continue publishing this series. CPAG argues that one possible poverty line is the income support/supplementary benefit level. LIF uses: income based on the *Benefit Assessment Unit* (see above) (rather than **household** income, as used in HBAI). The latest edition of LIF makes a number of methodological changes to the series; it uses **current** income (as is used in HBAI). It no longer makes an allowance for travel to work costs for full-time workers and it includes Northern

Ireland. Income is defined as: net earnings after tax, national insurance, and superannuation, gross profit from self-employment, all social security benefits *excluding* housing benefit, maintenance, investment income, and some income in kind, such as luncheon vouchers, less tax and national insurance paid direct. The statistics show incomes after housing costs. Housing costs are defined as: rent and rates (net of rebates), water rates, mortgage interest, maintenance costs etc., less housing benefit. LIF also uses different equivalence scales from HBAI (*see* Equivalence Scales).

**Low pay:** defined by the Council of Europe as 68% of full-time mean earnings. In 1991/92, this was £193.60 a week, or £5.15 an hour.

**Median:** *see* Average.

**Poverty definitions:** CPAG uses two possible definitions of poverty: the numbers living on and below income support/supplementary benefit and the numbers living below 50% of average income after housing costs.

**Quintile group:** successive fifths of all households arranged by income from bottom to top.

**Lone parents:** throughout the text we use lone parents to refer to anyone who is bringing up children on their own whether they are divorced, separated, widowed or never married.

**Single payments:** were grants for one-off needs such as cookers, beds and furniture, which provided extra help for people living on supplementary benefit. They were replaced by the discretionary social fund in April 1988 as part of the 1986 Social Security Act (*see* Social Fund).

**Social Affairs Unit:** a research and educational trust which analyses social affairs in order to promote 'a free and orderly society in which enterprise can flourish'.

**Social fund:** replaced the single payments scheme in the Social Security Act 1986 (*see* Single Payments). The first part of the social fund wa implemented in 1987 and provides grants for cold weather, maternity and funeral needs. It is governed by regulations and there is a legal right of appeal. The second part of the social fund was implemented in 1988;

this mainly provides interest free loans and has a small budget for community care grants to prevent people going into institutional care or to help them when they leave such care. Loans are repayable directly from income support at rates of 15% in most cases (though it can be lower). This part of the social fund is discretionary and cash-limited and there is no right to an independent appeal, only to a review.

**Social Security Act 1986:** was the outcome of the 'Fowler Reviews' set up to examine the options for the major reform of the social security system. The Act brought in a new structure of social security that was fully implemented in April 1988. Income support replaced supplementary benefit, the social fund replaced single payments, family credit replaced family income support and housing benefit was reduced.

**Social Security Committee:** is a House of Commons Select Committee composed of MPs from all parties. Its responsibility is to monitor issues related to social security.

**Supplementary Benefit:** was paid to people who were not in full-time work and who met certain conditions. It was replaced by income support as part of the Social Security Act 1986 in 1988. Supplementary benefit/income support is used by CPAG as one possible poverty line.

**Unemployment Unit:** is an independent body which campaigns on, and does research into, unemployment and training.

**Wages Councils:** known as Trade Boards, were first set up in 1909. Trade Boards determine minimum rates of pay and conditions, backed up by the force of law, in certain low-paying industries such as retailing, hairdressing, laundries and clothing. The Councils are made up of members from the eployers, and trade unions, and independent members. Their powers were weakened in 1986 and the government proposes to abolish them entirely under the Trade Union Reform and Employment Rights Bill.

---

*Sources: DSS, Households below Average Income: a statistical analysis, 1979- 1988/89, Government Statistical Services, HMSO 1992; DHSS, Low Income Families 1985, Government Statistical Service, 1988; Social Security Committee, Second Report, Low Income Statistics: Low Income Families 1979-1989, HMSO 1992; J Hills, Changing tax: the tax system and how to change it, CPAG Ltd, 1989.*